Cereal for Dinner,

Cake for Dessert

A True Story
to Inspire You
to Be Yourself

Laura Wells McKnight

LAURA McKNIGHT PUBLISHINGS, LLC
LEAWOOD, KANSAS

Cereal for Dinner, Cake for Dessert

A True Story

First published, 2012, in the United States of America

LAURA McKNIGHT PUBLISHINGS, LLC
Visit our website at www.laurawellsmcknight.com

Cereal for dinner, cake for dessert, a true story / Laura Wells McKnight.
Library of Congress Control Number 2012904739
ISBN 978-0-9853524-0-0 (PB)
ISBN 978-0-9853524-1-7 (E)
12   1

Printed by Spangler Graphics, Kansas City, Kansas

Edited by Melinda Wells McKnight, Philip Charles McKnight II and Sarah Mosher

Book and cover design by Sarah Mosher, moshdesigns, www.moshdesigns.com

To my mother

Thank you for buying this book. And thank you for reading this book. And, if you purchased this book directly from my website, thank you for making it possible for me to donate a portion of the proceeds to my favorite charities. My favorite charities that are referenced throughout this book and listed in the appendix.

Cereal for Dinner, Cake for Dessert is my first book. Unless you count the two I wrote in kindergarten. And this book is the first edition of *Cereal for Dinner, Cake for Dessert*. And this book is self-published, by me and my wonderful team of friends and family who all pitched in to get it done. Even though we are not really publishers. We think the book is pretty good! Like my cakes, though, this book is not perfect. Especially in its first edition. And my magic wand can't erase typos. And neither can I cover them up with frosting or fondant. So, I would love nothing more than for you, the reader, to email me, at laura@diaryofagoodgirl.com, with any typos you find so that we can get them corrected in subsequent editions. I always want to get better!

A thousand profuse thank yous to my friends and family who graciously reviewed early-stage chapters of this book. Without the candid input of these wonderful people, this book would not be very good! Amy, Ann, Aurora, Carla, Caroline, Christine H., Christine K., Clay, Cristal, Dalton, Erin, Jill, Joanne, Judy, Katie, Kristy, Laura, Lori, Mary Nan, Michelle, Paige, Pam, Philip, Sandra, Shari, Stephanie and Tom, you are all so wonderful!

Thank you to Sarah. Actually, a double thank you to Sarah! This book looks as good as it does because of your talent!

A special thank you to Brenda, Debbie, Jackie, Janeen, Jennifer and Katie at the Greater Kansas City Community Foundation for much appreciated friendship and support.

And, last but not least, thank you thank you thank you to my mother and father. I cannot even begin to imagine how many hours you have invested in this endeavor. It's a good thing we all like cake. And cereal.

Table of Contents

Cereal for Dinner 1

Cake for Dessert 12

Fluffy White Cake 21

Vanilla Buttercream Frosting 32

Hand-dipped Celebration Bon Bons . . .43

Raspberry Peach Drizzle Cake 57

Coffee Cake 68

One Signature Birthday Cake 79

Pink Champagne Cake 91

The Magic Wand 101

Yellow Cake 111

Cheerful Chocolate Peanut
Butter Cake 124

Paw Print Cake .135

Recycled Cake. .146

Barbie Cake 158

Mummy Cake 169

Studio Cake. 179

Chocolate Chip Cookies with a Twist . . .194

Happily Ever After. 207

Once upon a time,
every month or so,
three girls and their mother
put on a little lipstick, just for fun,
and get to work.

They bake a cake,
the more layers the better.
And they do something good for others,
like give to **charity**.

Occasionally the cake falls over,
but it is still A+ delicious.
So they make a wish,
blow out the candle

and live
happily ever after.

Chapter 1

Cereal for Dinner

I suppose I should not have been the least bit surprised to look around one day and find myself living a life filled with cereal. In my pantry, of course, in cereal boxes where cereal belongs. And in other places, too, outside of the cereal box. Like in the car, between the driver's seat and the console, the same impossible place that grabs lipsticks and never lets them go. In my salad. In the tub of Legos that seems to exist solely to be dumped all over the floor at least once a week by little girls. In a few of my cakes when I am attempting to be nutritious. Even stuck in a princess's hair when the cereal is the sugary kind.

It was cereal that got me thinking one morning as I was drying my hair and getting ready for work, attempting to keep an eye on what the round brush was doing to my bangs while little girls raided my lipstick drawer instead of getting ready for school. Which is what they should have been doing. "Please go eat breakfast," I asked for a third time, raising my voice enough to be heard above the screaming hairdryer. Actually a little louder than that because I was getting irritated. At least I said please. "Fix yourselves some cereal and then put your shoes on." No please that time.

Cereal again. What is it with cereal, anyway, I thought. My heart sank as I remembered a mother I saw a few weeks earlier at a business lunch. She was describing the pumpkin pancakes she had made her kids for breakfast that morning. Of course this mother looked like a cross between a supermodel and a Disney princess, and she was really nice, too, which made her all the more threatening. I listened to her real-life fairy tale in awe. Pumpkin pancakes. Wow. My three kids living at home eat cereal. Every day. So do the two in college. After all, they learned from me.

What kind of mother am I, anyway, having my kids eat cereal for breakfast every single day? Cereal is a perfectly fine breakfast food, I reassured myself. Most of the time it is even fortified with vitamins and minerals. Then my heart sank further when I considered the fact that I serve cereal for dinner a lot, too, and sometimes even for lunch on the weekends. That is probably not something that would earn me an A in the good mother category.

I kept thinking about the qualifications for a good mother as I added a sixth layer of mascara to repair any melting that the hairdryer might have caused. What does it take to be a good mother? How much cereal, really, can you serve and still qualify as a good mother? How many times do you have to make pumpkin pancakes before you get a lifetime designation of good mother? Can you never, ever, serve pumpkin pancakes for breakfast and still qualify as a good mother?

Then I started thinking about all of the other roles I have in my life and whether I was any good at those, either. A good sister? A good daughter? A good friend? A good employee? A socially responsible citizen doing good for the world? Was I a good anything? A good everything?

Think of the thousands of little but tricky decisions we make every day, all in an attempt to check our good girl boxes, I thought to myself. Swing by the grocery store, or stay at the salon long enough for the nails to dry? Meet a friend for coffee for her birthday, or fit in a workout? Show up at the school book fair, or show up at an office staff meeting? Serve cereal for breakfast, or make pumpkin pancakes? That last one obviously did not apply to me.

By 7:59 a.m. my hair was dry and I managed to load the princesses, now fortified with cereal, into the back of the car. Complete with backpacks and shoes that matched. Victory! We were on our way. I took a deep breath, backed out of the garage and opened up my can of all-natural grape soda. "Hurry, Mom!" said my ultra-responsible youngest child. "We'll be late!"

We had plenty of time. What she really meant was that she wanted the car to keep moving. She is the child who as an infant would scream as loud as she could whenever the car stopped at a traffic light. I put the car into drive. I took a sip of all-natural grape soda. I reached for the cup of fiber cereal that was my breakfast. The same breakfast I had eaten on the way to work every single day for almost ten years. And I hit the gas with enthusiasm to satisfy the anxious daughter. "We're off!" I declared. And we were. We were on our merry way. To our happy, busy days. Happy, busy days in the lives of a working mother and her three little princesses.

Ten minutes later the kids were safely at school and I had an empty back seat. And a 30-minute drive to the office. And a nearly full cup of cereal and a half-full can of all-natural grape soda. I also had a preoccupied mind. I was still thinking about cereal. And pancakes. And what it takes to be a good mother. And a good wife. And a good friend, a good sister, a good employee, a good citizen. I was thinking about what it takes to be a good girl.

Maybe, I thought, it would be worthwhile to start jotting down a few notes about what the definition of a good girl is to me, a road map of ideas for living life as a close-to-perfect—or even just good enough—modern female. Maybe this could be my next big endeavor, that next giant project after I finish cleaning out my closet, filing away that stack of cake recipes, getting rid of old lipsticks and reorganizing the basement. Actually, maybe I should just skip the closet and the basement altogether and get down to business right away.

And so I did. I started that night. Well, sort of. I started with something small. Very small. I started with a simple definition, my own definition, of what "good girl" means to me. I wrote it down just before I went to bed. After I had kissed the girls good night and thanked them for fixing their own cereal for breakfast that morning and for eating cereal for dinner. And after I had kicked off my heels, dress pants and blouse, rumpled from a day of sitting behind my desk and at tables in meeting rooms in the office. And after I had carefully removed six layers of mascara, still perfectly intact after more than 14 hours on the job.

I pulled a little pink notebook out of my purse and I found my favorite pen. Here is what I wrote: According to me, in no particular order, a good girl has good ideas. A good girl makes good cakes. A good girl is good at work. A good girl does good. A good girl looks good. A good girl has fun.

It looked pretty good to me.

Anyone who knows me will tell you that I am never without a little notebook in my purse. The notebook is usually pink. When I fill one up I immediately replace it with a new one. I keep all of the completed notebooks in a secret place in my closet where I hide things like chocolate and Sharpies and birthday presents to keep them safe from curious little girls. But the notebooks are always where I can reach them. Easy access is important because I review a notebook or two every once in a while when I need a dose of self-referential inspiration or self-reassurance that I really am making progress in life.

Each of my notebooks is filled with things I love. Regular things, of course, such as to do lists and grocery lists. And other things, too, like cake designs and ideas for fun ways to give to charity and varieties of wines I hope to try and notes about lipstick colors. And names I could have named female children if I somehow had wound up with eleven girls instead of just five. And lots of other little things and big things, all sorts of life's gifts, from the gloriously mundane to the nearly outrageous. I love the purse-size pink notebook. It is my diary.

A definition of "good girl." That was what I wrote in my diary that night, at the end of that day, once upon a time when my princesses had eaten cereal for breakfast. And dinner. Again.

When I put down my pen that night, I was actually excited to give this whole good girl thing a whirl. I promised myself that at least two or three times a month I would write down an idea in my notebook about some aspect of being a good girl, according to my own standards. A diary of a good girl would be fun. And it might raise my game just a bit, as a mother, as a stepmother, as a daughter, as a sister, as a friend, as a wife, as an employee, as a giver to charity, as a cake-baker, as a writer, as a socially responsible citizen, as an aspiring good girl. And it would give me something to think about on my commute downtown every morning, adding a little interest to my fiber cereal and all-natural grape soda.

Before I dozed off I had a drowsy, fleeting thought that an effort to be better might even convert me from a cereal mom to a pancake mom. I quickly came to my senses. No way could any amount of self-improvement ever make that happen. Cereal is everywhere in my universe. And not only in the present. I can safely bet that cereal is sprinkled into the nooks and crannies of my future. And it is absolutely swept underneath every sofa cushion of my past. Which means that any diary of a good girl I were to dream up for myself and write down in a series of purse-size pink notebooks would have to include a few ideas about cereal. For breakfast, lunch and especially for dinner.

"Maybe I am not really worried about the cereal," I said, talking it over as my mother and I snacked on a few Lucky Charms one Sunday afternoon, not long after I had started my diary of a good girl. We were sitting at my kitchen counter, which is where most of our best conversations occur. I was beating myself up a bit about the amount of cereal our family consumes. Really, how many families devote three full shelves in a pantry to dry cereal? I even have my very own shelf.

"Maybe my cereal guilt is just a cover up for something else, a way for me to avoid addressing what's really bothering me." My mother did not get a chance to respond because one of the children burst into the kitchen requesting Cinnamon Toast Crunch for lunch. Which, of course, I fixed right away. Which my daughter ate, but not very gracefully. Which meant that most of the cereal ended up on the floor. Which, of course, required three wipe downs because a mixture of cinnamon and sugar is really sticky. After all of that, my mother had to leave to get home for dinner. Not cereal. My mother and I would have to finish our cereal conversation another time.

I woke up the next morning still thinking about cereal. What was the matter with me? Cereal seemed to be taking over. My first recollection of cereal is so vivid that any day now I expected to discover a tattered photograph tucked underneath old baby clothes and birthday party invitations, buried in a box in a corner of the basement.

There I would be in that picture, perched on a chair in the kitchen, once upon a time when I was barely 3 years old, happily eating a bowl of Quisp and watching the sun come up with my dad, wondering why in the world he would rather eat Raisin Bran than Quisp. Quisp is so delicious! It is like a flattened Cap'n Crunch, only with fewer calories. Then again, Raisin Bran is still in every grocery store and Quisp is often hard to find, so he was probably right. Fathers are mostly right, even when it comes to cereal.

My mother is a cereal expert of sorts, too. She is one of those cereal blenders. Her mornings start with Special K and Cheerios with a little All Bran mixed in, the whole thing sprinkled with two spoonfuls of sugar scooped from the Armetale bowl that still sits in the cabinet in the white house with black shutters on the street where I grew up in Lawrence, Kansas.

So cereal is everywhere! No wonder I am not a pumpkin pancake mom. "I really do need to figure out what's eating me," I muttered to myself as I merged onto the highway into the Monday morning traffic, my fiber cereal clutched in one hand and the steering wheel clutched in the other. I am surrounded by cereal. Raisin Bran, Quisp, all of it. It dawned on me that the box of Quisp that was etched permanently in my memory at the age of three might have been the last box of sugar cereal I was allowed to eat until high school. Which was when I got a driver's license. And a job at the Dairy Queen drive-through window. Which meant that I could drive myself to the store to buy Apple Jacks with my own money. And believe me, I did.

"It is perfectly understandable that I am cereal-obsessed," I said out loud in the car to make myself feel better. "Things like this always start during childhood." In a household managed by a Raisin Bran dad and an All Bran Cheerios Special K mom, sweet cereal fell into the category of non-nutritious. Which is actually true, as much as I hate to admit it. Sweet cereal was not invited into the house. With one glorious exception. My parents rewarded my brother and sister and me with one box, each, of our choice of sweet cereal if we brought home good report cards. This perk was available for every other grading period, the ones attached to parent-teacher conferences. That meant two whole boxes of sweet cereal every year. And we did not have to share! It was better than Christmas.

The three of us plotted for months which type of cereal we would pick if we got good grades. And we always got good grades. How could we not, with such an irresistible incentive? We would eat two huge bowls of our bounty the moment we arrived home from the store. Then we would stash our boxes in the cereal cabinet, high above the stove, tucking the top of the stay-fresh bag into a secret fold so that we would be able to immediately detect any invasions from siblings or otherwise. Years later, as embarrassing as it is to admit, I checked a 20-pound bag of serving-sized boxes of Apple Jacks and Fruit Loops on an airplane, taking them home from college as a Christmas gift for my cereal-loving brother and sister. They were still living at home at the time and therefore still subject to the sugar ban, which was thoughtfully lifted for this occasion.

My mother is full of good ideas. She made an interesting observation. "This cereal for dinner concept is bigger than just cereal, you know," she said when I called her on the drive home from work that same Monday. I wanted to continue the kitchen counter conversation from the day before, picking up where we had left off when the Cinnamon Toast Crunch had interrupted our Lucky Charms. My mother continued. "You should run with the cereal for dinner idea in that new diary of yours."

Really? It turns out, according to my mother, that serving yourself the same thing over and over for dinner, and even for breakfast and lunch, has many advantages that extend well beyond the cereal category. This is mostly because you are creating useful patterns for meals that are easy to replicate. Fixing cereal for dinner means that you will develop the ability to establish meal traditions that easily can save you countless hours of cookbook scouring and menu deliberating. You will find yourself happily settling into a welcome routine of preparing the same five or six recipes every time you are charged with hosting a gathering.

My mother said not to worry about the food getting boring. "There is magic in repetition," she assured me. And I had to agree with her. After all, I really did enjoy eating a cup of fiber cereal every morning on the way to work. I saw no reason to change my breakfast plan. "Lose the guilt over the fact that you repeat yourself," my mother said knowingly. She explained that at first you might worry that you will feel bad about constantly repeating your menus, wondering whether your guests are thinking, chicken salad again? But you can easily avoid this concern from the very beginning, declaring early in your entertaining career something dramatic and sweeping and fun like "It's a tradition! Barbara's famous chicken salad at my house, every time!" In general, people appreciate certainty. Your regular guests actually will look forward to your traditions. They might even be disappointed if you stopped.

I think my mother is exactly right. We spent a full twelve minutes on the phone that Monday evening discussing how much we loved the wild rice soup we used to have for lunch every year on Christmas Day at my aunt's house. That was before our family converted to brunch on Christmas instead of lunch. I have the most incredible aunt who really could be a caterer, and not just the pretend kind like me. Everything she makes, brunch or lunch, could be served at a five-star restaurant.

I do have wonderful aunts. Another of my aunts is also a devotee of the repeat menu plan. Every spring, she rounds up all of the cousins and the cousins-once-removed for a picnic in the park. It is quite a crew! Between my three little girls and my aunt's five grandsons, we pretty much take over the park. My aunt always brings a big box of bagels and cream cheese. It is one of the highlights of our year. I hope she never switches to quiche.

"What about the All Toast Dinner?" my mother asked when we both had wiped away a few wistful tears lamenting the end of the wild rice soup era. I was still on the phone in the car fighting the rush hour traffic and at that point I really didn't care if I messed up my mascara. My mother continued, "You know, the dinner where you serve nothing but toast. Can you add that to your diary of good girl ideas?" I told her that was a little tricky because of toast's lack of nutritional diversity. The good girl ideas were supposed to be healthy and wholesome, at least in theory. Unless the idea concerned cake, which breaks all of the rules.

"You should add the All Toast Dinner," my mother insisted. "Once, the morning after I served an All Toast Dinner, I saw a cartoon in *The New Yorker* with a picture of a man tossing a toaster and two pieces of toast out the window and a caption that read 'The Last All

Toast Dinner in Apartment 5B." You have to add it to the diary."

How could I argue with *The New Yorker*? By the time we got off the phone, my mother had convinced me that the All Toast Dinner was a close enough cousin to cereal for dinner to make it into the diary of a good girl. Use the All Toast Dinner sparingly, though, because even my mother admits that it does not work as well as cereal for dinner. And no girl ever wants her Prince Charming to catapult a toaster into the backyard. Or does she?

For the record, my dad has never thrown a toaster or any other appliance into the yard, or anywhere else for that matter. Neither has my husband. My husband has, however, had to dig our own toaster out of the trash, twice, following one of my near meltdowns over little girls spilling cinnamon and sugar all over the kitchen floor after fixing themselves something other than cereal for breakfast. As I explained to my own Prince Charming on one of those occasions, in self-defense, "As useful as a toaster may be for making cinnamon toast, I have never seen a recipe for cake that requires a toaster. Plus, toast tastes better when it's made under the broiler because one side of the bread stays a little soft." He still rescued the toaster.

I was almost home. "Okay," I said to my mother. "Give me that recipe and I will write it in the diary tonight." Here is how my mother described the All Toast Dinner: "You must serve at least a dozen slices of toast, arranged beautifully on a serving platter with sides of jams, cinnamon, sugar and butter. Feel free to add variety to the meal by cutting the toast into triangles, rectangles and squares. Consider even using multiple types of bread. But French toast does not count." Got it!

Cereal for dinner is such a good idea! At least it is in my opinion. And my mother thinks it is a good idea, too. Which counts for a lot. That evening I consulted our kingdom's expert-in-residence, my husband, Prince Charming, to see if I was way off. My husband knows something about everything. Truly. I do not ever need to read a newspaper or watch a news program or check out a news website because Prince Charming tells me everything I need to know in the morning as I am drying my hair in front of the mirror and the princesses are eating cereal in the kitchen. And my husband eats cereal for dinner, too! He really is Prince Charming.

"Don't you think cereal is underestimated?" I asked Prince Charming in our closet as I clipped my favorite black pants back onto the hanger. "Surely there is no food category that comes in as many varieties as dry cereal. It takes up at least one side of an entire grocery store aisle! Not even canned soup does that! This means the possibilities are endless." He looked at me a little funny. "Are you still worried about the pumpkin pancake thing?" he asked. Quite insightful of him. Impressive, actually. "Oh, not really," I said, fudging because the truth was that the pumpkin pancake thing had rocked my world. "But I sometimes wonder if we eat too much cereal around here." Bless his heart, his cheerful response was simply, "I like cereal."

So do I. Over the years my favorites have included Buckwheats (remember those?), Grape Nuts Flakes and the truly exceptional Kashi line of breakfast products. Go Lean and Go Lean Crunch are standouts. All of those are nutritious cereals. Among the quasi-nutritious cereal greats are Frosted Flakes, Honey Bunches of Oats and Alphabits. Then there are the decadent varieties, like Fruity Pebbles. And Cookie Crisp. And, my true love, my calorie-counting nemesis, Peanut Butter Cap'n Crunch.

Never, ever insult cereal by assuming that it must always be paired with milk and served in a bowl with a spoon. The culinary options for cereal are wide-ranging, to put it mildly. For example, cereal has many exceptional qualities when called upon to serve as a fiber-booster to a health-conscious main course. I highly recommend experimenting with cereal whenever possible. One idea is to consider adding seven-grain puffs, at a mere 70 calories per cup, to your salad to add an entertaining crunch. Or, even better, stir a little cereal into Greek yogurt and sprinkle it with cinnamon, and artificial sweetener, too, if you refuse like I do to believe all of the terrible things they say about those magical substances. Presto! You can enjoy a treat as close to a McDonald's McFlurry as you can get for a fraction of the investment in calories.

I studied my diary entries before I crawled into bed. Cereal for dinner. Not bad! Not bad at all. A diary of a good girl. Starting with cereal. Who knows where this could lead? I put away the pink notebook with a little more respect than when I had opened it just ten minutes before. And then I turned on my laptop. Even though it was way past my bedtime. I opened up a new Google page. Out of curiosity, I typed in "diary of a good girl." Well, well! The domain had not been taken. Surely this was a sign? "I'll reserve it tomorrow," I said to myself.

And I did. I figured it was one of those things that might come in handy someday. Kind of like the two hundred lipsticks stored in a yellow hat box in my closet. And the dozens of cake recipes stacked carefully on a shelf in the kitchen cabinet between the crystal cake stand from Tiffany and my stash of birthday candles. Domain names, lipsticks, cake recipes. You just never know when things like that might prove to be the keys to the kingdom of your future.

Chapter 2

Cake for Dessert

I don't really eat cereal for every meal. I eat salad and soup and fish and chicken and multi-grain flats and turkey and chocolate and nuts and vegetables and other things that normal people eat. And I eat cake. A lot of cake.

I love cake. I have loved cake for almost as long as I have loved cereal. Maybe it is because I have always loved to bake anything and everything, from cookies by the hundreds to gingerbread houses by the dozens. Maybe it is because I love to celebrate even the smallest joys in life, and what's a celebration without a cake? Maybe it is because there is no such thing as a problem so daunting that it cannot be cured with a big piece of cake. Maybe it is because cakes are for parties, for dressing up, for having fun. Maybe it is because cake really is delicious. Especially if you know how to open up a box of Betty Crocker cake mix and adjust the recipe just a tiny bit. I promise, there is no better place to start making a really good cake than with Betty Crocker. Made from scratch is just hype.

Cake for dessert. This is always a good idea. Cake works well as a dessert, anytime, even following a dinner of cereal. The cake idea prompted me, a few weeks into the good girl project, to call my mother. As I so often do when a good idea pops into my head. No one is better at discussing a good idea than my mother.

"Hi!" I said. That's the way I start every conversation with my mother. Followed by the briefest of pauses to allow her to say "hi" back before I launch right into the idea, barely taking a breath. "Remember that diary? The one I am keeping in my pink notebook? The one about being a good girl? Well I've started jotting down all sorts of ideas about cake. I think cake will be the second major topic in my diary of a good girl, right after cereal." The sting of the pumpkin pancakes was wearing off just a bit. And I was beating myself up a little less about serving Cinnamon Toast Crunch as a main course. I deserved to move on to cake.

"I love cake!" said my mother. That is precisely what I had hoped she would say. My mother is wonderful. "Do you happen to have Grandmother's cake recipes?" I asked. "I thought it would be fun to test a lot of different cakes to see which ones are best. We can find out if I am really right about a Betty Crocker cake tasting better than one from scratch." My mother loved this idea. She kindly did not say anything about the fact that switching my food obsession from cereal to cake was not going to solve whatever it was that was really bothering me. Although I am sure she was thinking it. "I'll look for the recipes this week!" she said. "It would be so much fun for you to make them."

Prince Charming was more direct. "What's with all the cakes?" he asked a couple weeks later after I had spent three days in the kitchen testing recipes. "Are you okay?" He looked at me curiously. "I am fine," I said cheerfully. "I just love cake." Thankfully he did not ask any more questions and we just left it at that. After all, Prince Charming was enjoying the cakes, too. He really likes cake. He prefers the moist ones that involve fruit and not much frosting.

And it was true, of course, that I really do love cake. Which was at least part of the explanation for my prolific baking. Even now, many months after this whole thing started, I still bake a lot of cakes. I try to keep at least three boxes of cake mix in the pantry at all times. And I store my cake pans in the oven because it is so convenient. Sometimes there is so much cake in the house that I sit down for dinner at the kitchen counter with a big slice of fluffy white cake with buttercream frosting as my main course while my three littlest children dine on macaroni and cheese or Cinnamon Toast Crunch. "Why do you get to eat cake for dinner?" they ask. "Because I want to," I reply. "And when you are old, you can, too."

Something I know for sure is that cake has mystical powers. For example, one of the best ways to ensure that all of your wishes come true is to keep a little cake on hand at all times. Frequently all you will need is a bite of cake before bed to send you off to sweet dreams of castles and kings and queens and fairy tales. Other times a small slice after dinner does the trick. And every so often, when the dragons are roaring or your job at the office is wearing you down or Prince Charming is out of town or has temporarily lost the charming part, you just might need the whole cake.

If you are a girl who loves cake as much as I do, or even almost as much as I do, one of the best ideas I can share is to never, ever allow your cake supply to dwindle. The best way to guard against a cake shortage is to host frequent parties. Even if the guest list is comprised only of people who live with you. Always bake a cake for the party no matter what the occasion. And be sure to bake a big cake. This will ensure that there will be plenty left over for you to wrap and freeze for future desserts and emergencies. Better yet, bake an extra cake.

Just recently my mother had a cake emergency. She knew who to call. "Hi!" said my mother. She starts our conversations with a cheerful "hi," just like I do. "Do you still happen to have that raspberry red velvet dark chocolate cake in your freezer? The one that is shaped like a rose? I am having people for lunch on Tuesday and I really could use a delicious dessert." See? Bake and freeze plenty of cake.

If, heaven forbid, after dinner one evening you discover that you do not have any leftover cake hidden away in the back of your freezer, you can have cereal for dessert. Even if you ate bran flakes for dinner. Just select one of the marshmallow types so you will satisfy your craving for something sweet. A good choice is Lucky Charms, which my mother and I both love. Or, during Halloween season, Boo Berry, Frankenberry or Count Chocula. Most of these marshmallow-enhanced cereals are surprisingly low in calories, considering that they are impressively sweet and crunchy. Often an entire cup contains fewer than 150 calories.

I throw out all of my calorie rules when it comes to cake for dessert. Cake is completely exempt. Aside from cake, though, I generally stick with a 150-calorie benchmark for desserts. This is the calorie count of not only a cup of many sugar cereals, but it is also the calorie count of the beloved McDonald's ice cream cone, perhaps the world's most satisfying low calorie dessert. Although it could never rise to the level of cake, a special quality of the McDonald's ice cream cone is that it comes with an opportunity to do good if you drop a little change in the Ronald McDonald House collection box at the drive-through window or inside the store.

I know my mother likes McDonald's ice cream cones, too. Once I saw her in the drive-through after we had both been visiting my grandmother at the retirement home. We had driven separate cars. My mother had left just a couple of minutes before I did because I had to buckle the girls into their car seats. My mother had a head start on the road. "There's Gran!" my daughter had said when she spotted my mother's tan Volvo turning into McDonald's. We were stopped at a red light. When the light turned green, I slipped into the drive-through line a few cars behind my mother. She never knew I was there. All the girls had ice cream that day.

An ice cream run can be almost as magical as cake. The Ronald McDonald House people have told me that friendly customers give more than $25 million to Ronald McDonald House Charities each year, just by tossing a little spare change into these drop boxes. That is a lot! And for such a great cause!

An additional do-good bonus of the McDonald's ice cream cone is the fact that your children will witness an act of generosity every time you tell the drive-through attendant to put the change in the box. Honestly I think I have eaten a McDonald's ice cream cone at least every week for the past eleven years. My girls know the drill. "Did you give the money, Mom?" one of them always asks. I love it that they check up on me.

So the ice cream does good. And it tastes good. But I like cake better.

"I'm really getting into this cake project," I told my mother when I called to recruit her to help me try a few more of the recipes I had gathered. Of course, my mother cheerfully agreed to pitch in. And she still did not ask why I was doing so much baking. Just as she had never asked why I was suddenly so worried about serving cereal for breakfast, lunch and dinner. Or why I was feeling guilty about never making pancakes. Or why I had decided to fill my diary with an analysis of whether I was good enough. And, really, there would not have been much point in her asking any of those questions. Because I did not know the answers myself. At least not then.

We had so much fun with the cakes. The best part was that it gave my mother and me a lot of time together at my kitchen counter, mixing and stirring and testing and layering. And chatting. "Don't you think the repetitive meal patterns you establish with cereal and favorite recipes can apply equally well to cake for dessert?" I asked one afternoon when we were figuring out how much vanilla we should add to the batter. The batter we had started from a box of Betty Crocker white cake mix. The batter we were doctoring up with our own ingredients. Not haphazardly, of course. We were using a few of the scratch recipes for general guidance.

"Don't you think," I continued in leading question format, "that if you have a lot of children, or a lot of people in your life for whom you are assigned the birthday cake, you should stick with the same thing every year for each person? As long as you make sure the recipients actually like what they get since they'll be getting those cakes from you for decades?"

Of course my mother concurred. She had to agree! I had been repeating cakes for years and she is too nice ever to hurt my feelings. At my house when the birthdays roll around, each of my three daughters and each of my two stepdaughters has her own signature birthday cake. One daughter has chosen an ice cream cake, another picks out a delicious torte from our favorite Swiss bakery, another actually likes the grocery store variety and two of the girls love a multi-layer homemade extravaganza.

As fantastic as the repeat menu plan is for cereal, cake, special recipes and so much more, you must be careful not to overdo it. According to my parents. And they are pretty smart. "Moderation in all things," my dad says, quoting Aristotle. "Including moderation," he always adds. That last part is not Aristotle. That's my smart dad. My mother reminded me of my father's wisdom as we added just a tad more vanilla to the test batter. "There is such a thing as too much," she said. "Too much cake. And too much cereal." I said nothing. I said nothing because I'm not so sure about too much cake.

But I do think you can go overboard on the cereal. I once confessed, live on the radio, that I had served my houseful of good girls Trix cereal for breakfast, lunch and dinner. All in the same day. Granted, it was a Saturday, and granted, Prince Charming was out of town. But based on the disapproving reaction from radio listeners, Prince Charming's absence was probably not a good excuse for a cereal triple play. Especially with the same cereal. And not a nutritious cereal, either. Especially considering that the last meal of the day was self-serve for the children whose mother was parked at the kitchen counter, working hard on the good girl diary. And skipping the cereal for dinner. And clutching a very large 70% cacao dark chocolate bar in one hand and a can of all-natural grape soda in the other. Obviously there was no cake in the freezer that weekend.

After spending a few weekends hovering over the mixing bowl, with several dozen cakes under our belts, my mother and I decided that we were ready to test a really big idea. A big idea involving cake. My dad's birthday was just a week away. What if we came up with a way to celebrate this milestone, adding a little generosity to the usual menu of cake and ice cream? I had recently heard about a national organization based in Kansas City that provides tips, programs and training for fathers who want to be better dads. Perfect! We would make a donation in honor of my dad, who really is the best dad in the world. And I would bake a really big cake. We would turn his birthday party into a celebration that gives back. This would be fun! With a thumbs up from my mom, the plan was in action.

"I have an idea!" I said to my mother when we were at my kitchen counter making plans for the party. "Let's use dad's birthday party as an excuse to host a good old fashioned cake-off! We'll see whose cake is better. Grandmother's, or Betty Crocker's." Naturally, my wonderful mother agreed. "Dad would love that!" she declared.

And it was fun! We invented the Retro Birthday Cake, a six-layer extravaganza, its sides dotted with little purple fondant circles and its top adorned with brightly-colored plastic candle holders from the 1950s. The 1950s was when my grandmother was baking cakes for my dad's birthdays. I was pretty sure my grandmother would not have approved of cereal for dinner. This is because she was a fabulous cook. She used her stove for breakfast, lunch and dinner. But my grandmother most certainly would have approved of cake for dessert. And Betty Crocker would, too, of course. I was becoming Betty's best customer.

"You should try this idea!" I recommended enthusiastically to my friends. The ones who are not afraid to tell me when I am getting too thin. I was telling them about the cake-off after it was all over. "Whose cake do you think was better? Betty Crocker's, or my grandmother's?" They could not answer the question.

So, I explained that a cake-off like this produces real competition. Betty Crocker has reigned as Queen of Cake since 1921, when Marjorie Child Husted, a home economist and businesswoman, dreamed up the image of Betty for General Mills.

"But my grandmother is a force to be reckoned with," I said as we sipped our buttery Chardonnay. My own grandmother, Margaret McClymonds (later Margaret McKnight), was born in 1910 in Walton, Kansas. She graduated from college with a degree in home economics. Her career included writing a regular newspaper column offering recipes and culinary advice and later conducting cooking classes on how to use the appliances in the new All-Electric Health Kitchen promoted by the local utility.

"You're really getting into these cakes," remarked one of my friends. I did not acknowledge the comment and instead just carried on. My friends did not mind. They are very dear friends. And they are used to my enthusiasm for new projects.

Of course, as I told my friends, if you want to try a cake-off at home, it will require baking two cakes, one made from Betty's box and one whipped up from scratch according to your grandmother's recipe. But, as I always say, the more layers the better. Why bake just one cake when you can bake two? You've got to bake the same kind of cake, though, to really compare apples to apples, cake to cake. So, for my dad's birthday cake-off, I baked Betty's white cake and Margaret's white cake. Incidentally, it is my recreational pastry chef opinion that white cake is by far the best type of cake in the universe. Although my cereal preferences come and go, I am a die-hard fan of the white cake.

Follow your grandmother's recipe very closely to give her the best odds you can. If you are a brave girl, you can stack all of the layers into one cake, alternating each recipe. Do this only if you are willing to assume the risk of the cake falling over. In my experience, the likelihood of the collapse of a six-layer cake is 19%. Those are not bad odds, considering that 81% of the time you will produce the most dramatic and unusual cake your guests have ever witnessed, for it will be whimsical and lopsided and magically stay standing. And it will be delicious.

Another word to the wise on the cake-off: Be prepared to question the strength of your own family loyalty. My grandmother's formula produced an authentic taste, with a delightfully delicate hint of meringue baked into a traditional structured crumb. But texture reigned in Betty's layers, which boasted a moistness that was most impressive for a cake baked out of a box, supercharged by substituting whole milk for the 1¼ cups of water called for in the package instructions. So, although family loyalty would have declared Grandmother the winner before votes were counted, it turned out that Betty's texture tipped the scales, eleven to one. Indeed, although the contestants were evenly matched at six and six on flavor alone, the net result was a victory for the cake out of the box.

And a final note about the cake-off, in case you do try this at home: Be sure to record the comments for reference during future recipe experiments. "Grandmother's cake tasted more real," commented one party-goer. "Grandmother's cake would have been better with more frosting," was another guest's observation. "And soaked in rum." Of course. As with any cake, especially if there is rum anywhere in the mix, be sure to package up the remaining slices and tuck them away safely in the freezer, behind the frozen vegetables where no one cares to venture. Otherwise you will end up eating an entire chocolate bar some Saturday night when Prince Charming is out of town and you've just made the kids fix their own Trix for the third time in twelve hours.

A few days after the cake-off I was thumbing through my grandmother's cake recipes and I noticed something very interesting. There was not a single recipe for cupcakes. Not one! Of course not! I don't think cupcakes had been invented in the 1950s. Even if they had been invented, I am sure cupcakes would not have counted as cake. And I am sure my grandmother would have felt that cupcakes do not count as cake.

That's right. Cupcakes do not count. Please do not allow yourself to be fooled by the cupcake. As convenient, cute and trendy as the cupcake may be, only cake in all its glory will stand the test of time. Since the dawn of pastries, well before Betty Crocker arrived on the baking scene, cake has reigned unchallenged as the most revered icon of celebration, the trademark of a real hostess, the ultimate metaphor for happiness, the most aspirational form of decadent culinary artistic expression, a talisman for wishes coming true and the centerpiece of all of life's events from babies to birthdays, weddings to graduations, and everything in between.

Cake is the perfect dessert, whether it follows a dinner of prime rib or a supper of dry cereal. It is a fact that a little cake or a lot of cake every evening practically guarantees a life full of dreams come true. And, if you wish hard enough, you probably do not even have to blow out the candle to get what you want.

And finally, and perhaps most importantly, I must tell you that the process of cake making is itself worthwhile. As the eggs crack and the mixer whirls, your mind hums along too, dreaming of the future. Dwelling in the gifts of possibilities that this cake and every cake hereafter will bring to your life. Pour the batter into the pans, bake at 350 degrees, lick the bowl and do the dishes.

By the time you pull the layers from the oven, your soul will be filled with lots of good things to add to your own little pink notebook. Ideas for your own diary of a good girl. Good things like the hope of finding your favorite lipstick from a decade ago buried somewhere in the box in your closet. Or a mental sketch of a thorough grocery list for tomorrow's supermarket run. Or new ideas for making it fun to give to charity. Or a great idea for teaching your children to be generous and help others. Or a grandiose plan for reinventing your job so that you can bake more cakes with your kids.

Chapter 3

"This is the best cake I have ever tasted," my mother announced as we sampled the layer we had just pulled from the oven one Sunday afternoon. "It is delicious."

I agreed with her completely. We had done it. Weeks and weeks of testing and tasting and practicing and tinkering and changing and adjusting and tweaking had finally paid off. My mother and I had figured out the magic combination of a handful of easy changes to the recipe on the back of the box of Betty Crocker white cake mix to produce the most fantastic white cake we could have ever imagined. The cake was not just good enough. The cake was perfect.

Easy, fast, inexpensive. And yummy. I wrote that in my diary under the heading Fluffy White Cake. The recipe was so simple that the whole thing fit onto a single page in my purse-size pink notebook. I was writing it down one morning before work. Taking a break between the mascara and the hairdryer. I wrote the recipe so I would not forget: Blend the oil with the cake mix before adding anything else. Use whole milk instead of water. Bring the egg whites and milk to room temperature before adding them slowly, alternating between egg whites and milk, mixing well in between. Add a little vanilla. Add a pinch of salt. Add a little almond extract. Bake according to the instructions on the box.

What a relief, I thought to myself as I willed the round brush to do magic with my hair. What a relief to have accomplished something as simple as creating a recipe using cake mix and a few extra ingredients. I could check the makes-good-cakes box in my good girl diary. A small but meaningful victory.

And I needed that victory. I needed it because I was still wondering whether I was good enough. The dinner menu had not changed much since I had started the good girl diary months ago. I was still serving cereal, often more than once a week. I was still not making pancakes.

No, I was not convinced. Even with all of my cake success, I was not convinced that I was good enough. I was not convinced that I was a good enough mother. Or a good enough stepmother. Or daughter. Or sister. Or friend. Or a good enough anything else for that matter. I still did not think I met even my own simple definition of good girl.

Then I had a new thought as I was putting away the hairdryer. And putting on my earrings. And making sure my phone was in my purse before I attempted to round up three little girls and make my way to the door. This new thought was not about cereal or pancakes or cake. It was about bacon, of all things. Bacon, and work. "I wonder if I am good enough at work?" I asked out loud. I must have been asking the business clothes in my closet because I was all alone. Prince Charming and the princesses were still finishing their cereal in the kitchen.

I called my mother on the way to work that morning. Usually I call my mother in the evenings or on weekends. But every once in a while I call my mother on the way to work. Such as when I have an idea to share that simply cannot wait. Or when I have a strange pain in my side that can be diagnosed and cured only by a mother on the other end of a telephone. Or an interesting situation involving food. This time I was calling my mother with an interesting situation involving food. Specifically, bacon. I took the side streets instead of the highway so that I would be sure to have enough time for a really long conversation. And enough stoplights to eat my cereal.

"Hi!" I said to my mother. I gave her just enough of a window to reply with her own "hi" before I launched into a series of questions.

Questions I had been asking myself several times a day. On that day and on other days, too, once upon a time. Once upon a time when I was stressing about serving too much cereal and never making pumpkin pancakes. And when I was baking all of those cakes. And doing my best to be cheerful by day and cheerful by night. Once upon a time during a time that now seems like a long time ago.

My mother was such a good sport on the other end of the phone. I tend to talk way too fast and use complicated words when I am distraught. So all of the questions came out like one big, messy, academic sentence. Kind of like the sentences I had attempted when I used to practice law.

"Is it really possible for the air in an office to be filled with bacon grease when the bacon is being fried more than 500 yards away? Is it really possible for a well-meaning sub-subcontractor doing renovations to an office building restaurant to construct, accidentally, a ventilation system with an exhaust hood above the grill and deep fat fryer that is somehow directly connected to the ceiling blower in a nearby office? Is it really possible for bacon grease to travel from an office building restaurant to an office on the opposite side of the office building?"

There was a long pause on the other end of the line. I knew my mother well enough to catch on that her silence meant that I was not making sense. I tried it again, slowly, without all of the lawyer-speak. And I used statements, not questions. "There is a bacon smell in my office at work," I told my mother in the most normal voice I could muster. "And the smell gets in my hair. And it makes it hard for me to do my job."

She got it. "Oh," she said. "That really is bad. That's worse than sitting next to someone wearing bad perfume." My mother was right. I would have given anything at that point for bad perfume.

As funny as it sounds, your office really can smell like bacon. This can happen when an exhaust hood above the grill and deep fat fryer in an office building restaurant is connected, through the ventilation system, directly to your office. Which means that everything cooked on that grill and by that deep fat fryer in that restaurant ends up in your office. Not literally, of course, but in aromatic form. The french fries, the onion rings, the fish, the hamburgers. And the bacon. Especially the bacon.

I complained for seven minutes. Then I felt bad about being negative. So I tried to look on the bright side. "Maybe I am lucky that this is happening," I said to my mother as I waited at a stop sign for another mother pushing a stroller and wearing cute workout clothes to cross the street. "After all, I am lucky to have a job. I am lucky to have a job I love. I am lucky to have a job I love in an office I love in a building I love. Even with the bacon. Besides, the bacon is giving me a lot of ideas for the good girl diary."

And the bacon really was giving me some great material. I had started jotting down all sorts of good ideas in my pink notebook. Under a heading I titled Why Bacon Exhaust in Your Office is a Very Good Thing.

The first item that appeared on this list is one of the most noticeable and useful perks of having this situation happen to you. You are free to remove all of the clocks from your office, releasing yourself from traditional notions of time. Instead of looking at the clock, you can rely on the nature of the fumes coming through the ceiling vents to keep track of the hours.

For instance, bacon fumes signal it is 7:30 a.m. to 9:00 a.m., followed by the daily lunch special, which typically is deep fat fried between approximately 9:30 a.m. and 11:00 a.m. Fish seems to require near real-time preparation, so the seafood wave usually hits your desk at 11:30 a.m. French fries and onion rings mark the midday rush between 11:30 a.m. and 1:30 p.m. The remainder of the day is more of a mystery, but in general you can be pretty sure that it is later than 1:30 p.m. but earlier than 3:00 p.m. if you are catching a whiff of grill cleaner mixed with lingering grease. By 3:00 p.m., the flow is down to nothing, and that's how you know there are only two business hours left in the day.

"The bacon has its benefits," I told my mother. "I no longer need to wear a watch to the office. So much more room on my wrists for cute bracelets!" My mother agreed. What else could she do? Then she added, "I am sure it will all be just fine." For the record, when mothers say that, it is almost guaranteed to turn out to be true. Mothers just know. "Keep writing about the cakes," she recommended. "The bacon is just a distraction."

And I did. I kept right on testing and mixing and tinkering and wrote it all down in my diary. By this time I was working on inventing frosting to go with the fluffy white cake. "I think my cake obsession is here to stay," I said on the phone the next time I called my mother. It was Saturday night. The princesses were asleep. I was celebrating the weekend by sitting at my kitchen counter with a big slice of fluffy white cake. Which I had carefully hidden in the freezer for just such a celebration. "This cake even freezes well. It is delicious."

My mother made a very good point. "Deli exhaust blowing into your office actually reinforces your diary idea that eating cereal for dinner and cake for dessert makes so much sense," she said. "Cereal involves no grilling and frying. And neither does cake." Right!

And it was true. I really had developed a much greater appreciation for cake. Baking a cake smells so good! There is a reason every line of glass jar candles includes a scent that smells like birthday cake. Pure heaven, those candles. Candle people are savvy. I know this because I have a dear friend who used to work for a candle company. Make no mistake, there is margin in candles. People will pay a lot for aromatics.

Cereal for dinner, cake for dessert. My mother was right. Neither requires a deep fat fryer or a grill. It is the perfect formula for avoiding bacon fumes altogether.

"Here is another benefit," I said to my mother. We were having fun looking on the bright side. "I wrote this one in the diary, too." I told her about my idea that if you happen to be a cereal for dinner and cake for dessert girl who sometimes is tempted to stray to the french fry food group, a glitch in the ventilation system at work could be the very best thing that ever happened to your diet. Just as the deep inhalation of dark chocolate has been suggested as an appetite suppressant, breathing fried food aromas for eight hours a day will leave you feeling full. And satisfied. And craving a workout. "In fact," I said, "my lunch of spinach leaves wrapped in 90-calorie multi-grain flats tastes so delicious that I feel like I've just eaten Grandmother's fried chicken." I elaborated, "Especially if I spread a little butter on the flats."

I also shared with my mother that my desk is always shiny. "It's grease, yes, but it looks and feels so much like furniture polish that

I am sure my visitors are impressed with my sparkly work environment." I did not share with her the rest of that idea because it was a little odd. But I did write it in my diary. The rest of the idea is that your hair will be shiny, too. It is possible that you will be able to stop using hair conditioner altogether, creating a modest savings to your beauty budget or giving you extra cash to spend on cake mix, more frequent pedicures and donations to your favorite charities.

I chatted on about this for another 11 minutes. Then I could tell my mother was just listening politely, pretending to be interested. At that point in the conversation I think she was ready to get off the phone. Bacon exhaust in an office. As if this would ever happen to my mother! It was highly unlikely. Especially in light of the fact that her office building does not have a deli. "I am not worried that the bacon fumes will make me gain weight," I continued. I had to get in just one last idea. "They will not. You can't gain weight just by smelling something fattening. Breathing bacon is not the same thing as eating bacon."

On that hopeful note we said our goodbyes. I put down my phone. I finished my cake. I thought about everything my mother had said. And I thought about everything my mother had not said. I am sure that what my mother had wanted to say during that conversation but did not was that I really should try to figure out why the bacon exhaust was pouring into my office in the first place. Not the mechanical reason, the lowercase "why." The lowercase "why" is always a construction or engineering problem, relatively easy for the building people to eventually fix. I am talking about the capital "Why." Why is this happening? What kind of a sign is this? What is this situation telling you about your life? But my wonderful mother did not go there. She has always been so smart about letting me solve my own problems.

I was not quite brave enough to ask myself the "Why?" question. But, to my credit, I was savvy enough to recognize that the bacon infiltrating my office probably was the universe's way of getting even with me. Getting even with me for all the times I prohibited my brother from making bacon, sausage and pancakes before I went out on dates in high school. He has never quite forgotten it. So I figured I had to suffer the consequences for a while, showing up at business meetings reeking like a skillet. My only hope was that all of the knights in shining armor who usually show up at very important meetings—make that Very Important Meetings—were off fighting battles somewhere else in the kingdom on the days that the deli was operating at full throttle.

And it was so wrong of me to deprive my brother of bacon. Borderline mean, actually. He loves bacon. Or at least he did as a kid. Admittedly, I have not asked him recently how he feels about bacon. Maybe I should, just to check for scars. Bacon really was his thing. In fact, when my brother was two, he broke ranks from his nap, climbed out of his crib and sneaked downstairs to get into the refrigerator to eat bacon.

I was thinking about my brother and the bacon a few days later, wishing I had thought to ask my mother about it. But I dared not call her to bring it up myself. The bacon was getting old. Two minutes later, though, my wonderful mind-reading mother actually called *me*. Just to check on the greasy situation in my office. So nice!

I asked my mother if I had remembered things correctly about my brother and bacon. "That is a true story," she confirmed. "I found him, sound asleep on the kitchen floor, surrounded by the remains of an entire package of raw bacon, the refrigerator door wide open." She says he looked so cute, nestled on the linoleum with all of that meat.

"Food can be so confusing," I said to my mother on the telephone. "Why do I love cereal and cake so much but can't stand the smell of bacon frying? And why does a slice of cake taste so much better than a cupcake?" Sometimes my mother and I have the oddest conversations. We sorted this one out, reaching a conclusion logical enough to allow us both to get off the phone feeling satisfied. We decided that, just as cakes should not be confused with cupcakes, bacon should not be confused with turkey. Which is a slightly complicated notion because everyone knows that there is such a thing as turkey bacon. Turkey is a main course, a meat that stands alone. But you can't really lay out a big platter of bacon and call it Thanksgiving. No matter how fancy the platter may be.

Indeed, turkeys have their own style. I learned this when my daughter once proudly showed me her completed homework assignment for school, a drawing of a bright orange bird with numbered buttons all over it. The assignment had been to decorate a paper turkey and disguise it as something else. "Look Mom," she had said. "It's your phone." There was that job again, sneaking into the holidays.

Bacon does have a way of bringing out the best in people. The facility manager at my office building worked diligently for weeks, bringing in various contractors to re-route the vents above my desk so that the grease would pump out somewhere else. In an environmentally friendly way, of course, or at least I assumed so. I worked at a charitable foundation, and I hated to think of diluting all of that doing good with any kind of air pollution.

Really, the building maintenance people were fantastic. They negotiated with the deli to replace the faulty exhaust fans with new ones. They brought in ladders and flashlights to explore what was going on above the ceiling tiles. They checked on me and the bacon at least every other day. All that attention made me feel like a princess in my own castle of bacon. So much so that I kind of missed it when it was all fixed. No more bacon. But that also meant no more knights in shining armor climbing tall towers and rearranging things in the ductwork to eradicate serpents and grease. What girl should be so lucky?

As it turned out, the end of the bacon adventure was only the beginning. In some ways, the bacon grease eventually led me to a new chapter. To a life filled with cakes. And doing good at home and in the workplace. And starting a business. And blogging and writing. And lots of other good things. But the real story is that I had started my adventures as an entrepreneur once upon a time, many years before the bacon grease in my office. Once upon a time when I was a little girl.

That same brother who had put up with my ban on bacon was also the first person to volunteer to test every new product I dreamed up under the auspices of LM Associates, the company I launched in sixth grade with my allowance money. My gracious, bacon-loving brother did not complain at all when the LM Associates team of one converted his bedroom into a library, forcing my brother to check out his own books. And, as he claims, requiring him to pay to use his own toys although I do not remember that part. Nor did that gracious brother complain when I twisted his arm to become my test student for LM Associates' math and reading curriculum, created mainly because I wanted to staple pieces of paper together and fold them into textbooks.

I did not limit product testing to my immediate family. Every Thanksgiving, and a few other times each year, I published a newspaper called *The Family Times*, a collection of updates submitted by parents, siblings, aunts, uncles, cousins, grandparents and extended family. I think I even asked a few people to ghost write updates from their pets. This project lasted seven years, from the time I was in sixth grade through the fall of my first semester in college.

I published the final issue just before my mother served Thanksgiving dinner. This was when *The Family Times* was distributed by my sister whom I had dressed in a turkey costume. Bless her heart, she never asked why she was the one who had to wear the turkey feathers. If she had asked, though, my answer would have been something like, "The publisher is in charge. The publisher not only gets to pick which articles make it into the final copy but the publisher also gets to decide what the distributor wears."

Sometimes my projects involved creating costumes for both my brother and sister. And not just turkey costumes. Once, I produced a living room version of the Blues Brothers in concert. My little sister was a perfect Jake in a white t-shirt with a pillow stuffed underneath it around her stomach. My brother was taller than my sister and looked exactly like Elwood. Especially with the tie we found in my dad's closet. And the glasses we borrowed from both my father and my mother worked perfectly to complete both costumes.

My sister recently reminded me about this. She has always been so supportive of everything I have ever done. Business and otherwise. The Blues Brothers concert fell into the category of otherwise. "You taped black construction paper to the lenses to make sunglasses," she said. "They weren't real sunglasses. That's why all the dancing to 'Rubber Biscuit' was a little shaky. We couldn't see."

My sister and I both recalled that the audience of two loved it. My mom and dad gave the Blues Brothers performance a standing ovation. Although that was probably due to their relief that the singing and dancing had not appeared to have damaged the expensive (and necessary) glasses. As well as the fact that they could not really see the performance without *their* glasses.

Who knows where I would be today if my brother had kicked me out of his room when I was 10 and he was 8? And where would I be today had my little sister not permitted me to throw parties on the patio several times each summer in her honor (and her birthday is in January), so that I could invite all of the neighbor kids over for cake and ice cream and more cake?

And where would I be if my sister had not willingly volunteered to be a client of my before-and-after beauty spa? A brave act, indeed, considering that the photos taken after the makeover were scarier than the ones taken before. Yes, I think perhaps those special people, siblings especially, who indulge our creativity as children give us the greatest gifts of all.

"I'm going to write down just a few more ideas in my diary about Why Bacon Exhaust in Your Office is a Very Good Thing," I told my mother toward the end of the whole episode. "And then I will call this case closed." At this point she and I both were pretty done with bacon. We wanted to get back to cake. Fluffy white cake. And frosting. I still had not come up with a frosting that was quite good enough for such a delicious cake. My mother and I were getting anxious to get back into the test kitchen. And soon.

"A little grease in the ductwork is not all bad," I observed during what would turn out to be our final telephone conversation about the bacon. "In fact," I said, "charitable giving seems to be going up."

Kansas City always ranks high on the list when it comes to generosity. During the bacon months, though, Kansas City boasted some pretty incredible statistics. Individuals in Kansas City with an income of $100,000 or more gave almost twice the national average to charity annually, and the average annual household charitable gift in the Kansas City area was 50% greater than the national average. Coincidence? My enthusiasm for the great work of my colleagues was probably the best thing that ever came out of that corner office.

In the end, exhaust from the office building deli venting directly above my desk turned out to be a very good thing for me. If this happens to you, perhaps your own bacon experience will mark an era of introspection and good ideas. Good ideas that lead to a very good and very happy ending.

If this happens in your life, though, you must also consider the rather scary but exciting possibility that the grease pouring out of the ventilation system into your office is a sign that you are either in the wrong office, in the wrong job, or both. Bacon never lies.

Chapter 4

Test. Taste. Practice. Tinker. Adjust. Change. Tweak. Frosting is much more an art than it is a science. Creativity is required to make a good frosting because you have a wide range of latitude in dreaming up the recipe. Which actually makes it tricky because there are so many options. Options for the type of shortening. Options for the amount of shortening. Options for the type and amount of sugar. Options for the liquid. Options for the extracts. And options for secret ingredients.

By contrast, cake is more science than art. In fact, baking anything, cake or otherwise, involves a lot of chemistry because whatever you are baking has to change form in the oven, not just heat up. No one wants to eat hot cake batter. I take that back. Hot cake batter would be really good. It would be like cake batter soup. Ooh la la! But to convert a liquid cake into a solid cake by putting it in the oven for 22 minutes, the ingredients and proportions have to be just right.

Frosting is an art. There is nothing exact about frosting. That is why it was taking me weeks and weeks of testing to get even remotely close to a product I could fall in love with. I needed a frosting that would beautifully complement the heavenly, delicate flavor and the moist, light crumb of my fluffy white cake. A frosting with enough personality to balance my cake's subtle layers but not too much bravado that the frosting would diminish the cake's gentle elegance.

Frosting is as much about the texture as it is about the flavor. Frosting must melt in your mouth. But not before its flavor emerges. Frosting must taste decadent. But not greasy. Frosting must be sweet but not sugary. Frosting is best when it delivers just a hint of a crunch.

I was making a lot of frosting. I tried lots of recipes. Even my grandmother's recipe. Which was delicious. But it was way too high maintenance according to my busy girl standards. Grandmother's frosting required heating things up on the stove. That is a no-no for any frosting recipe of mine. I have my limits on how much complexity I am willing to take on in the kitchen. Obviously that is the case, considering I sometimes serve cereal for dinner.

I tried a few of the frosting mixes you can buy at the grocery store. I did not like those either. That is another difference between cake and frosting. Cake out of a box is fantastic. Frosting out of a box is not fantastic.

I was out of ideas. Almost. I decided to consult a professional. "What's the best way to make a really good frosting?" I asked the wonderful woman who owns my favorite baking supply shop. I was out on the town on a Saturday afternoon. Prince Charming was at home with the princesses watching the History Channel.

"Just make a standard buttercream. It's the best," the lady said as she rang up three boxes of curly birthday candles and put them into a bag. "The key is to use high-density shortening."

Oh. Well that will not work, I thought to myself. You can only buy high-density shortening in baking supply shops. Which are wonderful places to visit. But my favorite baking supply shop is way across town. And it is full of enticing candles and cookie cutters and cake toppers and candies. And it is dangerous when little girls visit a baking supply shop. Not dangerous for the little girls but dangerous for the contents of the shop. And going out on the town alone was not something I did very often. I prefer to shop with at least one princess. Otherwise I get lonely. High-density shortening simply was not in my realm of possibility.

I was a bit crestfallen. If high-density shortening was the key to a good recipe, I might be out of luck. My dream of the perfect frosting was fading.

But wait! "And add a dash of salt," the store owner continued. Ah ha! Salt? My ears perked up. High-density shortening? No can do. Salt? Can do. I could do salt. "Why salt?" I asked. "It cuts the sweet," she answered knowledgeably. "You will be amazed at what a little salt will do for your frosting." I was on it!

"Girls, today I will teach you how to make frosting," I declared one Saturday afternoon a few weeks later. We were gathered around the kitchen counter where I was ready to whip up my masterpiece. I had been practicing. And I was pretty sure I had arrived at just the right formula for a frosting worthy of my cake. Today was the day. I was ready. And I was surrounded by three helpful princesses who were eager to learn. And eager to lick the beaters. And lick the bowl. That is just part of the deal.

The girls watched, borderline amused. I dramatically unwrapped a stick of unsalted butter. The butter was just barely starting to get soft from sitting out on the counter. Perfect. With a flourish I tossed the butter into my pink mixing bowl. I flipped on my trusty hand mixer and beat the butter until it was just slightly fluffy. "Can we do that?" the littlest girls asked. "No," I replied. "Mixers are electric appliances. You cannot use them until you are older. Just like hairdryers."

But I did let them carefully add a little more than a pound of powdered sugar. Slowly. Slowly so that the sugar dust would not form a cloud above our heads and land in our hair. The girls also helped by adding splashes of whole milk between each addition of powdered sugar. The milk helps minimize the sugar dust cloud, too.

"How much milk?" my oldest daughter astutely asked. "I have no idea," I said. And that is true. The amount of milk you add depends entirely on how you like your frosting. I like mine to be easy to spread. That means not runny and not stiff. You just have to keep adding splashes of milk until you get what you want. But you cannot take milk out once you have added it to the bowl. So be careful. A good artist keeps going. A great artist knows when to stop. As goes art, so goes frosting.

The most fun part of the frosting is to add the flavors. That would be vanilla and almond. Vanilla is fun. It smells so good! One of my daughters loves the smell of vanilla. I always let her add it to the bowl. I let her pour it in the bowl straight from the bottle. Dangerous, I know. But like I said, frosting is an art. If you really want to measure your vanilla, I suggest adding somewhere between one tablespoon and two tablespoons. Finally, add the almond extract. This you should do yourself because a child might pour in too much. You only need about a teaspoon.

And then add the salt. Somewhere between a dash and a dash and a half of salt is probably best. But it all depends on what you like. Salt really does cut the sweet. Just as the bake shop expert said it would. Which means that your frosting will be sweet but not sugary. Add the salt to the frosting in increments. Keep tasting the frosting until you arrive at the perfect amount of sweet.

Mix it all together. Scrape the sides of the bowl. Mix again. And then add the magic. That would be the baker's sugar. "The crunch is important," I told my girls, holding a carton of baker's sugar up to my left cheek and smiling broadly. Trying to look like I was starring in a food commercial. Which is something I have always wanted to do. "Baker's sugar is the key to the crunch. It is the magic ingredient. Always add it last."

A healthy dusting of baker's sugar over the top of the frosting does the trick. "Here comes the crunch," I told the girls as I let them each try their hand at sprinkling the magic into the bowl. The frosting was shaping up nicely! Finally, I mixed it all together one last time. "Abracadabra!" I declared. "We've got frosting!"

I was pretty proud! I was especially proud about adding my own secret ingredient. I had figured out the baker's sugar all on my own. I thought maybe I should go back to the bake shop and tell the store owner about baker's sugar. As a thank you for her tip about the salt. One good deed deserves another. Oh but the bake shop is all the way across town, I reminded myself. So I decided to call my mother instead. Calling my mother is always a good idea.

"Hi!" I said. "Guess what?" It is so fun to start conversations with "guess what?" As long as it is good news that follows. "What?" asked my always cheerful mother. She is amazing. She is my role model for so many things. She is graced with an all-around good disposition. All the time.

"I figured out the frosting!" I announced, elated. "It is delicious! And it has salt in it, of all things. And baker's sugar. You'll have to come over and try it. I'll make a fluffy white cake to go with it. Why don't you and Dad stop by tomorrow afternoon?"

A visit from my parents is so often the highlight of my weekend. Sometimes I bake a cake just to give me an excuse to ask them to drop by. And my girls love it, too. Gran cheerfully plays Dogopoly. And Granddad always has a pocketful of peppermints.

It turned out to be a very good thing that I had an excuse to test the new frosting on an actual cake. The assembly process was not exactly a graceful exercise. That evening I baked my fluffy white cake, according to my perfect recipe. I placed the first layer carefully onto one of my favorite cake stands. The beautiful Tiffany cake stand, a wedding gift from my parents. I used a spatula to spread a little bit of vanilla buttercream frosting over the top of the first layer. Oops. The frosting was spreadable, just as I had planned. But it was also adhesive. Meaning that the frosting picked up the entire top three millimeters of the cake layer. The frosting was inviting the crumbs to come along with it on its journey across the cake. Hmmm.

According to the cookbooks, this adhesive phenomenon relates to something called the crumb coat. Creating the crumb coat is something you usually do on purpose. You create the crumb coat just before you put the layer of cake into the freezer for a while so that the next layer of frosting you spread on top of the nearly frozen crumb coat is perfect and crumb-free. But I did not have time in my life to mess with a three-step process for frosting a cake. I would just have to live with a messy crumb coat.

I added the second layer of cake and frosted it just like the first layer. The same thing happened. The cake mixed with the frosting to form a layer of cake-frosting blend between the two layers.

I licked the spatula, now covered with cake-frosting blend. I stopped dead in my tracks. It was absolutely delicious. The top three millimeters of cake, blended with frosting, was exquisite. "This might be the best thing I have ever tasted in my life!" I declared this to the spatula. Prince Charming and the princesses were again watching history programs in the bedroom. "Perhaps I am on to something here!" I said to the spatula.

I added the top layer of cake. I got out a new, clean spatula. I lifted the spatula. And then I paused. I didn't want messy-looking frosting on the top of the cake. I could live with cake-frosting blend between the layers. But I really did want the top of the cake to look good. How could I avoid stripping the top three millimeters of cake from the top layer and still frost it generously?

Then I had an idea. What if the frosting were just a little bit runnier? Just runny enough for me to pour it over the top instead of spreading it over the top? Kind of like an icing, but not quite that thin?

On a hunch, I put the rest of the frosting in the microwave. I set the timer for just 15 seconds. I did not want to wind up with frosting soup, as delicious as that might be. I poured the slightly runny frosting over the top of my cake. Like magic, the frosting covered the top of the cake without disturbing the delicate crumb coat. And some of the frosting dripped over the sides of the cake, creating several gorgeous, cascading waterfalls of frosting, perfectly decorating the sides of my creation.

I stood back and took a look. The cake was beautiful! Just the way it was. The cake was graceful. The cake was authentic. The cake was fun. The cake had personality. It carried a casual elegance. Classy and stylish, yet realistic. And it was easy. I could do this cake again. And often. Any girl could do this cake. You would not have to be a real pastry chef to create a cake like this. Any recreational pastry chef, including me, could do this cake. I loved it.

A final touch, I thought to myself. That is all this cake needs. I pulled the shopping bag from the bake shop out of the pantry and opened up one of the packages of curly candles. Curly candles are my favorite. I picked out an orange candle. A bright and cheery color most appropriate to celebrate this momentous occasion. I placed the candle carefully into the top of the cake. Right in the middle.

Beautiful.

A cake does not need to be perfect to be beautiful, I wrote in my diary of a good girl that night before I went to bed. A cake just needs to be itself. Yes, I thought as I removed the persimmon-colored lipstick from my lips and the six layers of mascara from my eyelashes. Beauty does not require perfection.

I wish I really believed that, I thought to myself as I put away the bottle of professional-strength eye makeup remover. "I wish I looked better," I said to Prince Charming. He was straightening up the pillows on the bed. Pillows that the now-sleeping princesses had used to build a castle. Earlier that evening during the historical education marathon. "You look good," he said. Which is what he always says. Which is so nice. "You look great!"

Maybe I did look great. Maybe I did not look great. All I knew was that I wanted to look better. It was one of those things that was nagging at me. That, along with all the cereal for dinner. And the worries at work. And the relentless pursuit of perfect cake and perfect frosting. My pink notebooks were filling up with all sorts of ideas that I was hoping would help me meet my own definition of a good girl.

It was about this time that I notched up my exercise routine. Maybe it was because I did not think I looked good enough. Maybe it was because I was getting a little restless and unsettled and I needed more physical activity. Maybe it was because I had a feeling that good things and new ideas and big opportunities were ahead of me and I wanted to be in good shape to be able to seize them. Maybe it was because it is impossible not to feel two pounds heavier after sitting under a bacon cloud for eight hours a day. Especially if you are baking cake every weekend and eating cake for dessert most nights during the week. And sometimes even for dinner. At the same time you are eating your cereal.

It was about this time that I dreamed up a new workout idea. I called it the Good Girl Workout for a Good Enough Figure. This workout is really pretty simple. Anyone can do it. If you want to try it yourself, keep in mind that, like every new worthwhile endeavor, this workout idea starts with making time in your life to do the things you *want* to do. Otherwise you might fill your life with things that are not really the things you want to do. And that might not be fun. That was what I was just beginning to figure out.

To test out the Good Girl Workout for a Good Enough Figure, start by setting aside 30 minutes, three times a week, to devote to exercise. Using a little math you can quickly figure out that this is 90 minutes a week. Note that 90 minutes also happens to be about how long it takes to mix a cake, bake the cake, make the frosting, clean the kitchen and stack up the layers. You might not want to compare the time required for exercise to the time required for cake baking, though. Exercise does not stand a chance against cake and you might end up skipping your workouts altogether and making a lot more cakes.

Instead, consider the fact that 90 minutes a week is about one-and-a-half television shows. Or at least I think so. My girls know that I watch not a shred of television because I cannot sit still for more than two minutes. And not much on television is very good, really. I have to confess, though, that my little princesses watch fairy tale movies and history shows, especially during those times in my life when I am in the middle of a writing frenzy or a baking marathon.

The Good Girl Workout for a Good Enough Figure does not have to be logistically complicated. For example, do not worry about leaving your house to go to a health club, abandoning your baby chicks for an hour, to be able to pull this off. Sure, this workout can be done in a gym, but it is perfectly fine to do the routine in your bedroom wearing an old t-shirt from college and investing in a few $5 elastic exercise bands.

If you are going for the A+ workout, you could splurge and invest about $50 to do a single session with a professional trainer who can show you exactly what exercises to do at home. Strength training is one of those things where online resources can be tricky. Even if you watch the video versions of training tutorials, you still cannot quite tell what the models are really doing. This is the is-her-right-leg-my-left-leg-or-is-her-left-leg-my-left-leg paradox. And there probably is no one at home with you who can watch your every move to be sure you are doing it right. It is not only a waste of time but it is also potentially injurious to do this stuff wrong.

My at-home version of the Good Girl Workout for a Good Enough Figure includes lifting hand weights and doing lunges, sit-ups, squats and waist-twists with resistance created by wrapping the elastic bands around the handle bars of my treadmill. I also do some push-ups, a few basic yoga moves and, of course, leg lifts, which are my favorite.

I learned about leg lifts from my mother. She is a whiz at leg lifts. All those years of high school drill team paid off for her. She still can lift a mean leg. Or, in the case of my mother, a nice leg. Don't we all have Jane Fonda to thank for the at-home workout with minimal equipment? The audio tape was only $7.99. My mom and I wore it out when I was in high school. In fact, we did so many aerobics in our family room that the floor began to sag from all of that jumping and bouncing.

My parents eventually had to bring in the foundation experts. "Fortunately, they were able to install jacks under the floor joists, avoiding a more expensive mud jacking repair," my dad explained when he joined my mother and me for one of our cake taste tests. We were also having fun testing our memories of stories about my high school years. "I guess it is easier to crank up joists than mud!" I told my parents. As my dad pointed out, that neat Jane Fonda tape cost a lot more than $7.99. "But that's okay, Dad," I said reassuringly. "Sure, the infrastructure was a little beat up, but the women were in great shape."

If you have little girls I promise that they will delight in watching you do squats and lunges and twists with elastic bands. Even a kindergartner can start going through the motions. Leg lifts are not all that different from eyelash sweeps with the mascara. Legs are a great place to start.

Thirty minutes three times a week seems to be just right for the Good Girl Workout for a Good Enough Figure. This duration is short enough to prevent schedule-fatigue-based self-cancellation. But it is long enough to check the I-really-do-exercise box. And it is frequent enough to see results. But it is not so frequent that the workouts infringe on time allotted for coffee drinking. And wine sipping. So as not to compromise the good of my workouts, I limit myself to three-fifths of a glass of wine. That is 90 calories, which is the same as a light beer. But I treat myself to a little more than three-fifths of a glass on special occasions.

Even now, months and months later, I sometimes look back on the days when I was testing the good girl workout idea. Upon reflection I realize that I really must have been stressed and pressed for time. "I was in a funk," I recently told my mother. "Why else would I have come up with such strict rules about what to wear for a workout?"

When I dreamed up the workout idea, one of the most important conditions was the dress code. Here is what I had written in my diary of a good girl: Your ratty t-shirt is fine for at home. But if you happen to exercise at a gym, do not change out of your regular clothes. If you have a job that requires playing dress up, just wear slacks, not skirts, on workout days. Changing clothes would require an extra fifteen minutes, each way, which would add onto the total time of the workout.

What a pathetic thing to have written! Clearly I had secretly longed to be one of those girls who had time to change into designer work-out clothes before exercising. Even if changing clothes was not an efficient use of time.

As unusual as that workout was, I sure did learn a lot from the Good Girl Workout for a Good Enough Figure. The risk of wearing office clothes during a workout at a gym is that the other people working out in the gym will look at you funny. They really will. But that might be the best part of all. The stares of curiosity will build psychological muscles you never knew you had. Smile back at the stares. Repeat the workout, three times a week, month after month. Watch your self-confidence grow with every smile. You will become a stronger person. You will have more self-esteem. You will earn the respect of the other gym-goers for having the guts to be yourself.

The mind plays a big role when it comes to lifting weights. Just as it does when it comes to other things, too. Such as bacon grease in your office and frosting for your cake and having more time to change clothes. Believe that the knights in shining armor will fix the ventilation situation in your office. Believe that you might someday be living a fairy tale that gives you the time to change clothes before you go to the gym. Believe that you will invent a recipe for frosting that is as good as your recipe for cake. The mind is a powerful tool. All the best self-help books say that you should believe you have it and then you will have it. And I believe it.

Mind to body. And the reciprocal benefits are impressive, too. Body to mind. There is a direct correlation between physical strength and mental strength. As my arms bulked up, even just a tiny bit, my emotional stamina had increased. I had started to feel a tiny bit better about myself. After a couple of months, I was able to endure "you said we could get a lizard" and other assorted verbal arrows from each of my three little girls simultaneously without changing my facial expression from regally stoic to almost scary. And I was able to easily withstand a day in the office surrounded by greasy air without getting the least bit grouchy.

A little heavy lifting every couple of days really does pay off over time. Even if you never quite make it to super model status. At some point, good enough really is good enough. Believe you look good and you will look good.

And it actually might work, I thought to myself. I had started to become a tiny bit more generous with my self-evaluations. In the mirror and in my diary.

Love my new eyeshadow, I had written one night in my pink notebook. Adding: The stylist was right about lightening up the lid color. I had also noticed that I filled out my jeans a little better. No doubt thanks to the leg lifts. And brighter lipstick colors really are better, I noted in the same entry. And a final thought: I still love my six layers of mascara. Some things should never change.

When it came to fluffy white cake with vanilla buttercream frosting, though, good enough was an understatement. Truly the cake was perfect. "This is delicious!" my father exclaimed. He and my mother had just arrived for a Sunday visit. I wasted no time before slicing into the cake I had made the night before. I served them each a big piece. "This is really, really good," my mother agreed. So did my husband. So did the girls. And so did I. The cake was scrumptious. And of course the very best part was the yummy layer of cake-frosting blend nestled between tier one and tier two and between tier two and tier three. The cake was a dream come true.

I ate another piece of fluffy white cake with vanilla buttercream frosting before I went to bed that night. Then I wrapped up the rest of the cake and carefully tucked it away in the back of the freezer. I tucked it away because I had a feeling I would need it in the weeks and months ahead.

And I was right. I had invented the fluffy white cake with vanilla buttercream frosting just in time. Things were about to get interesting. And challenging. And exciting. Things were about to get good.

Chapter 5

Hand-dipped Celebration Bon Bons

Is a hairdryer a cooking appliance? Typically it is not. But it becomes one instantly when you need to heat up four dozen baked chicken breasts. When your oven is already occupied by four dozen biscuits. And your house is already occupied by four dozen hungry guests. Guests who arrived two hours earlier for your sister's rehearsal dinner. Which you are hosting. And catering. Even though you are not really a caterer.

But do not worry. This can be done. Especially in a laundry room. With the clothes dryer running. With the chicken on top of the dryer. With the laundry room door closed. And locked, safe from curious guests looking for dinner. Yes. Chicken warms up in a jiffy under the blasting heat of a hairdryer operating at high speed. Even in a laundry room.

Practice makes perfect. Or close enough. I was so grateful that my sister had allowed me to cater her rehearsal dinner. Even though I was not really a caterer. The laundry room experience proved to be a valuable test run. A pilot. A practice session. A textbook example of experiential learning. Experiential learning of the culinary variety.

If you find yourself someday in your laundry room with your

hairdryer, catering your sister's rehearsal dinner even though you are not really a caterer, consider yourself lucky. Very lucky. You will be so glad you learned how to serve a lot of chicken when you find yourself, three years later, catering a rehearsal dinner as a gift to one of your favorite office colleagues whose son is getting married. Even though you still are not really a caterer.

"Hi!" I said to my mother when I called to recruit her for my latest kitchen adventure. "What are you doing in May?" "May what?" she asked. "All of May," I answered. "I volunteered to cater a sit-down rehearsal dinner over Memorial Day weekend at a lakeshore clubhouse."

My mother is wonderful. She did not hang up. She did not hesitate. She did not shriek. She did not ask what in the world was wrong with me. She did not demand to know what in the world would cause me to throw myself into a project like this. Especially now that the bacon smell was gone from my office. And now that the cakes seemed to be keeping me relatively happy. And now that I had found a lipstick color I really loved. Instead she said, "Oh that sounds fun!" My mother is wonderful.

"This is a good idea," I was assuring my mother. And reassuring myself. "Actually, this is not just a good idea," I said, pumping myself up. "It is a great idea."

I was on the spot. I owed my mother an explanation. Especially now that she had agreed to help. "The main reason it is a good idea," I continued, "is that it is a nice thing to do. It is a great example of doing good by helping others." And that was, in fact, the case. I had been in the business of charitable giving long enough to know that the point of philanthropy is to help others. Helping others is the whole idea behind doing good and charitable giving and giving back and being socially responsible. Or whatever it is you prefer to call it.

And it really was true that this was a good idea. Weeks later, after the clubhouse rehearsal dinner was over and I had closed my diary for the night, I went to bed a very happy girl. And satisfied. And inspired. And motivated. It always feels so good to do good.

"Originally I thought it was for 50 people," I explained to my mother on the phone as we started to mentally calculate the shopping list for a headcount of 100. Never offer to cater a rehearsal dinner, or anything else for that matter, if you know well in advance that the total number of guests is really 100. That is just too scary. Unless, of course, you really are a caterer. Real caterers are among the most noble knights and ladies in the kingdom. Real caterers willingly and cheerfully assume responsibility for the happiness and satisfaction of every single guest at the royal ball. That is very, very brave. Big numbers do not scare real caterers. But I was scared.

"One hundred people is a lot," said my mother. "But don't worry. It will work beautifully. We'll just make something with chicken." My mother and I were lucky. We already knew about the power of chicken. We knew about chicken thanks to my experience in my laundry room with the hairdryer and my sister's rehearsal dinner a few years earlier. Chicken, particularly in large quantities, seems to have mystical properties that practically guarantee that the story will have a happy ending.

Good friends are critical to any catering adventure. This is true whether the chicken is served from your laundry room or from the galley kitchen of a lakeshore clubhouse. You need good people. When I catered my sister's rehearsal dinner from my laundry room, one of my good friends pitched in to help. Hairdryer and all. That dinner served 40. Serving 100 people at a lakeshore clubhouse was a little different.

With careful planning, though, I knew my mother and I could do it. For sure we would be able to handle the food preparation. And the transfer of the food from my kitchen to the clubhouse. But then the logistics would get complicated. "There is no way we can *serve* the dinner without extra help," I told my mother before we hung up the phone. "I will need to recruit a few friends."

And I was right, as it would turn out. This situation calls for truly good friends. Only truly good friends will still be your friends after you subject them to six hours on their feet under your chaotic, sleep-deprived leadership. And after you subject them to so much chicken grease that they will have to throw away their clothes after it is all over.

Luckily for me, six good friends at the office volunteered. They volunteered immediately upon learning about my bold offer to cater the rehearsal dinner. Probably they volunteered out of sheer horror at what I had just agreed to do. But volunteer they did.

Some of the people who work at the Greater Kansas City Community Foundation are accountants and attorneys. Some of the people who work there are people who know a lot about involving families in giving. Other people who work at the community foundation know how businesses can efficiently manage their corporate foundations. And all of the people who work there are talented. And smart. And dedicated to making Kansas City a better place. But not one of them is a caterer.

That little detail did not stop six brave ladies from saying yes to the rehearsal dinner adventure. One of the volunteers was my fabulous executive assistant. Another was the energetic person who headed up a branch office. Another volunteer was the lovely lady in charge of our donor relations work. She even recruited her terrific husband to pitch in. Another volunteer was the smart woman who heads up the communications and customer experience department at the foundation. And the sixth member of the royal team of volunteers was our general counsel and chief operating officer. She is the woman who is now running the foundation. The rehearsal dinner team was an illustrious group!

A few weeks later, my mother and I were deep into the rehearsal dinner planning. We were sitting at my kitchen counter. Enjoying a little Cap'n Crunch. And something suddenly dawned on me. Something important. Something challenging. "You know, Mom," I said. "The trickiest part of this whole thing is that we will have to develop a dessert that is not cake."

And I knew I was right. "Just as bridesmaids should not compete with the bride's beauty, a rehearsal dinner dessert must not compete with the wedding cake." I recited this rule to my mother. "I am just sure I read that somewhere in an etiquette book." She nodded in agreement. "Yes," she said. "It's just like the rule that a guest should not wear a white dress to a wedding. It might threaten the bride's beauty."

A dessert that is not cake? Hello! My mother and I had been practicing cakes for months! Cake is the very best dessert in the universe. Surely by now you believe me when I say that cake is at the epicenter of all human celebrations. Especially weddings because cake is one of the most effective ways to capture the heart of Prince Charming forever. But if you decide to volunteer to cater a rehearsal dinner, you are going to have to come up with a dessert that is something other than cake. Which, if you are cake-obsessed like I am, is a daunting task.

My mother and I solved the mystery. After all, we had become brave and fearless culinary souls after all of those hours at my kitchen counter. Testing and mixing and baking and frosting and tasting and chatting. "We might not be able to serve cake at the rehearsal dinner," I said. "But we can get pretty close."

We decided to go with a cake derivative. A cake derivative is a recipe that calls for plenty of butter, flour and sugar combined to create a dessert. A dessert that is not quite cake but that is enough like cake to still be delicious. Ideas for cake derivatives to serve at a rehearsal dinner could include cake balls dipped in white and dark chocolate. Or an amped-up brownie-esque chocolate nut torte. Or even hand-decorated, melt-in-your-mouth sugar cookies in the shapes of Xs and Os.

If you dream up a cake derivative, whatever you do, be sure to invent a fancy name for your dessert. For example, instead of cake balls or brownie or cookies, all of which are very pedestrian-sounding, dub your desserts Hand-dipped Celebration Bon Bons or Dark Chocolate Pistachio Drizzle Torte or Signature Iced Sugar Cookies. And whatever you do, make all of the desserts ahead of time and stash them in your freezer so you can focus all of your attention on the dinner itself during the entire week leading up to the big event.

My mother and I did just that. We spent two weekends during the month of May making Hand-dipped Celebration Bon Bons. I did not dare tally it up, but I would bet we spent more than 24 hours on those bon bons! Baking cake and making frosting. And then mixing the cake and frosting together. And then adding crushed candies like Reese's Pieces and M&Ms to different batches of the cake and frosting mixture to create a variety of flavors. And then rolling the mixture into little balls. Little balls that were not much more than bite-size. And then freezing the balls for two hours. And then dipping each one, by hand, into the melted chocolate. Sometimes white chocolate, sometimes milk chocolate, sometimes dark chocolate.

We needed help! "Girls, girls, girls!" I called to the princesses. "Come quickly to the kitchen! And get ready to have fun!" The princesses were quite responsive. They had been eyeing the M&Ms and Reese's Pieces all day.

I continued with the instructions for the special assignment. "I will dip each bon bon in melted chocolate. Watch closely, because the moment I place the dipped bon bon on the wax paper, you must shake a few sprinkles over the top. You must hurry, though, before the chocolate firms up. Otherwise the sprinkles will not stick." My daughters did a great job. They always love adding sprinkles to the treats I make in my kitchen. Who wouldn't? Sprinkles are fun.

The girls also pitched in on my mother's packaging assembly line. They all kept busy folding up little plastic containers, converting the containers from flat form to box form. One hundred little plastic boxes, each two inches square. The perfect size for wrapping up Hand-dipped Celebration Bon Bons for party favors. My mother tied a cute little bow around each one, even hand-labeling every box with the flavor of the bon bon inside. Lemon Pecan. Dark Chocolate Orange. Toffee. Vanilla Crunch. Milk Chocolate Peanut Butter. It was quite an operation we had going that day in my kitchen.

Prince Charming was such a good sport throughout the whole rehearsal dinner adventure. He even made a few emergency grocery store runs to get more cake mix. And eggs. And whole milk. And butter. And powdered sugar. My wonderful husband never complained about the fact that the kitchen in his castle had been taken over for weeks by a mother-daughter team of non-caterers. And he never complained about eating cereal for dinner every single night. Dry cereal really was his only choice. There was no room in the refrigerator or freezer for food that did not pertain to the rehearsal dinner.

And Prince Charming never questioned why I was doing this. Although a few times I did notice him watching me curiously when he thought I did not see him. He was watching me with his "What is she doing now and why is she doing it?" look. But he never said a word. Like I said, he really is Prince Charming.

"Good thing we planned meticulously," I said to my mother as we headed into the final week. My freezer was bursting at the seams with 100 Hand-dipped Celebration Bon Bons in little plastic boxes and 100 more in freezer bags to serve for the actual dessert at the rehearsal dinner.

Planning is always a good idea, of course. Sometimes too much planning is counterproductive because planning can be used to procrastinate the actual doing. In this case, though, too much planning is not a danger. You cannot plan enough when you are getting ready to cater a rehearsal dinner for 100 people, especially when you are not really a caterer.

The key to successful planning is to select recipes that are highly scalable and highly transportable. My mother is right. Some form of chicken is the safest bet for the main dish. Chicken is noncontroversial. It is fairly predictable in its cooking behavior. And chicken can be made to look beautiful simply by adding a sauce. Sauce on the plate makes the whole meal look more substantial. And it softens the unattractive rough edges of the chicken where the meat is a little mean.

I had decided to use my favorite chicken recipe. The same chicken I had served at my sister's rehearsal dinner. After all, repeating menus always brings good luck. And besides, how can you beat chicken breasts topped with white wine and brown sugar and baked in an olive and plum marinade? It is delicious.

One of the best parts of this particular chicken recipe is in fact the sauce. The sauce you get when the marinade, wine and brown sugar mix together during the baking process. "We can drizzle the sauce over the chicken when the chicken is being plated," I explained to my mother. "Just before the plates are ready to be served to the tables." That would be service to the tables by the team of co-catering friends who were not really caterers either.

We made a salad that was based mostly in hearts of Romaine. Romaine lettuce works well for large-scale gatherings. This is because Romaine is the type of green least likely to wilt when tossed three hours before it is served. "I think we can skip the dark, leafy organic greens here," I told my mother. "We are doing enough good with the gift of the rehearsal dinner itself that we should get a pass on buying organic. We will still qualify as socially responsible."

Indeed, when you are scaling to 100, bargain shopping at whole-sale clubs is fine for most salad components. Including not only the greens but also the edamame, red onion and zucchini. But go ahead and invest in the really good Parmesan cheese and just use it sparingly. Most of the time you really do get what you pay for in cheese.

The rehearsal dinner was getting closer and closer. It was time for a few final decisions. "We can't add a complicated starch to the menu," I said with conviction. I was telling my mother about the rice dish I had tested earlier that week. "Rice is way too tricky to cook in large quantities." My test kitchen attempt at a cranberry and celery rice dish had failed miserably. And not just because of the issues that come with tripling any rice recipe. The truth is that I am a much better baker than I am a cook.

"I won't have time on the day before the event to be dealing with potatoes or polenta or rice or couscous," I continued. And it turned out that I was right. I would have no time for that. And my mother would have no time for potatoes or polenta or rice or couscous, either. She was in charge of salad on the day before the event. This meant that she would spend a full seven hours washing and chopping lettuce at an off-site location. An off-site location that was her own kitchen. My kitchen was way too crowded and way too stressful. Besides, my mother would get plenty of time in my kitchen the following day. The big day. The day of the rehearsal dinner itself.

For the starch, instead of potatoes or polenta or rice or couscous, go with a bread. An already buttery and sweet bread, such as corn-bread or cinnamon rolls. Cornbread or cinnamon rolls can easily be placed on each plate, right next to the chicken. That way you are not dealing with arranging breadbaskets and butter platters on the tables before the guests arrive. There is simply no time for that.

The preparation plan you develop must include a strict, hour-by-hour schedule, with a very early start time. Remember that 100 is five times 20. This seems obvious. But when you are dipping chicken breasts in marinade the day before the event and you are on chicken breast number 25, you still have 75 chicken breasts to go. That is a lot of chicken.

It was the afternoon before the day of the rehearsal dinner. I was toiling away at my kitchen counter. My mother was toiling away, 40 miles away, at her kitchen counter. I placed a kitchen-to-kitchen call to my mother. I had just dipped chicken breast number 25.

"The number 100 is truly very, very big," I told my mother, trying not to get marinade on my iPhone. The number 100 was also very, very messy. I was under stress and I was talking fast. "I am on chicken breast number 25 and I have 25 more chicken breasts to dip after that and then 25 more after that and then 25 more after that. This is a lot of chicken." My mother sounded just slightly anxious too. "I've been washing lettuce for five hours," she said. "This is a lot of lettuce."

It was a lot of everything. "We'd better start early tomorrow," I said to my mother before I had to get off the phone. There was no time for a long conversation. "Come as early as you can."

If you take on an adventure like catering a rehearsal dinner for 100 people, start very early on the day of the actual event. Start as early as you can possibly imagine. So early that you are practically starting the day before the event. This means that on the day of the event you should plan to get up at 1:00 a.m. to start cooking. Or at 12:15 a.m. if you want to get in a run on the treadmill. Start early because, unless you have five ovens in your house, you will need every minute you can squeeze out of the event day to get the chicken cooked. And then get it cooled down fast enough so that it can be safely reheated later on site by you and your team.

By 4:00 a.m. on the day of the event your kitchen will be in full operation. And you will be getting pretty good at pulling aluminum pans full of hot chicken out of your ovens. To facilitate the cooling process, spread out the pans of baked chicken on the floor as they emerge from the oven. Immediately lay a well-sealed bag of ice on top of the aluminum foil covering each chicken-filled pan.

And absolutely do what I did and ask your mother to come to your house as early as she can. Ideally before 8:00 a.m. This is because your mother will end up having to make three trips to the grocery store to get bags of ice to cool the chicken you have been baking since 1:00 a.m. The six bags of ice you bought the day before will last only until 8:30 a.m. This is because the ice will melt faster than the Wicked Witch of the West. Baked chicken is hot, hot, hot.

Note that you will not be able to help your mother carry the bags of ice from her car into the laundry room where the chicken is cooling. You will need to leave your mother alone at your house, placing her in charge of chicken cooking and chicken cooling, soon after she arrives. This is because, for two hours that morning, you will need to be at the event site 30 miles away setting up the flowers. Assuming you are also playing florist even though you are not really a florist. In addition to playing caterer even though you are not really a caterer.

I got home from playing florist at about 10:00 a.m. on the day of the event to help my mother deal with the oven and the ice and the pans and the hot chicken. "I can't believe Aunt Susan does that five times every weekend," I told my mother. Aunt Susan is a real florist. And a really good one, too. I should have called her for advice. I will not make that mistake again. Hauling roses and hydrangeas was hard work. But, on the positive side, playing florist smelled great.

The chicken in my laundry room smelled good, too. I was loving the yummy aromas! My mother was more interested in safety. The laundry room floor was quite a scene. "Be careful," she said. "The floor is slick. Not from the ice but from the olive oil in the marinade and the chicken grease spilling over the edges of the pans onto the tile." Yikes!

Evidently, volunteer catering jobs for groups of 100 people are genetic. My mother's considerable catering skills undoubtedly were developed during her college years when she prepared a taco dinner for 100 people in her sorority house. She elaborated. "Tacos sound easier than chicken," she said. "But not when every single one of the 200 corn tortillas is deep-fat fried and folded by hand into a crispy taco shell."

Wow. My mother really is a rock star. I can handle the thought of baking 100 chicken breasts if I take a couple of deep breaths. But my thoughts become scrambled when I consider what the grease from deep-fat frying more than 200 taco shells must have done to the floor in the sorority house. Let alone to the air.

Timing is everything. To cater a rehearsal dinner for 100 people even though you are not really a caterer, you must plan your schedule so you and your mother have time after you finish chilling the chicken to toss the salad. Tossing salad for 100 is most efficiently handled by gently shaking it all together in big batches. To do that, simply divide the lettuce, red onion, edamame, chickpeas, zucchini, Parmesan cheese and salad dressing among 25 big Ziploc bags. And shake.

Watch those bags! We had a few of them break. Maybe the zippers were weak. Or maybe we were shaking the bags with too much enthusiastic gusto. All I know is that a lot of lettuce and chickpeas ended up on the laundry room floor, cheerfully joining the layer of marinade and grease. Quite the celebration it was that day in that laundry room. What with all of those salad ingredients and chicken drippings gathering in chaotic revelry on the slippery tile in front of the washing machine.

Do not forget that somehow you will need to get the chicken and salad and bon bons and cornbread and cookies and silverware and plates and serving platters packed up, out of your laundry room, loaded into your car and transported across town. Those are not minor details.

Plan to complete the loading process no later than 4:00 p.m. for an event that is scheduled to start at 6:30 p.m. This is especially important because you will need to leave your house early enough to swing by the grocery store to pick up two dozen pieces of fried chicken and four containers of pre-cut chunks of watermelon. Which is what you will serve to those guests who are under the age of 18. A person's love of olive and plum marinade and edamame salad usually does not emerge until college.

Beg the universe for no rain on the day of the event. This is primarily because your mother will need to navigate, out in the fresh air, while you drive. "Would you mind leaning your head out of the passenger side window?" I asked my mother as I maneuvered the vehicle out of my driveway and onto the road that leads from my house to the grocery store.

A rearview mirror is no help to you when you are driving a car loaded to its ceiling with chicken. And you do not have time to get into an accident. And your insurance company would never believe the accident was unavoidable because of chicken if you were to back into the neighbor's van. Which you should have borrowed in the first place. Chicken, salad, cornbread and Hand-dipped Celebration Bon

Bons for 100 people. Plus you and your leg-lifting mother. It all just barely fits in a Volvo sedan. Even the glove box will be full of chicken.

I have to tell you that the foundation where I used to work is in excellent hands. My smart lawyer friend who is now in charge of the Greater Kansas City Community Foundation is also a recreational chef of sorts. Remember, she was one of the six generous souls who happily volunteered to join the rehearsal dinner fun. At the event location, I put her in charge of solving the mystery of how we would bring 100 chicken breasts from an iced-down condition to the perfect amount of hot. Hairdryers might work for your family gatherings. But hairdryers are not appropriate for family gatherings of people who are not members of your own family.

My friend was a whiz at calculating precisely how many seconds each chicken breast would need to be submerged in boiling marinade not only to warm it up but also to ensure food safety. She and another dear friend and colleague, the one who is in charge of communications and customer experience at the foundation, toiled masterfully over boiling pots of plums and olives and olive oil. Dipping and plating with such skill and efficiency that they were more than able to keep up with the fast-paced team of servers. That would be the servers who were delivering 100 plates of chicken and cornbread to a dozen tables of hungry guests after clearing plates of salad. And keeping wine glasses at least three-fifths full at all times.

In the end, I suppose the rehearsal dinner story is a cautionary tale. Take on this kind of a project only if you have just a tiny bit of crazy in you. The kind of crazy that is related to boundless energy, not to insanity. Even if most people cannot tell the difference. Everyone, except for your mother and your husband, will call you crazy for doing it. So it is better if you start out that way.

In fact, you might actually find that you come out of the whole thing a little more sane. Not only because of your newly-sharpened culinary skills but also because of your much stronger friendships. Blood may be thicker than water. But the grease from 100 chickens is just about as close as you can get to a permanent bond of friendship. And you will gain new respect for your taco-shell-frying, chicken-cooling mother.

The only downside is that the grease lingers for a while. But not forever. The grease eventually will burn itself out of your oven. And eventually you will throw away the clothes you wore that night because the grease smell will not quite go away. Despite ten rounds in your washing machine. The washing machine in your now-legendary laundry room. Eventually the grease will wear off the tile in front of that washing machine. But in the meantime, you will be slipping and sliding on your laundry room floor.

And in the end, the rehearsal dinner idea really is a good idea. It is a very nice thing to do for another human being. I tried to explain all of this to my husband a week after it was all over. When he slipped in the laundry room for the third time in a twelve-hour period. I tried to explain that doing things like catering a rehearsal dinner for 100 people even though I was not really a caterer was one of the ways I give back.

"Gratuitous catering is a form of giving back that counts as doing good. Even though it is not tax deductible as a gift to charity," I insisted. His only remark was that next time I got the urge to engage in gratuitous catering in an effort to check my good girl boxes, perhaps I could consider sticking with something more traditional. Such as making dinner for a neighbor or volunteering at a soup kitchen.

"That was one of the best things I have ever done," I told my mother on Memorial Day, just 60 hours after it was all over. We were sitting happily at my kitchen counter. Having a little lunch. A little lunch of nothing more than a few of the leftover Hand-dipped Celebration Bon Bons that I had hidden in the back of the freezer. "Yes. It was one of the best things I have ever done," I repeated enthusiastically. "Now I am really inspired."

And that was the truth. The rehearsal dinner adventure had inspired me to think big. Even bigger than I usually think. Which is pretty big. It had inspired me to test my own limits. It had inspired me to dream up new ways to make things with cake. It had inspired me to more fully appreciate the wide range of talents of my colleagues at the office. Colleagues who were just as good at working outside the office as they were at working inside the office.

The rehearsal dinner had even inspired me to give a name to my gratuitous catering operation. I called it One Celebrations. And it had inspired me to design a logo for the business. And to order a roll of cute little logo stickers. Stickers my mother and I had put on the bon bon boxes. I love those stickers!

And the rehearsal dinner inspired me to continue to believe what I had always believed. Which is that almost anything is possible if you put your mind to it. And if you have really good friends to help you. And if you have an unbelievably wonderful mother who happily skates on chicken grease and dashes to the grocery store and back loaded down with bags of ice.

Anything is possible.

Chapter 6

What do you call a blue ribbon combination of two layers of oven roasted sweet peach cobbler? Stacked between three layers of fluffy white cake soaked in apricot brandy glaze? Topped off with a vanilla buttercream drizzle and studded with fresh raspberries? You call it the Raspberry Peach Drizzle Cake.

"This cake is really good," my husband remarked as he took a big bite of my latest creation. We were all out on the deck having dinner, picnic style. Branching out from dry cereal now that the refrigerator was no longer on rehearsal dinner duty. Tonight it was hot dogs. And grapes. And cheese. And a few Honey Bunches of Oats for the princess who does not like hot dogs. And cake for dessert. Of course.

"This is really, *really* good." Prince Charming added ten minutes later. He was already helping himself to another piece. My husband usually is not so effusive with his praise. But it is true that he really does love a moist cake that is heavy on the fruit and light on the frosting. In fact, I have noticed over the years that most men prefer moist cakes that are heavy on the fruit and light on the frosting.

As I am so fond of declaring, my favorite cake is fluffy white cake with vanilla buttercream frosting. Where dessert is concerned, fluffy white cake with vanilla buttercream frosting is the love of my life. But even I had to admit that the Raspberry Peach Drizzle Cake was delicious. I had dreamed it up that afternoon. Right after lunch when I was craving cake. Again. My test kitchen only had about a week of downtime after the rehearsal dinner before I started tinkering with cake again. I could not help myself. I love cake.

The Raspberry Peach Drizzle Cake is slightly more complicated than the standard fluffy white cake. But it is worth it. Especially for a special occasion. Or when a girl really needs to win the heart of Prince Charming. Or re-win it, as the case may be. I was going for the re-win. Our entire kingdom was still recovering from 100 chicken breasts, 100 salads, 200 bon bons and 100 pieces of cornbread. Especially Prince Charming, who was looking just a tad too thin from spending three weeks on an involuntary all-cereal diet.

The Raspberry Peach Drizzle cake starts with baking a three-layer fluffy white cake. But you do not stack the layers together until after you have made two layers of peach cobbler. Bake both the cake and the cobbler in eight-inch cake pans. That is so the layers are the same size and stay stacked up nice and neat. At least in theory.

The cobbler itself is easy breezy. I got this recipe from a friend at work. One of my chicken-dipping friends. Whisk together three-fourths cup of self-rising flour, three-fourths cup of sugar and one cup of whole milk. Divide the batter between two cake pans. Cake pans that you have coated generously with melted butter. Yummy!

And when I say generously I mean generously! Use so much melted butter that the melted butter is about an eighth of an inch deep in the bottom of the pan. You have to pour in the batter carefully so that you do not disturb the butter. You want the butter to gently wrap around the batter. So that the butter practically cuddles the batter. I am telling you, this is yummy!

"Next time I make this cake we'll combine it with an organic field trip," I announced to the girls. They liked the cake, too. But not as much as Prince Charming. "What's an organic field trip?" they asked. "That is when you actually visit an organic orchard and pick the peaches off the trees yourself," I answered. "But peach-picking season does not start until later next month. So we couldn't have gone on a field trip this time around."

I made a mental note to record in my diary at least half a point for doing good that day. True, I had not hand-picked the peaches. But I did buy them in the organic section of the grocery store. That counts. I was working on being socially responsible. Even with cakes. It was all part of my quest to be a good girl.

Slice up about five or six peaches. Incidentally, I never follow any rules for slicing up food. Rules about slicing wear me out. I always end up with hunks, chunks, slices, pieces and slivers. And it all tastes just fine to me. Toss the peaches in some brown sugar and a splash of vanilla. Grease a cookie sheet with a little butter and roast the peaches. Twenty minutes at 350 degrees should do the trick. Let the peaches cool so they are not super hot.

Gently add the cooled peaches to the top of the cobbler batter. Gently, so that the batter cuddles the peaches. Just as the butter cuddles the batter. This cake is full of love. There is a lot of cuddling going on in that cobbler.

Bake the cobbler layers for about 37 minutes, give or take. You just have to keep an eye on it. You want the cobbler layers to be firm, but not dry. Every oven is different. If the cobbler starts to smell really, really good, it is probably done. Baked goods always smell really, really good just before they start to burn.

Make an apricot brandy glaze. This is not as hard as it sounds. Just heat up some vanilla buttercream frosting in the microwave and stir in apricot brandy. Presto magico, you've got apricot brandy glaze.

Place one layer of fluffy white cake on a gorgeous cake plate or a lovely cake stand. The more gorgeous or lovely, the better, I always say. "What would you like for your birthday?" my mother always asks. "A lovely cake stand," I always answer. When you bake a lot of cakes, you simply cannot have enough lovely cake stands and gorgeous cake plates. A good-looking cake stand or cake plate will add an air of elegance to your cake. Which is always a good idea. Especially if your cakes are a little funny-looking. Like mine.

Pour half of the apricot brandy glaze onto the bottom layer of fluffy white cake. Carefully add one layer of the cooled cobbler. Add another layer of fluffy white cake. Pour the rest of the apricot brandy glaze on top of it. Add the second layer of cobbler.

Add the top layer of fluffy white cake. This time pour vanilla buttercream frosting over the top. Just like you do with the regular fluffy white cake. Except maybe warm the frosting just a little bit longer so that the frosting flows over the sides of the cake like a drizzle instead of a drip. After all, the drizzle is the reason this cake is called the Raspberry Peach *Drizzle* Cake.

The raspberry part comes last. Top off the cake with about 15 raspberries, cuddled together in the center of the cake. Tuck seven more raspberries around the edges of the cake where the drizzle has pooled beautifully onto the gorgeous plate. It is all so beautiful! You will fall in love.

The sun was setting. That meant it was time to do the dishes and send the princesses off to sweet dreams of peaches and orchards and of castles and cakes. Picnic dinners in the summer out on the deck are one of my favorite family traditions. I love to eat outside. I especially love it because I don't have to clean the floor afterward. The birds and the rain take care of that. It is recycling in its purest form. All very organic and sustainable and socially responsible. A dinner plan that does good! I would write that down in the diary.

Years ago I had figured out that the trick to avoiding cleaning the kitchen floor in the summertime is to eat outside. The birds really do eat whatever pieces of cereal fall onto the deck. Some birds even eat grapes and cheese. But I think birds like cereal better than grapes and cheese because the cereal disappears overnight. The grapes and cheese take a little longer. They sometimes do not disappear until it rains.

You can even eat dinner outside in the rain if you are really, really not in the mood to clean your floors. I did this a lot once upon a time when I was eight months pregnant with the littlest princess. When Prince Charming had been out of town on business for so many days that summer I had lost count. A few of those times when we were eating outside it had started to sprinkle. But only lightly. The cereal and grapes were unaffected.

When that happened I just pretended it wasn't raining. One of my daughters once asked "Mommy, is it raining?" I cleverly answered the question with a compliment and said "What a good question!" Then it really did start to rain. So I sent one of the girls inside for umbrellas and we carried on with dinner. Only at the first sign of lightning did I move the party inside. And get down on my hands and knees 15 minutes later to clean the cereal off the floor.

The weather cooperated tonight, I thought to myself as I carried the Raspberry Peach Drizzle Cake back into the house, bringing up the rear of a line of three little princesses led by a Prince Charming. And the weather had indeed cooperated. It had been a perfect night for a new cake.

I found the roll of plastic wrap in the pantry. I started to pull out a piece big enough for the cake. Then I noticed something very curious. The cake, which by then was just two-thirds of a cake, was leaning. As in tipping. As in nearing collapse. "This is odd," I muttered. Then I looked a little more closely. The cake wasn't just tipping. It was sinking. The moist, delicious layers of cobbler were weighing down the more delicate fluffy white cake layers. Not cuddling, but crushing. The whole cake was in the process of converting from a cake to a heap.

Well, well, I thought. Maybe five layers is too much for the Raspberry Peach Drizzle Cake. After all, I noted, two of the layers contained moist, delicious fruit.

As silly as it sounds, this whole discovery made me sad. I wanted to believe that I could build a five-layer dessert out of peach cobbler and fluffy white cake. A five-layer dessert that would stand tall and proud. A regal dessert that was strong enough to handle the weight of raspberries and peaches but gentle enough to cuddle delicate fluffy white layers. Perhaps it was not meant to be. Then I cheered up. "I'll just keep testing!" I told the cake. "You might fall apart on me. But I won't fall apart on you."

With that, I lovingly wrapped up the rest of the cake and put it in the refrigerator for my husband to eat for breakfast. No back of the freezer for this cake. Cakes with fruit do not freeze well. I turned off the lights in the kitchen. I went upstairs to kiss the girls goodnight. And I made my way back downstairs and headed straight for my closet. And my purse. And my pen. And my diary.

I had to write down the recipe for Raspberry Peach Drizzle Cake before I forgot how I had made it. That would have been a shame. It is so sad when a good idea is lost forever. That's why I love the purse-size notebooks. When you have a good idea you can write it down immediately.

I was thinking about the layers. I was still a little sad knowing that my beautiful cake would probably sink into one big pancake by morning. I wondered how many layers I could really put onto a cake plate? Five might be too many for a fruity cake. But what about a regular fluffy white cake? How many layers could I get into a single cake using that particular recipe? Could I add different flavors? Six layers of white cake had worked pretty well for the birthday cake-off. The cake had tilted a bit, yes, but it did stay standing. Would six layers work if I alternated fluffy white cake with chocolate cake? Could I build a seven-layer cake? Eight layers? More?

"Maybe cakes are like lipsticks," I said to my husband. He was in the closet, too, taking off his shoes and placing them neatly onto the shoe rack. "Maybe cake layers are like lipstick *and* mascara," I added, expanding the concept. It is always fun to observe and connect and combine more than one favorite thing into a new idea.

Prince Charming did not see the connection. "Are you talking about your cake? Or are you talking about your makeup?" Prince Charming always asks such good clarifying questions. Maybe it is his Westpoint training. Or his ten years practicing law. Or maybe I give him lots of practice.

"I am talking about both," I said. "You know how I layer my lipsticks, right? I always carry at least three different colors in my purse. So that I can mix and match and create new colors. Just by layering them in a different order. It adds variety to my day. And you know how many mascaras I use every morning. Six different products! The layering is the key. The layering is always the key. The more layers the better."

By this time I was talking to myself. Prince Charming was checking his phone and pretending to listen. The two-way conversation was over. So I went back to my diary. Adding a question to my entry for the day: How many layers can a cake actually handle before toppling over? And adding an answer of sorts: Maybe I should find out.

Believe it or not, I rarely dream about cake. Usually I dream that I am late for work. Or that I have missed a Very Important Meeting. Or that I have arrived at a Very Important Meeting wearing all the wrong clothes and no makeup. Or that I say all the wrong things in a Very Important Meeting. But rarely do I dream about cake.

That particular night, though, I dreamed about cake. Lots of cakes. Cakes of many layers, all stacked up on top of each other. Brave cakes daring me to add just one more layer. Big and bold cakes, full of possibility.

I woke up with a new question to write in my diary. It was all of two words: What next?

With a lot of help, I had pulled off a rehearsal dinner for 100 people. I was having fun baking cakes with my kids. I was serving cereal to my family with a little less guilt. I was feeling slightly more optimistic that I might actually someday be able to live up to my own standards for being a good girl. A good girl who bakes good cakes. And who likes to do good. And who strives to be good at work. And who tries to look good. And who wants to be a good mother, daughter, sister, friend and wife. Especially a good mother. I was feeling a little braver. I was feeling a little bolder.

What next?

If you ask yourself that question someday, perhaps you will get an answer like I got. Which was "Do not stop." Do not stop taking on good work that seems impossible but which your instincts are telling you most certainly can be done. Do not stop dreaming up ideas to improve your cake recipes and add more layers. Do not stop dreaming up ideas for working with really good people. And ideas for having fun with your children. And ideas for doing good that go way beyond traditional notions of charitable giving. Do not stop.

I did not stop.

That said, my first project after I asked the "What next?" question was rather anti-climatic. I started with something easy. That something easy was cleaning out a hat box filled with more than 200 tubes of lipstick. That hat box had been sitting in my closet for a very long time.

"Girls, girls! Come quickly!" I called out to the princesses. This time there were extra princesses in the house. The oldest princess had a few friends over. Eight friends, to be exact. This was because I was conducting a camp in my basement. This camp was my attempt to infuse a little charitable giving education into Friday afternoons during summer vacation. Of course I had promised the girls that there would be cake. So far it was working. I was serving cake. And the girls were showing up. I think they were even learning a few things about doing good.

"Today's lesson is all about corporate social responsibility." The girls stared at me politely. Most certainly they were thinking how boring that sounded. I tried it again. "Companies that give back are companies that move forward! Today you will start a business that does good."

That went over a little better. I explained the rules. There were only two. "First," I said, "the business must involve lipstick." This was my clever idea for re-purposing my 200 lipsticks in a socially responsible manner. "Second," I continued, "the business must give to charity, even in a very small way. After, of course, it has begun to turn a profit." In my opinion that is the first rule of corporate social responsibility. To make money. To make money to stay in business. To keep people employed. And to keep customers happy.

The girls got busy. The results were impressive! In just four hours, two businesses were launched. One was called Lipstick Love and the other was called Sticks. And each business had a plan to make money and each business had a plan to do good. And we all had cake to celebrate. Not bad for a day's work. Especially at the beginning of summer on a Friday afternoon. In a basement.

It was a relief to finally let the lipsticks go. As much as I loved them, they were not doing any good sitting all alone in that hat box in my closet. Most of the colors in the box were not my best colors. As much as I wished I could wear Peaches 'n Cream and Raspberry Twist, I had to admit that they washed out my skin tone, making me look tired or sick or both. I had moved on to brighter colors, like Apple Berry and Give Dreams. And even just regular Red, which is never boring.

Many of the old lipsticks were artifacts from one of my previous business ventures. A business venture I had delved into once upon a time when I fell in love with network marketing. I absolutely loved that business idea! What could be more fun than inspiring other girls to get into the business of making themselves money and making themselves look good? And then inspiring even more girls to do the same thing? My skin care regimen was never better than it was when I was using the products I sold and selling the products I used.

And the product samples and logo bags and brochures were better than candy. At least I thought so.

I was a little sad when I got promoted at work and had to get out of that business. But, on the bright side, for years after that, the princesses enjoyed hours and hours of make-believe entrepreneurship using all of the product samples and logo bags and brochures. And that promotion at work meant that I had landed a good job. A really good job. A job that I would love for a long time.

"I would love to do network marketing again someday," I told my mother on the phone. I had called her late Friday afternoon to report on the cake and lipstick camp session that had just ended. "Along with, of course, baking cakes. And blogging and writing about doing good at home and in the workplace. And maybe even starting a more traditional business, too. All socially responsible, of course. It is all so fun!"

"Did you at least save a couple of lipsticks?" my mother asked. "Just for memory's sake?" I assured her that I had. The now-empty hat box had contained every lipstick I had ever owned. Since the time I was 20 years old. That was a lot of lipstick. But before the campers arrived I had pulled out the few good-looking colors. The ones I really loved.

If you happen to have your own box of lipsticks, it is a good idea to keep the box tucked away in a safe place. You probably will need it someday. Especially if you have a houseful of girls. After all, lipstick is useful for so many things. Like playing dress up. And putting on Halloween makeup. And lipstick makes a terrific prize for good behavior.

And lipstick is a handy substitute for Magic Markers when every single one of the 233 Magic Markers in your castle is hiding between sofa cushions and under beds and at the bottom of junk drawers and in all of those other secret places where Magic Markers end up when they go on vacation. The vacation they take with the 14 pairs of scissors in the house.

Obviously, up until that Friday afternoon at cake camp, I had followed a strict rule that I would never throw away any lipstick. I love lipstick so much that I could not bear to part with a single tube. Even if I was not crazy about the color. And I had learned over the years that it was a good idea to keep a lipstick even if the product is so low that it is deeply recessed into the metal. You will need that almost-gone tube of Rosy Roses you wore on your wedding day when you are nostalgically browsing the cosmetics counters years later, attempting to find the perfect matching color. A color that coordinates beautifully with the red dress you plan to wear on your date with Prince Charming. A color that is sure to bring back fond memories of champagne and smiles and wedding cake.

Once upon a time, when we had moved castles for the third time in three years, weary from lugging furniture and cake stands and books and clothes and lipstick from apartment to house to apartment to house, Prince Charming asked me why I kept the box of lipstick. "Keeping lipstick is the female version of the male idea that you should never throw away any can of paint," I said.

Ah ha! My husband nodded enthusiastically, understanding my point completely. Any Prince Charming worthy of his title knows with absolute certainty that the queen of the castle will someday request that at least one room be repainted precisely in its original shade, no substitutes allowed. That's just the way it is. And that was the end of my Prince Charming's line of questioning about the lipstick.

"Never pass up a chance to buy a new lipstick," I advised my mother. I was still chatting away on my phone. Which I was clutching in one hand. I was using my free hand to pick up paper cake plates and plastic forks from the basement floor and toss them into a big yellow recycling bag.

"A great new shade of lip color is a reasonably-priced pick-me-up on one of those frazzled days," I suggested. My mother agreed. She added her own diet idea to the lipstick idea. My mother and I love to share diet ideas. "And, at zero calories," she said, "a treat like a lipstick is a figure-conscious substitute for a dip into the candy jar. Which in turn allows you to eat a little more cake for dessert that night." My mother is so clever.

Keeping lipsticks really is a great idea, I thought to myself after my mother and I got off the phone. Maybe, though, forever is too long. Maybe a box of lipstick has a shelf life of something closer to 20 years. After 20 years, I think it is okay to let it go.

I wrote it all up in my diary that night. All of my good ideas about lipsticks. And how long to keep them. And how long to keep other things, too. Twenty years is plenty long to keep a lipstick, I wrote. Adding: And a pair of jeans. And probably a cake recipe cut out of a magazine. And anything else that starts to look a little tired and a little faded after two decades. Except for Prince Charmings, I thought to myself. A good one of those is something you should keep forever. Even if yours happens to look a little tired and a little faded every once in a while. Particularly after he has hauled your box of lipsticks from castle to castle. Again.

Keep the Prince Charming but recycle the lipsticks, I wrote as I nearly completed the diary entry. I circled back around to cake as I so often do. Lipsticks are no help when it comes to the stability of cake, I added. I was almost ready to close the pink notebook for the night and put away my pen when I was struck by another interesting application of the lipstick idea. I jotted down one final thought in my diary entry for the day: Twenty years might also be too long to keep a job. Even the most magical and wonderful job. Especially if you are the type who tends to ask "What next?"

Actually, twenty years might be about two times too long.

Chapter 7

Every girl needs a go-to coffee cake recipe. Even I have one. Even though I never actually eat coffee cake for breakfast. I do, however, make coffee cake when I serve brunch. And I do drink a lot of coffee. And I don't want any gaps in my cake portfolio. So I have a go-to coffee cake recipe.

"I wonder why I've never bothered to give my coffee cake a fancy name," I said one Sunday as I was working away in the kitchen. I was in the mood to bake. Again. Still. Always.

Neither of the two princesses who were in the kitchen with me that morning had an answer to that question. But they did ask an even better question. "When do you add the coffee to the cake?" So smart, these princesses! "You don't," I explained. "Coffee cake is something you eat when you drink coffee. "You don't actually add coffee to the cake," I explained. "Although I suppose you could dip the cake into your coffee. Kind of like some people do with biscotti or donuts." The girls still looked a little puzzled. Then they became more interested in the idea of helping me add the vanilla to the cake batter and less interested in the idea of the cake itself.

Coffee cake is a wonderful invention! It is like eating dessert before noon. Which is always a fun idea. Plus, many coffee cakes are baked in Bundt pans. Which automatically gives them an air of legitimacy. There is something about a Bundt pan that says "I am trustworthy. Your grandmother had one of me. I have been around for a very long time."

I make my coffee cake using Betty Crocker white cake mix. Of course I do! In my favorite pink mixing bowl, I blend a stick of melted butter into the cake mix. Then I add one egg at room temperature. I mix up the egg a little bit first so I can add the egg slowly, in three parts, mixing in between each addition. Then I add vanilla. Oh how I do love vanilla! I always let the girls add about a tablespoon. Next I add a dash of salt. Finally I fold a cup of sour cream into the mix. In baking, to fold means to mix very slowly, using a lifting motion with a spatula so you are pressing the ingredients together. This is different from stirring. Which is a circular technique. Stirring adds more air to the batter than folding. I like my coffee cake dense without much air.

The girls watched as I poured the coffee cake batter into the Bundt pan. Which I had greased with butter and dusted with flour. I love a buttery coffee cake! So I use the real thing to grease the pan instead of using non-stick cooking spray. Out of the corner of my eye I caught a glimpse of my littlest princess swiping the extra butter from the side of the Bundt pan. She licked it off her finger with a look of pure joy. She is the princess who views bread as a condiment for butter instead of the other way around.

The distinguishing feature of coffee cake compared with other types of cake is that coffee cake includes some sort of crumble or crunch or streusel. I just call it crumble. Crumble is the best part! Crumble is kind of like frosting. Meaning that the ingredients do not have to be precise. It is hard to go wrong when you are combining butter, sugar, nuts and cinnamon with a little flour and spreading it all over the top of the cake batter to form a yummy bottom crust for your coffee cake. Delicious!

A good crumble usually happens when you follow the general guidelines of folding one cup flour, one cup firmly packed brown sugar and a tablespoon of cinnamon into a stick of butter cut up into at least 12 pieces. And then mixing in a cup of chopped nuts. I like to put walnuts and pecans in my crumble. Almonds don't work so well in a crumble.

"Girls, girls!" I declared. "Add the crumble!" Crumble is a great way to involve children in coffee cake. It is fun to scoop out the big, yummy, nutty, buttery crumbs and sprinkle them all over the top of the cake batter. The top of the cake batter becomes the bottom of the cake. After it is all baked for about an hour at 350 degrees and the cake is flipped over onto a gorgeous cake plate.

No matter what my husband says, I cannot stand the thought of a cake with no frosting. Even a coffee cake. So I always drizzle vanilla buttercream over the top and toss on a few extra nuts to make the cake look pretty.

"There!" I said to the only princess who had stuck with me in the kitchen to see the happy ending of the coffee cake-making story. "We now have a coffee cake for Sunday brunch." Of course this was purely theoretical. I was not actually serving brunch. We all had finished our cereal four hours ago. And the girls and I had already made a round trip to my favorite coffee shop, LattéLand. Where the littlest princesses had eaten an early lunch of plain bagels, toasted. With butter. Of course. And where I had lovingly sipped my café Americano. Which I do every day. A large Americano with Splenda and two tablespoons of half-and-half. So the coffee cake was just for show. I took pictures.

Summer was in full swing, with dinners on the deck and Saturday afternoons at the swimming pool and camp sessions in the basement and cakes in the kitchen. And cake was still filling up a lot of pages in my diary. But I was branching out a bit. I had started to jot down a few more ideas about doing good. In my pink notebook. And in my blog posts, too.

Truth be told, my literary adventures in cakes and charity began a couple of years before I fell in love with pink notebooks. My literary adventures had begun while sitting behind my desk at the office writing articles, brochures and blog posts about charitable giving and all of the easy, fun and rewarding ways to do good. It is an understatement to say that the blogging took on a life of its own when I also started doing it at my kitchen counter. I suppose magical things happen when you bring your day job into a house full of girls, generosity and lots of Betty Crocker cake mix!

I was still at my kitchen counter. Staring at the coffee cake. Wondering what I should do with it. Eat it? Freeze it? Invite a few friends over for four o'clock tea? Give it away? I called my mother. "Hi!" I said. "Hi!" she replied, even though she had already said "hello" when she had answered the phone. That's just the way it works with me and my mother.

"Do you and Dad want a coffee cake?" I asked my mother. I was developing quite a reputation among family and friends for finding good homes for good cakes. Sometimes I even left them, anonymously, at neighbors' doorsteps. By this time, though, most people had figured out that it was I who was the recreational pastry chef behind the One Celebrations label.

"Oh, no thanks," said my mother. "I still have some of your cake from Mother's Day in the freezer." My mother is so sweet. She saves my cakes for months. At any given time I am sure she has remnants of at least five cakes in her freezer. But, as I always say, there is no such thing as too much cake. I guess I could just eat this one myself.

"How's the diary coming?" my mother asked. She is always so thoughtful to check in on my various endeavors. "Great," I answered. I'm starting to write a little more about charitable giving." That was true. I was writing more frequently on that topic.

I did not mention that I had also started to seriously wonder whether I was doing enough good in the world to qualify as a socially responsible citizen. True, I was trying to recycle as many cans of all-natural grape soda as possible. And I was tossing coins into the Ronald McDonald House donation box on ice cream outings. And Prince Charming and I were writing checks to a few of our favorite organizations. But was all of that good enough to add up to being a good girl? Was that good enough to count as giving back? Was that good enough to teach my girls about the joys of being generous and helping others?

I was still feeling a bit insecure about looking good. About work. About doing good. About myself.

I shared a few of my initial ideas with my mother. Launching into the ideas with high speed and enthusiasm. Which is what I typically do whenever I dream up a new idea and test it on my mother. "Some people do good by volunteering to pick up trash in their neighborhoods," I said. "Some people give back by donating canned goods to a food pantry. Some people recycle because they want to be socially responsible. Some people write checks to charities. Some people help others by making dinners for families going through tough times."

Even through the silence on the other end of the phone, I could tell my mother was listening. So I went on. "I think all of these things are good ideas! My ideas about doing good are a lot like my ideas about making a cake. There is no such thing as a bad way to do it. And no amount is too little or too much. It is all good."

"Well," said my always supportive mother. "You are certainly qualified to have an opinion. It would be next to impossible to spend more than ten years working at a charitable foundation and not come up with a few ideas about doing good."

And that was true. My wonderful job had taught me a lot. A lot about giving to charity. About giving back. About being socially responsible. About helping others. Whatever words you use—giving to charity, giving back, being socially responsible, helping others—all of it is doing good.

Some of my ideas about doing good are big ideas, some are little ideas, some are interesting ideas and some of my ideas are probably not all that interesting to anyone other than me. My favorite idea, though, is that good, like beauty, is in the eye of the beholder. Meaning that any sort of definition of what qualifies as doing good is entirely personal. It may even be useful only to the one who created it.

Bolstered by my mother's validation, I kept right on going. Writing down my ideas about doing good. The following Saturday morning I ventured out alone to the coffee shop. I pulled out my pink notebook. And I started making a list of all the ways a person can do good. After only 15 minutes the list was getting so long that I decided to switch from the diary to the iPhone. A list like this was worth putting into electronic format, I thought. It might come in handy.

Balancing a Splenda-spiked large Americano in one hand and my iPhone in the other, I typed as fast as I possibly could with the few fingers I was not already using. I called my list of ideas Easy Ways for Every Girl to Do a Little Good. Not quite as catchy as a few of the names I had given some of my cakes. But the words said exactly what I meant. It really is easy to do good. And everyone can do it.

I want to qualify as socially responsible, I thought. Whatever that means to me. And that was true. And that is still true. I want to do good. I want to give back. And I want to inspire other people who like to do good to do good, too, and give back in their own ways. Whatever their own favorite causes might be.

You really can do good. Even if you do not work for a charitable foundation. Even if you do not have socially-responsible-citizen-in-training printed on your business card. Even if you do not idolize Angelina Jolie. Even if you do not write checks to charities. And even if you do not believe in recycling. No matter who you are or where you live or what cereal you eat or what you believe, it is easy for you to do good if that is what you want to do.

Coincidentally, one of my favorite ideas for doing good is somewhat related to coffee cake. And bacon, of all things. And even pancakes, I suppose, if you are a pancake girl. And donuts. And quiche. And coffee. Lots of coffee. And even cereal. Bacon, pancakes, donuts, quiche, coffee and cereal are all things you could serve at a Breakfast for Bedspreads. A Breakfast for Bedspreads is a wonderful idea for doing good.

The credit for the Breakfast for Bedspreads idea belongs to one of my friends. My smart friend who started a really great communications firm. A communications firm that does a lot of good. This firm is so good that it gives every single one of its employees a charitable foundation. Wow! This very good firm is called Global Prairie. And my friend who founded Global Prairie is also very good. And creative. And generous. She dreamed up the Breakfast for Bedspreads.

The idea started one Saturday morning. My friend and I were visiting Ronald McDonald House with our daughters. As we were saying our thank yous and our goodbyes, the Ronald McDonald House director just happened to mention that the comforters in the rooms at the house were getting old. "This is a home away from home," she said. "A home away from home for families of children who are in the hospital. We want the rooms to be as comfortable as possible." The director and the mothers and the daughters checked out a few of the rooms. The director was right. Some of the bedding was looking a little tired.

"Let's host a Breakfast for Bedspreads," said my friend. She is always so innovative and entrepreneurial. "We can invite mothers and daughters. And we can raise money to buy new comforters for Ronald McDonald House." What a great idea! "I'm in!" I said. And our daughters were smiling. They were in, too.

A Breakfast for Bedspreads is something any girl can do to do good. A little bacon is just about all you need to pull it off. You will also need a handful of little girls who are beginning to appreciate how good it feels to do nice things for others.

It is that easy! Truly, just pick up some donuts and coffee. And, if you want, fry up some bacon. Gather your friends and their children around your kitchen counter on a Saturday morning. Just for an hour or so, in a come-and-go format. Take up a small collection of coins from piggy banks and allowance money. And maybe a few checks from the mothers who are willing to skip the pedicures this month.

"The whole breakfast adventure warmed my heart and soul," I said to my friend when I thanked her for dreaming up the idea after it was all over. I had loved watching that special do-good glow of pride work its magic in my daughter. Sparking a new little twinkle in her eye. And making her cheeks rosy up to the most beautiful shade of princess pink.

"Thank you for hosting it," I added sincerely. My friend had been so generous. She had opened her home to three dozen mothers and daughters that morning. And she had served gourmet quiche, not donuts. The whole thing was such a lovely affair. My oldest princess was just sure that she had stumbled into the domain of royalty when we arrived at the party. There is no substitute for lovely antiques and quiche when it comes to converting even the youngest and most independent good girl to act like a lady for a day.

I was still sitting in the coffee shop. Typing away into my iPhone. Host a Breakfast for Bedspreads, I added to my growing list of Easy Ways for Every Girl to Do a Little Good. I kept going with the list. I was taking advantage of the fact that Prince Charming was at home with the little girls, bless his heart. Setting up the pink princess tent in the basement. And serving cereal for breakfast. And unloading the dishwasher. And breaking up inter-princess disagreements. I had the whole morning to myself.

I put away my phone and switched back to the pink notebook to give my fingers a break. I opened my diary to a new page. I added an entry about parties. Building on the whole idea of the Breakfast for Bedspreads. Parties are a great excuse to do good. The magic is that the reverse is true, too, because doing good is a great excuse to have a party. It really is a palindrome of sorts: Have a party, do good; do good, have a party.

Parties come in all shapes and sizes. If you love dressing up and going to the charity ball each year, do it! If you love tossing coins into the fountain at the art museum on summer afternoons, do it. If you love hosting a block party to eat all of the Girl Scout cookies purchased by the families who live on your street, do it. And if you love baking cakes with your kids, picking a charity and making a donation, do it.

Wow! That was an awful lot of good thinking for a Saturday morning at the coffee shop. I closed the diary of a good girl and slipped the pink notebook into my purse. I left the coffee shop. Heading to the grocery store to buy cereal, cake mix and a few non-essential groceries.

I felt a rush of euphoria as I approached the baking aisle at the grocery store. I was surrounded by the things I loved. It felt so good! Dozens of flavors of cake mix. Six types of sugar. Cooking oil in bottles of every possible size and shape. Vanilla extract in eight varieties. Almond extract. Birthday candles. Candy sprinkles.

Heaven.

I scanned the cake mixes. I was feeling a little sheepish for having taken the easy way out the weekend before, making a simple coffee cake that did not involve layers. Surely I had not let the Raspberry Peach Drizzle Cake experience get the best of me? Surely I was not afraid to go beyond five layers? Surely I was braver than a crumbled fruity cake, now reduced by a dashing Prince Charming to just a few bites left in the refrigerator?

No. Not me! I was not scared of layers. "Bring it on," I said to the cake mixes. And with that, I loaded up my cart with thirty boxes of cake mix. White cake mix, yellow cake mix, lemon cake mix and various chocolate flavors of cake mix. German Chocolate. Devil's Food. Dark Chocolate. Milk Chocolate. I even tossed in a few boxes of Red Velvet. I was inspired!

I pushed my cart down the aisle, attempting to gently maneuver around a woman and her granddaughter. They were analyzing the Jell-O and trying to figure out which size box they needed for a recipe that called for cherry gelatin. The grandmother took one look at my cart as I tried to pass and immediately stopped me in the middle of the aisle.

"Are you a baker?" the grandmother asked. She and her granddaughter were staring, wide-eyed, at my cart full of cake mix. I thought about saying, "No, I work at a charitable foundation. I am a lawyer." And then I realized how utterly silly that would sound coming out of the mouth of a woman pushing a grocery cart full of Betty Crocker.

"Yes," I said instead. I repeated it with a little more confidence. "Yes, I am!" And then the woman and the granddaughter and the recreational pastry chef—that would be me—had the most delightful, ten-minute conversation about cake.

"We are making the Poke Cake," the grandmother explained. She was pointing to a recipe cut from a magazine. The paper was yellowed. The well-loved recipe had been folded and unfolded so many times that I could barely see the print. "You know, the yellow cake you make in a 9 × 13 pan? The one you poke holes into with a straw when it is hot out of the oven? And pour Jell-O down the holes? The Poke Cake."

Of course I knew all about the Poke Cake. I do not make the Poke Cake myself because I like to bake in round layers, not flat rectangles. But that's just my architectural preference when it comes to cake. The Poke Cake is a very fine cake. I told that to the grandmother. "Oh the Poke Cake is wonderful! It will be delicious. You have done such a great job figuring out the ingredients. It is not your fault that Jell-O has changed its box sizes since your recipe was printed."

The grandmother and the daughter looked genuinely relieved. I pushed my cart back into the aisle's right lane and made a left turn toward the butter section. I was smiling from ear to ear. It had felt so good to be able to help.

I was still on a Poke Cake high when I loaded the groceries into the trunk and got back into my car, heading for home. I kept thinking about doing good. And I kept thinking about my definition of a good girl. "I sure am spending a lot of time thinking about what it means to do good," I said to myself. "And what it means to be good. And what it means to be a good girl."

And that was true. I was thinking about it not just when I was sitting in coffee shops. Or driving to the grocery store. Way more than that. I was thinking about what it means to do good, and I was thinking about what it means to be good, practically every single day of my life. I was thinking about doing good and being good as much as I was thinking about cake. "I really am obsessed!" I said aloud. A car is a wonderful place to engage in a good conversation with yourself.

Most of us want to do a little more good and be a little more good than just waking up every day. I am sure that is what I was thinking when I had been compelled to write down my own good girl definition in the first place. Admittedly, I frequently question whether I am measuring up. And not just measuring up in terms of pumpkin pancakes versus cereal. More like a global "Am I good?" Or an "Am I good enough?"

I bet I am not alone in asking myself this question.

I see that question in the brown eyes of my two stepdaughters as they begin to think about launching careers after college. Wondering just how far their talents and their stunning beauty will get them. And wondering if they will be good enough to make enough money to eat at Chipotle three times a week.

I see it in my oldest daughter, in her big green eyes, as she wonders whether she is good enough at hitting the softball. Or good enough to be friends with the kids who wear Justin Bieber t-shirts. Or good enough at keeping her room clean to earn her allowance.

I see it in the blue eyes of my middle daughter with the curly blonde angel hair as she tries desperately to make friends on the playground. Something that will be a lifelong challenge because of her special needs.

I see it in my youngest daughter. Especially when she stops dead in her tracks in the middle of a sprint toward the soccer goal. Pausing to adjust her ponytail and then looking around to see who might have noticed that her hair had been slightly out of whack.

Yes. Like daughters, like mother. I spend a lot of time wondering whether I am living up to good girl expectations. Whatever that means for a woman who is in relentless and humorous pursuit of being a better mother. A better stepmother. A better wife, daughter, sister, friend. A better entrepreneur, cake-baker, giver to charity, writer, connoisseur of coffee and mascara, fairy tale chaser, lover of wine (limited to three-fifths of a glass unless it is a special occasion). A better non-practicing lawyer, self-proclaimed recreational pastry chef, socially responsible citizen-in-training and, of course, lipstick's biggest fan. Which requires the ability to select a really good color. Something I am always studying.

And then I laughed at myself. I really was obsessed with being good! And, even funnier, I had to admit that I was starting to enjoy the obsession. What girl wouldn't? Good looks, good cake, doing good. It was all good!

I got home from the grocery store. I re-stocked my pantry with cake mix and cereal. And then it dawned on me that I might be okay. Maybe I am good after all, I thought to myself. Maybe I am already a good mother, a good daughter, a good stepmother, a good wife, a good friend, a good do-gooder. Well that would be a relief! All of this self-help might be paying off. "Maybe I am getting closer to living up to my own definition of a good girl," I said to the empty kitchen.

Maybe. But I still had a feeling that I could be better.

Chapter 8

One Signature Birthday Cake

Even I will admit that chocolate cake is seductive. That is because chocolate cake is much more about the chocolate than it is about the cake. And chocolate is compelling. Chocolate is compelling in a way that no other dessert is compelling. White cake, though, is all about the cake. Therefore, because I love cake more than I love chocolate, it makes sense that I would love white cake more than I love chocolate cake.

But I love chocolate, too. And every so often I find it absolutely necessary to make a chocolate cake.

"What are we doing this weekend?" asked my middle daughter. She is the daughter who was born with Williams Syndrome, which is a rare genetic condition affecting one out of approximately 7,500 to 10,000 people. A rare genetic condition that causes a handful of mostly mild physical and mental disabilities. A rare genetic condition that is present at birth and so there is no cure.

"Well," I said, looking her straight in the eyes to increase the likelihood of focus and retention. "On Saturday, we will wake up and get dressed and eat cereal. And then we will go to LattéLand." Explaining future events in chronological order is very important when you are talking with a child who has Williams Syndrome. Abstract concepts of space and time are really hard for them to grasp. But they are pretty good with sequences.

"And then what?" my daughter asked. "And then what?" is one of her favorite questions. "And then," I said, "we will come back home. I have to make a chocolate cake." I paused to let all of this sink in. "Oh," she said. And then she asked, "Why do you have to make a chocolate cake?" The answer was simple. "Because I just have to."

That is how it is with chocolate cake. Call it a craving. Call it a compulsion. Call it a calling. Whatever it is, when it happens, you really have to make a chocolate cake. The only legitimate questions from that point forward are questions that pertain to what kind of a chocolate cake you will make. Not whether you will make one.

Saturday morning unfolded precisely as I had promised my daughter it would. We woke up. We ate cereal for breakfast. I drove myself and two princesses to LattéLand to pick up my favorite coffee. And I drove us all back home.

I surveyed my pantry to check on the cake mix supply. "Oh, good!" I said to the girls. They were ready to roll up their sleeves and get to work on chocolate cake. "We have lots of choices!" How could I have forgotten? I had stocked up on Betty Crocker cake mix the weekend before. What a relief. Otherwise I would have had to make a polite request of Prince Charming to make a grocery store run. And I was not sure it had been long enough since the rehearsal dinner to be able to get away with that.

German Chocolate. Devil's Food. Milk Chocolate. Dark Chocolate. It was all sounding pretty good to me. So I let the girls pick. "Devil's Food!" They were all in agreement. Only one of them actually likes chocolate cake, though. So I am pretty sure they picked the cake flavor based on its name. Which is itself worth noting. A good name can get you pretty far. If you are a person or if you are a cake.

Any variety of Betty Crocker chocolate cake mix is a good choice. I have tried them all. And they are all tasty. Doctor up the recipe a bit, though. Blend the oil into the mix first, before you add anything else. The box calls for water, but use whole milk instead. And be sure to bring the eggs and milk to room temperature before you add them. And add the eggs one at a time, alternating with the milk. And add a little vanilla. Vanilla in chocolate cake is yummy! Sometimes I also add a dash of cinnamon. Or coffee in place of a tablespoon or two of milk. Or a little cocoa powder. Playing with the flavors in a chocolate cake is fun.

"Girls, you may now lick the bowl," I announced as I placed three round cake pans of chocolate cake batter into the oven. "Lick" "the" "bowl" were the three words the girls had been waiting to hear. I gave each of them a spoon and let them have at it. And this time I got out my own spoon and jumped right in myself. I actually like chocolate cake batter better than baked chocolate cake.

I licked my spoon and surveyed the situation. It was only 11:00 a.m. The day was young. And the pantry was full. Why bake just one cake when we could bake two?

"While we're at it," I said to the girls, "let's make a white cake, too. We could get that done and still have time to make the frosting. And maybe even go swimming." It was a pretty day outside. Sunny and warm but not too hot. One of those textbook days in mid-June without a cloud in the sky. A perfect day to go to the pool.

Two hours later I had six layers of cake cooling on my kitchen counter and a big bowl of vanilla buttercream frosting to go along with it. And I had six little feet pattering along behind me, single file like little ducklings, their flip-flops flapping as we made our way down the sidewalk and across the street and to the pool.

What mother could ask for anything more, I thought to myself. Cakes in the kitchen. Kids at the pool. Sun in the sky. It is all so good! I answered my own question. "Me, that's who," I said out loud. The girls kept walking. They were used to me talking to myself. "I am a mother who could ask for something more. I am a mother who wants more. I am a mother who could do more."

But more what? That was the real question. I thought about that as I stood watch over the swimming pool. Attempting to keep an eye on all three girls at the same time. Supervising children who are bobbing around in a pool has got to be one of the most challenging exercises for a parent. Way more challenging than supervising children when they are adding vanilla to cake batter. Bodies of water are far more treacherous than hand mixers.

"What more could I do?" I said quietly to myself as I took a few steps closer to the edge of the pool to get a better view. Surely I could do more. My life has given me so much. A good husband. A good job. Five good girls. I am so fortunate, I thought, with a rush of gratitude.

The girls and I talk a lot about gratitude. I always tell my daughters things like "We are so lucky to have a house." And "We are so lucky to have each other." And "We are so lucky to be able to go to the swimming pool." I try to explain that some little girls and little boys never learn to swim. That some girls and boys do not have a swimming pool nearby. "And even if they do," I added the last time we had the conversation, "there is no one around to take them to be sure they stay safe." My girls always listen and nod. As young as they are, they do understand they are lucky. And they are grateful.

Maybe I could start by doing more good, I thought. A shark toy flew out of the pool and hit me on the toe. I checked to be sure it hadn't chipped my pink nail polish. No time for a pedicure today! The polish was unscathed. I tossed the shark back into the water. Yes, maybe doing more good would be a good place to begin. Besides, I thought, it would be a good excuse to start testing the ideas I had written down in my pink notebooks. The ideas in my diary entry about Easy Ways for Every Girl to Do a Little Good. Yes, I thought. I could test a few things. Kind of like I had been testing recipes for cake. It sure couldn't hurt to try.

I called my mother from my laundry room. The girls and I were back home from the pool. Safely. "Hi!" I said. I got ready to throw two wet towels into the dryer and realized the dryer was already full of already dry clothes. "I have a good idea to run by you." My mother loves ideas. "Oh good!" she said. "What is it?" "Actually," I said, "it is an idea about doing good. I have decided to try to do more good. By trying out new ideas for ways to do good. Some of the things I've been adding to my diary lately."

My mother liked the idea. "How nice that your hobby can help your job and your job can help your hobby," she said. "Not many people get to do good at work and also do good at home. You're checking a lot of boxes with that diary of yours." I stopped moving laundry around for a moment to consider what my mother had said. "You know, you're right," I remarked. "And to think! I also get to eat a lot of cake."

The cake! I had almost forgotten about the layers of Devil's Food and fluffy white. My mother and I said our goodbyes. I called out to the girls. "Girls, girls! It is time to assemble the cake. Come quickly!" No one showed up. I guess I'd been calling on the girls a lot lately. Maybe there really is such a thing as too much cake. Then again, maybe there isn't.

The assembly was all up to me. Three layers of fluffy white cake. Three layers of Devil's Food cake. A bowl of frosting. I dug around in my pantry until I found a package of white fondant and little circles of pastel candy and I set them on the counter next to the bowl of frosting. I got out a clear glass cake stand. My decorating materials were spread out in front of me. I was ready for six layers.

Surely I could manage six layers, I thought. The Retro Birthday Cake was a six-layer cake and it had stayed standing just fine. This might work. Then I thought about the five-layer Raspberry Peach Drizzle Cake. And the fact that chocolate cake is a little more dense, and therefore a bit heavier, than fluffy white cake. This is because chocolate cake contains egg yolks as well as egg whites. It's all chemistry.

"This will be a good test," I said to the materials on my kitchen counter. "I suppose I will find out if chocolate cake is heavy like cobbler or light like white. Or somewhere in between."

Mindful of the relative weight of chocolate versus white, I started with a layer of Devil's Food on the bottom. I worked my way up, alternating chocolate with white. I frosted the top of each layer before I added the next. Intentionally disturbing the crumb coat. I wanted to make sure I got that delicious layer of cake-frosting blend. Even if it fell over I wanted the cake to taste good. So far, so good, I thought as I added the sixth tier. The cake was not even wobbling. Amazing. I warmed up the rest of the vanilla buttercream frosting in the microwave. I poured it over the top. Cake still standing. Like magic. Perhaps wishes really do come true!

I still did not quite trust the cake. So I kept watch out of the corner of my eye as I rolled out the white fondant onto a plastic mold. A plastic mold covered with a pattern of little indented circles. "What a fun touch to make the fondant look a bit like a pebbly beach. Perfect for a post-swim celebration." I was still talking to my decorating materials.

I got out my circular cookie cutters. The small ones. And I cut 25 or so circles, in three different sizes, out of the rolled fondant. Using a little extra frosting as the glue, I stuck the circles all over the sides of the cake, randomly, in no particular order. And then I stuck the little circles of pastel candy right in the middle of the fondant circles.

I stepped back. I raised my eyebrows. This was not your run-of-the-mill cake. The cake was off-beat. It was slightly eccentric. And friendly. Authentic. Unusual. Colorful. Still classy, in a casually elegant sort of way, like my other cakes. And this cake was even a bit artistic. I liked it! "I am the cake-baker," I reminded the voice in my head telling me that my cake was not good enough. "And the cake-baker gets to decide how the cake is decorated. And it does not have to look like the pictures in cookbooks and magazines."

Right. This cake was my cake. This cake was mine to decorate. This cake was mine to eat. Or to share. Or to give away. This was my cake. Whoever said that real cakes have to look like the cakes in the magazines anyway? Beauty is in the eye of the beholder. Just because a cake does not look like the super model cakes in the magazines and on television does not mean that the cake is not good.

I took a few steps toward the opposite end of the kitchen counter to get another look. An alternate perspective. A second opinion. A view of the cake from a different angle. Just to see if I was right. Ah. From my position at the other end of the counter it was clear that the cake had started to tilt. It was leaning to the right. Noticeably, I might add. Noticeably leaning to the right.

My heart began to sink. Then I noticed something else. The cake was tilting, yes. But it was not actively tilting. That is, the tilting had stopped. The cake was not moving. The cake was stable. In a tilted position. Well, well, I thought. Isn't this interesting? The cake actually looked rather appealing, leaning a bit to the right. Imperfect, but lovable. This cake was not afraid to be itself.

"I love you!" I said to the cake. It was a good thing the girls had scattered after we returned from the pool. "I love you" is an unconventional thing to say to a cake. But I really did love that cake. I loved that cake for what it was. Tilt and all.

I loved it. And I had no idea what I would do with it. I thought about calling my mother again. This time to ask if she wanted a six-layer fluffy white and Devil's Food cake with vanilla butter-cream frosting decorated with white fondant and pastel candies and leaning slightly to the right. I decided that was not a good idea. My mother had turned down a coffee cake less than a week ago due to a freezer already full of cake. There was no way she would be interested in opening her home to a cake twice that size. Except out of pity. And this was not a cake to be pitied.

"I'll think about it tomorrow," I said to the cake. "But I promise to find you a good home." I thought about adding "or I'll eat you myself," but I kept my mouth shut. I got out the roll of plastic wrap and carefully covered the cake.

And then I went back to doing good. Or at least thinking about doing good. Picking up where I had left off earlier that day with my new plan to test out different ways to do good. I started with a little market research. Which meant that I tracked down Prince Charming. I found him in the office.

"I need your help," I said. "I need a little research on the overall idea of doing good and charitable giving and giving back and social responsibility and helping others and whatever else people call it. I've got a few ideas written down in my pink notebook that I'd like to test."

Prince Charming is wonderful. He always knows how to find the best information. Fast. "Sure," he said. "Give me just a minute." I sat down on the chair in front of his desk. Tap tap tap tap tap tap tap. My husband typed away on his computer. Staring intently at the screen. I think I got smarter just watching him. "There," he said, decisively lifting his fingers off the keyboard. "Here's some information to get you started." "Wait," I said. "Let me get my diary. So I can take notes."

I was back in a flash. "Go ahead," I said. And he did. I had to write quickly! My husband talks almost as fast as I do when he is full of good ideas. "I suppose you have noticed that everyone is doing good?" he commented. I jotted that down in my diary. A question is always a good place to start. "Well, a clear majority is doing good," Prince Charming continued. "More than 70% of Americans give to charity, shelling out $300 billion or so every year to the one-and-a-half million charities across the nation."

"That's a lot!" I said. I did not tell him that I already knew that statistic. That it was my job to know that statistic. I was just glad to be engaged in a conversation with someone other than a cake. My husband continued. "Apparently, most people think giving back is fun because consumer spending on charitable giving totals almost 60% of the amount Americans spend on recreation." Well that was interesting. "I did not know that!" I said to Prince Charming. "I guess that means that giving is fun? Or that it should be fun? Or that it is fun to do good?" "Makes sense to me," he replied.

Yes. It really did make sense. Come to think of it, I had in fact noticed that it was becoming much more fun to give than it used to be. "Remember when we used to feel arm-twisted into giving?" I asked Prince Charming. "Well I think the tide is turning! It seems like scarcity and guilt are caving into an abundance mentality. Like giving has become part of popular culture." I paused for a moment to think about this. "And," I continued, "it certainly doesn't hurt that just about every celebrity has adopted a cause. Or at least one orphaned child. I say more power to them. Plus it means that I can read *People* magazine and count it as continuing education."

That was the end of the conversation. Prince Charming does not read *People* magazine. He reads *The Economist* and *The Wall Street Journal* and *WIRED* and the *Atlantic* and *The New Yorker*. That is why he is so smart. He is the smartest person I know. And those are all very good publications. And I like them just fine. But I love *People* magazine.

That night I sat down to study my diary. I flipped back to my entries from the coffee shop. The entries about all of the easy ways to do good. There really are so many ways to check the I-did-good box! Just because your favorite method of giving doesn't show up as a tax deductible contribution to a charitable organization does not mean it is not good. Sometimes the best way to do good is to support a school fundraiser. Or buy a product where a portion of the proceeds supports a charitable cause. Or buy a ticket to a fundraising dinner. Or purchase something fun at a charity auction. Or, of course, to drop your change in the McDonald's drive-through box. Or remember to turn off lights. Which, in my opinion, includes telling your children to do it. Or to deliver a cake to a neighbor for no particular reason. Or to cater a rehearsal dinner as a gift to a colleague. Or to recycle as many cans of soda as possible.

I spent the next few days doing more research on the subject of doing good. It turns out that there are lots of interesting theories about why people give. And lots of research to help explain the behavior. Some people cannot bear to see other human beings suffer. So they give out of a desire to help the less fortunate. Some people give to make the whole community better because they love where they live. Some people give out of a sense of equity and fairness, believing they should give some of what they have to those who do not have as much. Some people give out of a sense of gratitude, so thankful for what they have that they want to give away a little or a lot as a thank you to the universe, as a statement of appreciation to the human race. Some people give because of social pressure, wanting to be sure they measure up to the standards of good achieved by their neighbors, colleagues, fellow club members, parents and grandparents and professional competitors. My head was spinning!

"It looks like doing good probably even makes you happier," I said to Prince Charming one evening after a couple days of research. We were sitting at the kitchen counter. Prince Charming was not thinking about doing good. He was thinking about cake. "What are you going to do with this big cake?" he asked. My six-layer masterpiece was still sitting on the counter. Three days after I had made it. Carefully covered, of course. And it was still tilting. But it was still standing. And I still loved it.

"I'm working on that," I assured my very patient husband. "First I need to get this research done. So that I can start testing ways to do good. In addition to testing cakes." That seemed to only partially satisfy Prince Charming. "Well, okay," he said. "As long as you keep testing cakes. I really liked that peach one."

I continued sharing the results of my research. "Plenty of studies are emerging on this," I said. "Researchers are finding that extra endorphins are actually released when you do things for other people." For Prince Charming's sake I added "Of course eating a huge piece of fluffy white cake with vanilla buttercream frosting will make you happier, too. And it definitely produces a positive chemical reaction in your brain." So, why not do both, I thought. Have your cake and give, too. I kind of liked that idea.

"The best way to do good," said Prince Charming, "is to employ people." Prince Charming is very involved in politics. The kind of politics that lean the same way the cake on the counter was leaning. "Every human being deserves to do meaningful work. And to be paid for it. That's the whole point behind free enterprise. It's the best form of doing good out there."

Hmmmm. I do not really get involved in politics. I tend to prefer universal truths to policies and regulations and laws and committees and platforms. Universal truths about the value of each human being. And the potential of diverse talents. And the power of the mind and the soul and the body and the heart when they are all working together. And the importance of treating people with respect. And the beauty of managing your own affairs so you have something to give to others. Things like that.

But I did not dismiss what my husband had said. He is very smart. And usually very right. That night I pulled out the pink notebook from my purse. I opened the diary to a new page. I wrote: Can a cake do good? And below it I answered the question: Yes. I was sure I could figure that one out. So I wrote down another question. A more specific question. A question inspired by Prince Charming. The question was: Can the six-layer cake sitting on my kitchen counter do good by translating into meaningful work for a talented human being? I did not have an answer. I drew a complete blank. I would have to sleep on that question, I thought as I climbed into bed.

At 2:45 a.m. I was wide awake. I had an idea. An idea for the six-layer cake. An idea for meaningful work. Meaningful work for a talented human being. I made my way into the closet in the dark. I did not want to wake Prince Charming and the two little princesses sleeping on the floor. I pulled my iPhone from my purse. And I headed for the kitchen. And for the cake.

I lifted the plastic. I carefully moved the six tilting layers of cake to the most attractive corner of my kitchen counter. I got out the box of curly candles. Orange. Purple. Green. And then, just for fun, I got out the box of regular candles. I pulled out one candle. Yellow. My favorite color. I stuck all four candles into the top of the cake. Three tall candles. And one short candle. The cake was darling! At least I thought it was. I loved the quirky look of the candles. A perfect complement to the fondant circles with the pastel candies stuck right in the center. It all coordinated beautifully.

I turned on and off various lights in the kitchen until I found a combination that brought out the cake's best features. And then I started snapping away with my iPhone. I photographed the cake from every angle. The angle from which the cake looked straight. The angle from which the cake looked crooked. And the angle in between. "This cake doesn't have a bad side," I said to the kitchen. "It looks good from every angle." I carried on with the accolades. "This cake is artisanal. This cake is a masterpiece." And I concluded my early morning pronouncements by giving the cake a name. "This is the One Signature Birthday Cake."

It did not matter to me that no one in our family was celebrating a birthday. Somewhere, in lots of places in the world, it was lots of people's birthdays. And every birthday is worth celebrating. "The One Signature Birthday Cake," I repeated. Just so the name would stick.

I covered up the cake with the plastic. I turned off the lights in the kitchen. I returned to my closet. I put my iPhone back in my purse. I went back to bed. And I thought about my idea. "You were right," I whispered to my sleeping husband. "You were right about meaningful work. Thank you."

The next day I was in my car. On my way to a neighborhood I do not usually visit. The kind of neighborhood where children do not get to go to the swimming pool because there is no swimming pool. The kind of neighborhood where 36 percent of residents live below the poverty level. The kind of neighborhood where, in a three-month period alone, police reported 20 homicides, recovered 66 handguns and confiscated $19 million worth of narcotics. The kind of neighborhood my mother would not want me to visit alone. I did not call my mother from the car.

I was not afraid. I was not afraid because my friend lives in this neighborhood. My friend who is a talented graphic artist. My friend who founded Euphrates Gallery, a studio deep in the urban core of Kansas City. My friend who was kind to me in the early days of my job at the charitable foundation. My friend whose words and designs and courage and perseverance inspire me. This was a beautiful neighborhood. It was beautiful because my friend lived in this neighborhood. And my friend is a beautiful person.

"This cake is beautiful," my friend said. We were in his living room. Looking at my 3:00 a.m. photographs of the six-layer cake. "I love this cake," he continued. "I understand this cake."

And he did.

That day I commissioned my friend to design a poster. A poster featuring a graphic rendition of the six-layer cake. A poster that told the story of this cake. A cake capable of transforming a perspective on life. In the words of my friend, this cake transformed a spirit of challenge into a spirit of creative problem solving and tangible creative innovation. My friend was an artist. An artist who deserves to be paid for his work. His work is meaningful work. Meaningful work because it is how he makes a living. And meaningful work because his business is a bright spot of free enterprise in the midst of poverty and blight. And meaningful work because he creates beautiful designs that delight and inspire the people who see them.

"This cake is a beacon of hope," he said.

And to be perfectly honest, the One Signature Birthday Cake was a beacon of hope for me, too.

Chapter 9

Pink Champagne Cake

I do not always bake my own cakes. Sometimes I buy a cake. A very specific cake. From a very specific bakery. A bakery that is very close to my house. That bakery is 3 Women and an Oven. That cake is the Pink Champagne Cake. And that cake is very, very good.

"I'll pick up a Pink Champagne Cake on my way home," I told Prince Charming on Friday morning as I prepared to dash out the door with a cup of cereal and a can of all-natural grape soda. "I won't have time to bake one this weekend." A statement like that called for an explanation. When do I not have time to bake a cake? "I am really busy at work. And next week I go to that meeting in New York."

My husband and I were discussing what to give a mutual friend for his birthday. "A cake is a terrific birthday present," I called out to Prince Charming before the door to the garage shut behind me. After the 3:00 a.m. photo shoot I had declared open season on the six-layer cake. That particular cake now was half eaten. So re-gifting the One Signature Birthday Cake was not an option.

I like my idea, I thought to myself as I backed out of the garage. A cake is always a good birthday present. Even if you buy the cake instead of bake the cake yourself. And especially if you tuck a single candle into the top of the cake so that your friend can blow it out and make a wish. So that your friend can get whatever it is that your friend wants. Just for such occasions I keep a box of birthday candles in my car. Along with a few black and silver seals printed with the words "One Celebrations Loves This Cake." Yes. A cake. With one candle on top. In a box. Sealed with a sticker. It is my go-to gift.

Of course this meant I had an excuse to buy a Pink Champagne Cake for myself, too. Why buy one cake when you can buy two? Besides, the next few days would be good days to eat cake for dinner. And for dessert. It had been that kind of a week at the office. And I always eat a lot of cake before I go out of town. It calms me down. I really don't like to be away from Prince Charming and the princesses. And traveling alone makes me anxious.

The Pink Champagne Cake is absolutely divine. I have no idea how three women and their oven make it, but whatever they do, it works. The crumb is light, like cake crumb should be. But the cake is a little more dense in all the right places. Selectively dense so you can practically taste the champagne popping out of the perfectly baked batter. And the cake itself is a light pink. Which matches the light pink frosting. Which sparkles. And crunches. And melts in your mouth. It is so yummy.

Of course the Pink Champagne Cake looks as good as it tastes. It looks to me like the frosting is hand-piped by all three women. The lattice detail is intricate and delicate and symmetrical. The cake is gorgeous. The cake is delicious. I love the Pink Champagne Cake.

I pulled into the parking garage at the office, still thinking about the Pink Champagne Cake. And thinking about going out of town. And wishing that I did not find it so hard to leave my children, even for only two nights. And wishing I knew how to better manage the rocky emotions of anticipation on the days before business trips. Mostly I was wishing I could come up with a better idea for coping than eating cake. Business trips always wreak havoc on my daily calorie counts.

Actually, I was looking forward to this particular business trip. New York is always fun. And the meeting about charitable giving would be interesting. And on this trip I would get to see a dear friend who would be at the meeting, too. A dear friend who lives in Palo Alto, California.

One of the things I loved most about working at a charitable foundation for all those years was the opportunity to meet wonderful people all across the country who know a lot about philanthropy and charitable giving and doing good and social responsibility. I always learned so much when I was with those wonderful people. And I was sure that the meeting with the people in New York would be no exception.

"I am amazed at the amount of advice floating around out there about charitable giving," I told Prince Charming a few days later. It was Monday night. The night before I would leave town. I was in my closet, surveying my wardrobe options for the trip. I folded up my favorite pair of black pants. That was easy. Now I was picking out a pair of sandals appropriate for a business meeting. I had wisely decided against waiting until morning to pack my bag. It is highly unlikely that I could squeeze in one more activity somewhere between the hairdryer and the mascara and the lipstick and the diary and the cereal and the princesses. And still make it to the airport on time. Pack early, I always say.

"So many smart people have ideas about why to give to charity. And how to give to charity. And how to determine what all of the different charities actually are doing with the donations," I said, chatting away to my husband. I recalled that my stepdaughters in college love to check out Charity Navigator. And I love to review the information on GuideStar. And I had just reviewed the packet of materials for the meeting. Giving was on my mind. "Have you Googled 'charitable giving' lately?" I asked Prince Charming.

"Not since I did it for you," he answered. Oh, right. I had almost forgotten about the research. "Interestingly," he said, "when I typed in 'foundation,' the first thing that came up was an advertisement for makeup and how to find the perfect color to match your skin tone."

"Really?" I asked. I loved that! Maybe charitable giving and makeup really were related! "Do you think I could apply doing good to cosmetics?" I asked my husband. "Kind of like I am trying to connect cakes and charitable giving?" Prince Charming gave me that look. "No," he said. I backed off and dropped the subject. Even I know when to quit.

"Well," I said. "I am always amazed that more people don't know about community foundations. Community foundations are one of the easiest and best ways to find good information about community causes. And community foundations are full of smart people who can walk you through your options for charitable giving." Prince Charming nodded in agreement. It is so wonderful to be married to someone who agrees with you on major points and on things that really matter. Prince Charming is that kind of someone. And the reverse is true, too. I agree with my husband on major points and on things that really matter.

I was a fan of community foundations even before I worked at the Greater Kansas City Community Foundation. I fell in love with community foundations when I was a tax lawyer at Spencer Fane Britt & Browne. Incidentally, that was also when I fell in love with Prince Charming who was practicing law at the same firm. So, when it comes to community foundations, my underlying opinion is completely unbiased.

"Maybe people just don't know where to find a community foundation," my husband observed. I had to admit that he was probably right. Which is a shame. There are almost 700 community foundations in the country. So it is not hard to find one near wherever you live. In fact, you could probably Google "community foundation" and in three minutes flat figure out who to call. Your community foundation might even be as nearby as your favorite bakery or your favorite coffee shop.

The technical definition of a community foundation is a tax-exempt, nonprofit, autonomous, publicly supported, nonsectarian philanthropic institution with a long term goal of building permanent, named component funds established by many separate donors to carry out their charitable interests and for the broad-based charitable interest of and for the benefit of residents of a defined geographic area, typically no larger than a state.

"Is that English?" my husband said when I showed him the definition. It was printed on a page in the materials I was taking with me to New York. "All of that sounds more complicated than it really is," I assured him. "In Kansas City, the community foundation is designed to offer services to people who donate to charity so the whole giving experience can be as fun, meaningful and rewarding as possible." That made more sense. Giving is one of those things that is sometimes hard to explain, I thought. I would have so much to think about on this trip!

Incidentally, the business trips I took during my years at the Greater

Kansas City Community Foundation were not only trips to big cities like New York, but also trips to other wonderful places. Other wonderful places like cities and towns in the Midwest, where people are more generous than almost any other region in the country.

"Remember when I went on that road trip to Bird City?" I asked my husband in the closet. "That was such an amazing place. The community foundation in northwest Kansas is doing incredible things to help people invest in the future of their communities."

Prince Charming actually remembered that trip. "Yes!" he said. "That was when you brought back those birdseed tree ornaments for the kids. The ones we hung in the backyard. The birds loved them." He was right. My husband has such a good memory. That birdseed really was pretty neat. Locally-grown and sustainable and organic and socially responsible and all of those good things. And the best part of that trip was that I went with one of my good friends. With one of my good friends at the foundation. We brought back birdseed ornaments for the entire staff. So that everyone at the foundation could experience social responsibility, right in her own backyard.

"It's not about how much you give," said my friend. I was in New York. The Very Important Meeting was over. My friend and I were sipping delicious wine and enjoying a delicious dinner. We were talking about the meeting. And we were talking about philanthropy. And we were talking about giving. "It's about *how* you give," she concluded. The statement was simple and succinct and strategic all at the same time. "You are so right," I said, nodding. "You will make it easier for people to be effective with their giving."

My friend was telling me about her new book. A book called *Giving 2.0*, which would be released in the fall. I could not wait. "The world needs a book like yours," I told her. "A book that celebrates every level of generosity." This was an opinion I believed I was qualified to give. By this time I had read every article, visited every website and scanned every book I could get my hands on relating to charitable giving. *Giving 2.0* would be a dream come true for my work at the community foundation.

"I am so glad you are writing this book," I told my friend. "Otherwise I would have to write it myself. And my book would not be as good as your book." My friend is a professor at Stanford. She is beautiful and brilliant and generous. "Besides," I added, "I'd rather write a book about cake."

Truth be told, my friend loves cake, too. We had almost as much fun discussing the pleasures involved in eating white cake batter as we had discussing charitable giving. Doing good and eating cake really do go together.

"Girls, girls, girls!" I called as I burst in the door. I was back. Coming home from business trips is always the best part. "I've brought presents!" It was past the girls' bedtime and I knew they would already be in bed. But I did not care. I had to get my hands on the sweet princesses. I had missed them so much.

I stood at the foot of the stairs waiting for them to come down. I did not, however, venture up the stairs. Curiously, the upstairs recently had become someplace I did not like to go. It was so odd! "What is the matter with me?" I said to myself as I bravely placed just one foot on the first stair. "I have become so jittery lately."

If we were all honest with ourselves, we might admit that from time to time there is a space in our house or apartment or recreational vehicle or castle that we simply do not like as well as the other spaces. That space could be the storage closet you cannot bear to open. After all, do you really want 13 years of clutter to come crashing down at your feet? Or that space could be the garage full of Prince Charming's paint cans. Or, if you are someone who does not bake cakes, I suppose that place could be your kitchen. In my case, at that point in my life, it seemed that place was the upstairs.

Naturally the upstairs had not always been distasteful to me. I had loved decorating three little girls' rooms with princesses and dolls. And pink curtains and pink flowers. And wooden letters spelling out each of their names. And monogrammed trunks to store dress up clothes. And baby pictures in sparkly frames. And neatly-arranged closets full of frilly jumpers hanging on pretty hangers padded with pink satin.

"If I really want to go upstairs," I said. "I can just go visit a few model homes." I was rationalizing my behavior to Prince Charming when this strange affliction had first hit me a few weeks before. "I can thoroughly check out the second floors of each one." He was giving me that look again. That look of concern mixed with amusement mixed with bewilderment.

That was not a bad idea, actually. Model homes are tons of fun. Model homes are full of endless opportunities for your imagination to invent whatever stories you want. Stories about the girls and boys and mothers and fathers and princes and princesses and kings and queens who might wind up living in that castle. And what they might do on the weekends. And what kind of cakes they might bake. And what fairy tale jobs they might venture off to do on Monday mornings. In fact, you can make a whole day of touring model homes. Bring along one or two of your children. Pack a lunch. Give yourselves new names. Dream any dream you want. The bigger the better.

I was still waiting at the foot of the stairs. One foot on a stair, one foot on the floor. Where were the princesses? They sure were giving me a lot of time to think about not going upstairs.

Maybe the hurry and scurry of life is making the upstairs just a little bit un-fun, I thought. But it was more than that. The upstairs was making me sad. It was making me feel like I had lost something. Something I could not get back. The pink decorations were looking a bit dated. And the letters kept falling off the walls because over the years most of the stickiness had worn away from the back of the wood. The dress up clothes were buried somewhere in the bottom of a drawer. That was because the monogrammed trunks were now filled with Legos. "Playing princess is for little girls and we are big," my daughters had explained. And the frilly frocks hanging in the closet were two sizes too small. And the baby pictures had started to look less and less recent.

On the flip side, as my trips upstairs became less frequent, the upstairs more frequently ventured downstairs. It did not take me very long to start climbing the stairs again on a regular basis. But some patterns, once set, are nearly impossible to break. For nearly a full year now the sleeping quarters on the first floor have been occupied not only by Prince Charming and me but also by two little princesses. And various dolls and puzzles. All of whom and all of which seem to come and go at odd hours of the night.

This is a health hazard! I now stumble around a lot in the dark. Navigating through an enchanted forest of sleeping princesses and blankets and puzzles and dolls and books and Magic Markers. To complicate matters further, one of the princesses has developed a habit of crawling into bed with me at 1 a.m. Which is wonderful for snuggling. But which is slightly uncomfortable because of the little girl's fondness for wearing cowboy boots with her Hello Kitty pajamas.

The lesson here is simple. No matter how sad your upstairs makes you feel, do not stop going there. Not even for three weeks. Be brave. Otherwise the upstairs will come downstairs and never go back.

"Girls, girls, girls!" I called out again into the stairwell. "I have presents!" This time it worked. All three of my children scampered out of their bedrooms and down the stairs and into my arms. Three seconds of a hug is all you get when you are a mother who has been out of town on business. "What did you bring us?" is what happens at second number four. I pulled out three t-shirts from my carry-on bag. "Here you go! Real t-shirts from New York City." The last thing any of the girls needed was another t-shirt. But they really do love them. And it's often not a bad idea to give a girl what she wants.

"How was the trip?" Prince Charming asked as I was unpacking in the closet. The girls were back in bed, at least until two of them would wander back down after midnight. They were wearing their t-shirts. "Good!" I said. "I got a lot of ideas about ways to be charitable. Ways that go beyond traditional ideas about charitable giving."

I sat down with my pink notebook. Instead of writing about charitable giving, though, I decided to add a little variety to the good girl diary and write down an idea about traveling instead. I have my own system for painless and stylish air travel. I wrote it in the pink notebook that night under the heading System for Painless and Stylish Air Travel. The idea had nothing to do with cakes or kids or charity or lipstick or work. But I didn't care. I needed a break.

My system works for one, maybe two, nights on a business trip. That's plenty long to be out of town unless it is a family vacation. Any more than two nights away from home creates too great a risk that upon your return your children will say "Mommy, you grew while you were gone."

The first part of the System for Painless and Stylish Air Travel is never check a bag. I wrote down that idea three times. Never check a bag. Never check a bag. Never check a bag. You really can pack an arsenal of cosmetics if you pick the right luggage and bring the right clothes. I have even figured out how to travel with all six mascara products in a quart-size plastic bag!

Pack only one pair of shoes in addition to the pair you are wearing, I wrote. That is the second part of the system. If you really need a third pair of footwear you can shop when you get there. You can bend the rules on this formula, just a wee bit, every once in a while. Like if you really need a third pair of shoes. Such as strappy taupe sandals with lots of buckles.

Once I had to go shopping for another outfit when I was out of town on a business trip that required three nights away from home. That was dangerous. I wandered aimlessly around the department store until my body was magnetically pulled toward a stunning dark reddish, quasi-fur, asymmetrical designer jacket with edgy zippers and a slightly cropped fit. I touched the jacket. And immediately yanked my hand away when I glimpsed the $6750 (no decimal) price tag. Yikes! I settled for an equally beautiful $16 lipstick, aspirationally named Rags to Riches. Which was much easier than a designer jacket to fit in carry-on luggage. On that note, if you do go shopping and therefore you are returning home with more outfits than carry-on space, just ship one outfit back. Or donate the least favorite of the outfits to a local clothing shelter. After you have worn it, obviously.

Next I wrote: One pair of basic but flattering pants is all that is required for the bottom component of each of your outfits. This allows you to preserve your precious carry-on space for a couple of really great tops. Trust the universe to ensure that no one will notice that you wore the same pair of pants two days in a row. Particularly if they are black pants. Everyone will be oblivious to your double-dip leg wear. Especially the women. Who are also wearing the same pair of pants two days in a row.

I really mean it when I say never check a bag. Use those little contact lens cases to stash must-have anti-aging products and professional strength eye makeup remover. I got that brilliant idea from a friend who travels more than any girl I know. The same one who worked for the candle company. And who was one of the noncaterers serving chicken at the big rehearsal dinner.

Every time I get on an airplane I wonder whether all of the people on the airplane really want to be going where they are going. Wouldn't they rather be home taking their kids to the coffee shop? Or discussing the news with Prince Charming? Or getting a pedicure?

Or even going to the office? "Am I the only one on this airplane who is still reeling from the goodbyes?" I always ask myself. I am always thinking about the little girls sitting on the garage steps in their pajamas. Waving and blowing kisses. Before the plane takes off I always find myself holding back tears. Remember the mascara, I tell myself. Always protect the mascara.

Do what you want to do, I added to my diary entry, attempting to circle back to what I had learned in New York. I needed to call it a night, and soon. Otherwise the rest of the Pink Champagne Cake hiding in the back of the freezer would call out to me to schedule an emergency meeting. An immediate emergency meeting. Do what you want to do certainly applies to charitable giving. I wrote down a few ideas on that. Explore your charitable giving options on websites or in books or in articles. Or contact a community foundation. Or discuss the options with your friends and family. Whatever you want to do.

Give to what you love, was the next idea I wrote. Then I really would need to wrap this up. I was tired. Give to what makes you feel good about giving, I added. Give to what makes you cry when you read about it in the newspaper. Or see it on television or on YouTube. Or hear about it from Prince Charming or wherever you get your news. Give to the organizations that employ the people who saved your child's life. Or the people who helped your colleague at work adopt a pet. Or the people who cleaned up your neighborhood. But do not overthink it. Your giving is your own. Kind of like your cakes. I thought I heard the Pink Champagne Cake. I chose to ignore it.

A final note in the diary. Then I really would go to bed. Go where you want to go. If you want to go to New York, go to New York. If you want to go to the salon to get a pedicure, go to the salon to get a pedicure. If you want to go to your favorite coffee shop every morning, go there every morning.

Indeed, on airplanes, as in life, it is always best to want to be going where you are going.

Chapter 10

"Here, Mommy," my youngest daughter chirped from her cozy spot in the cow print car seat. "You need this." She reached around the headrest and handed me a glittery, star-topped magic wand. A magic wand that was a favor from the late summer birthday party. The birthday party that had just ended.

And thank heavens it had ended.

The party had been at one of those blow-up bouncy places. The kind of place that is as jarring for the adults as it is fun for the kids. Especially when your child is the child who gets wedged into the top tier of the netted tower maze. And insists that her mommy climb up to rescue her. Which rescue attempt results in not just one but two girls trapped in an inflatable plastic box. A plastic box that is fifteen feet off the ground. Which, in turn, requires the princely teenage gymnast-esque attendant on duty to climb up, too, to help both girls get down. Give me poison.

"Thank you, thank you!" I told my daughter, blowing her a big kiss from the driver's seat. "Thank you for the magic wand!" Bless her heart. She could tell I was a frazzled mess. As could every other parent and child who had witnessed the brave tower rescue.

I was mortified.

"Why have I been so out of whack all summer long?" I asked my little girl. "I am just not myself. No matter how hard I try." And it was true. No matter how much I worked on my diary of a good girl. No matter how many cakes I baked. No matter how many lipsticks I tried on. I still did not think I was good enough. I was missing something important in this whole exercise.

"Maybe I just need to keep working on doing good," I suggested. My daughter said nothing. I glanced in the rearview mirror. The little princess was sound asleep. "Maybe it will help to keep testing ideas," I told her, even though she was napping. Perhaps. Or maybe I just needed a magic wand.

"I'll think about that tomorrow," I said to myself. There is only so much self-analysis a girl can take on any given day. I tried to turn my thoughts to something else. Like the upcoming birthday parties I would be hosting for various daughters. All of the birthdays in our family are bunched together. I love it. It is so much fun.

I considered the birthday party that had just ended. I gave the parents a lot of credit for ending the party on time. "Setting expectations and meeting those expectations is so important," I remarked. I could talk to myself the whole way home. The people in the cars next to me would just think I was talking to my daughter in the back seat. I doubted they would notice she was sleeping.

I would have to record a few of these ideas in the diary, I thought. Birthday party ideas always come in handy. Including ideas about how to end the party on time. Any good girl who has children knows that the precise conclusion of a child's birthday party is the moment when all of the party favor bags have been passed out to the little princes and princesses. Especially princes and princesses who have braved a haunted forest of red, blue and yellow contraptions.

"Everyone sticks around until the end of the birthday party," I told my sleeping daughter. "Everyone wants the party favor bag." And, on that day, at that particular party, it was a good thing we had stuck around. Otherwise I might never have had the magic wand.

I held up the magic wand in the sunlight as I waited for a light to turn green. The magic wand was really pretty, actually. I liked it. A lot. It was about seven inches long. The perfect size for a girl of any age. It had a shiny handle and a sparkly top shaped like a star. The star must be where the magic comes from, I thought. I could almost see sparks flying from each of the five corners. As it turned out, I would keep that little magic wand in my purse for a long, long time. Like for six months. Which was when my little princess would ask for it back. Smart girl. But by that time I wouldn't need it anymore.

The thing with magic wands is you have to know how to use them properly to get what you want. That much I know, I thought. I was recording the day's events in my little pink notebook. In my closet. Before I went to bed. Like I had been doing every night, for months now. The good girl diary had become a comforting ritual.

Magic wands have a limited bandwidth of capabilities and therefore there are many things they cannot do, I speculated as I started a new page in the diary. But I'll bet the capabilities they do have are impressive.

I paused. This diary entry could be interesting. I was in the mood for something different. I was in the mood for magic. And make believe. Why not dream up a few things about a magic wand? I checked the time on my iPhone. Which was in my closet with me. 8:15 p.m. Good! I had at least an hour before I would turn into a pumpkin and have to go to bed. It was a good night to try my hand at a little creative writing.

The proper use of a magic wand is definitely something every good girl needs to know, I thought as I carefully examined the glitter that was covering the star. Frankly I was in awe of the fact that a type of glue exists that is strong enough to hold glitter onto plastic or cardboard. Or whatever the star was made of. Glitter occupies every corner of my house. Kind of like cereal. The glitter, though, is not a culinary phenomenon. Rather, the glitter is thanks to years of little girl craft projects gone wild. I had never managed to find a type of glue that would hold glitter onto anything other than carpet.

Magic wands and hocus pocus are not as easy as the fairy tales make them out to be, I wrote in the diary. It takes a while to catch on to exactly how and when to wave the magic wand. And that much is true. You have to figure out by trial and error what a magic wand can and cannot do. Kind of like determining how many layers you can stack onto a cake without it falling over. You have to be willing to let a few cakes fall before you can appreciate the true boundaries of your recipe.

A case in point on the limits of the magic wand is a dinner routine gone bad. Cereal for dinner is all very well and good. But you still should practice and teach proper table manners to ensure that your princesses grow up to be ladies and queens. Magic wands cannot fix less-than-good mother habits. As when you paint your kitchen and move your family dinners from the table to the counter as a temporary measure. And then you never move them back. This is an especially bad habit if you let your littlest girls sit *on* the counter, rather than *at* the counter. Do not delude yourself into thinking that it is an okay thing to do just because it is so much more efficient to let the little lambs graze among the bowls of cereal arranged in a colorful dinner display.

And it is really, really not good if your children begin to teach the bad habits to others. Such as when you play tea party with your littlest princess. And you helpfully arrange the dolls neatly in their chairs. And you begin to pour the tea. And you get a scolding of "No, Mommy!" as your daughter lifts the dolls out of their chairs and plants them squarely on top of the table. Just like real life. Not good at all.

Indeed, habits like these are nearly impossible to unwind. No magic wand will save you from your own mischief. Even if your offspring is otherwise quite polite. Even naming the tea-drinking dolls lovely things like Princess Queen and Chunklyn (Chunquelynne, perhaps?) and other royal-sounding appellations. Countertop cereal dinners are a no-no.

I started laughing in the closet. Creative writing was fun! "What are you writing?" asked Prince Charming. He had come into the closet to gather up the dry cleaning. "I'm writing about magic wands." My husband stared at me. After about 12 seconds he finally said, "You must really be bored."

I put down my pen for a moment and looked up at him from my spot on the floor. The spot on my floor that is next to my running shoes. The spot where I always sit to write in the good girl diary. "You may be right," I said with a new spark of clarity. "Believe it or not, that hadn't occurred to me." My husband is wonderful. He knows me better than I know myself. "But this is fun," I assured him. I picked my pen up and kept on writing.

"Magic wands don't work well for getting your kids out of weird situations. And not just inflatable plastic mazes." Sounded like an accurate observation to me. Once upon a time my oldest daughter had casually said something like "I'm going to get a drink of water." And she began to make her way up the stairs from the basement. Moments later a panicked "Help!" rang out in the stairwell. When you find that particular child stuck between the railing and the wall, unable to move, do not reach for the magic wand. The magic wand will not get her out.

And that is true. To solve a dilemma like this you will need to remove one entire banister from a wall and one pair of jeans from a body. Neither can the magic wand answer how this happened to her in the first place, I continued in the diary. How does a 50-pound girl get herself wedged behind a stair rail? She can't tell you either. Unless you buy her story that she was "just walking up the stairs when suddenly I got stuck." Indeed.

Magic wands will not transform dangerous and damaging household items into toys appropriate for children. Common sense is your own responsibility. Be brave enough to ask yourself the tough questions. Like, is a screwdriver really an appropriate substitute for a hand-held video game stylus? And, can you really afford to pretend not to notice that your children are coloring with Sharpies? The big, fat, permanent kind? And the ever-popular question of should you or shouldn't you let your toddler select the kiddie nail polish from the dollar section as a reward for good behavior? No, the magic wand is no use for these things. Ignore these types of questions at your own peril.

And magic wands, as pretty as they are, cannot erase the embarrassing things your kids say to you in front of your friends. Or in front of the check-out girl. Or in front of your parents-in-law. Like, "Mom, you are too old to laugh." Magic wands will not make the temper tantrum in the appliance section of the home improvement store go away, either. The temper tantrum that occurs as your child is throwing a fit, pointing at the washing machines, screaming "I want one of those for my birthday" at the top of her lungs. When all you were doing was attempting to pick up a few paint samples.

"What about birthday parties?" I asked myself. I was already on the fourth page of this diary entry. I thought I should write down something about a birthday party. Considering that was where I got the magic wand in the first place. Magic wands do not convert cake into ice cream. But you don't need any hocus pocus to pull that off.

As hard as it may be to believe, not everyone likes cake. Astounding! Nevertheless it is true. If you are searching for birthday cake ideas that do not actually involve cake you will need to be creative. Try packing up a cake box with a dozen pints of ice cream in a variety of flavors. Tuck in a few bowls, spoons and even sugar cones. Magic! You have just created a do-it-yourself ice cream cake.

Once upon a time I gave the do-it-yourself ice cream cake to my bacon-and-ice-cream loving brother. He loved it. It might even have made up for the times I made him pay to use his own toys all those years ago. Incidentally, my brother once tried bacon ice cream. Just to see what it tasted like. He tried it in Las Vegas. His report was brief: "Not good." Good to know.

A magic wand cannot convert the kale chips baking in your oven into a delicious lemon cake. I knew this had to be true the moment I wrote it in the diary! Based on the time when I was trying to be organic. When I stood peering into my oven. To see if the edges of the greens baking at 350 degrees had turned, to quote my hip and trendy cookbook, "golden brown but not black." When I opened the oven door the kitchen filled with smoke. I guess golden brown and black look about the same where leafy vegetables are concerned. And through an organic smoke screen. Chalk that one up to going green gone awry.

The next idea I wrote was about disappearances: Magic wands probably cannot make things go away. Once, in high school, I had tried unsuccessfully to make a car go away. I didn't have a magic wand at the time, but even if I had, I doubt it would have worked. The vehicle in question was a 1979 Dodge Aspen station wagon with wood siding. It was our family car when I was growing up. It was okay in 1979. But by the time I was in high school a decade later I was so embarrassed about the station wagon that I named it the Big E. That would be E for Embarrassment. I begged my dad to let me park it at the neighbors' house when my friends came over. Or when dates arrived to pick me up. "Why is your car always parked down the street?" someone finally asked. Station wagons are stubborn.

Prince Charming ventured back into the closet. "Still writing about the magic wand, eh?" he asked with a playful smile. I nodded. "Just for a little bit longer," I promised. "And then I will get the kids to bed. I needed a little break from all of the good girl work."

While I had Prince Charming in the closet I decided to recruit him. "Maybe you have some ideas," I suggested. "Do you think I could use a magic wand to turn a bowl of Life cereal into a batch of pumpkin pancakes? Or wave it across my dress pants and silk blouse on the way to the gym to see if it could change my business outfit into super-cute workout clothes?"

Yes, I thought. That is exactly what I would do with my magic wand if it really worked! "I would for sure try it on cereal," I assured my husband. "Maybe I would try to cast a spell on Frosted Mini Wheats to see if I could create a nice piece of grilled salmon for dinner. Or even spaghetti. Or at the very least a big hunk of white cake with buttercream frosting." Prince Charming liked that idea. "That would be great!" he said. "Especially the spaghetti."

I was almost finished in the closet. Nor can a magic wand ensure that moments meant to be etched in your memory forever actually stay there, I wrote. This you have to do yourself. And that is true. It was something that had occurred to me a few years before as I watched my two youngest children walk into preschool together on a deceptively regular Friday morning, arm in arm, wearing their matching navy blue dresses covered with appliqued watermelons, the little tufts of fair hair catching every drop of the summer morning sun. As a wise colleague of mine often reminds me, "Enjoy the little things because someday you'll look back and realize that the little things were really the big things."

And with that I closed the diary. I tucked the pink notebook back into my purse. And I went to bed. Thinking about magic wands. And wishes coming true. And asking the universe for gifts. I fell asleep thinking about every girl's responsibility to use her gifts to the absolute best of her ability. Whatever those gifts may be. So that others can enjoy her gifts, too, and in turn be inspired to share their own gifts with others.

I called my mother the next morning. "Hi!" I said. "Hi!" she said. "I got a magic wand yesterday," I reported. I described the birthday party. And the rescue from the plastic tower. And a few of the ideas I had written down in my good girl diary the night before. "I am pretty sure you can ask the universe for anything you want," I told my mother. "And, chances are, it will not let you down."

"What a fun idea," my mother said. "I am so glad you are branching out a bit with your good girl topics." I could tell she wasn't quite with me on the universe thing. But she played along anyway. "The universe has never let me down when I have asked for a parking space at work," she remarked. "Sometimes I get the very last one in the lot." And this is true. My mother has a knack for parking spots. In fact, my father is happy to have my mother along with him in the car when he is headed someplace where he knows it will be hard to find a place to park. Who knows? Maybe my mother is his magic wand.

"Did I just hear you telling your mother about the magic wand?" asked my husband after I had hung up the phone. "Yes," I said. Adding, purposefully, "And my mother agrees with me about the power of asking for what you want and getting it." Which was probably not quite exactly true. But it was close enough. My mother and I are always on the same side.

"I suppose asking for gifts, believing you will receive them and behaving as though you have them could do the trick," he said. "But that is not the work of a magic wand. Or the force of the universe. Or any other form of mystery." Prince Charming is pretty firm on his position that there is a logical reason for everything.

"There is nothing magical about it at all," my husband continued. "Chance favors the prepared mind. When you can say what you want well enough to ask for it, of course you will naturally observe and use those things in your environment that reinforce your choice of whatever it is that you want." My husband is also very articulate. He could tell by my blank look that I needed a translation. "You know what I mean," he explained. "It is kind of like when you buy a certain kind of car. And after you buy it you suddenly see dozens of those cars all over town. Even though you had never before even noticed that those cars existed." That I understood.

I did something different that night. Instead of sitting on the floor of my closet I took my diary outside. And I sat on the driveway. Where I could watch the sun go down. The days were getting shorter. School would be starting soon. Along with all of the birthdays. Lots of opportunities to test my cake ideas.

I opened my diary to a new page. I wanted to write down a few final observations about wishes coming true. And getting what you want. And asking the universe for help. And the power of the magic wand.

Then I had an idea. "I wonder what all of this means?" I asked myself. On a hunch I went back inside the house. And into my closet. And I pulled out all of the other little pink notebooks. The entire diary of a good girl. I took the notebooks back outside to my spot on the driveway.

The sun was setting in that perfect place in the summer sky. That perfect place so that there is still plenty of light for reading. And that perfect place so it is not hot. Not hot but warm and comfortable and magical. I started with the first pink notebook. All the way back to the beginning of the diary of a good girl. And I read every single entry. In every single pink notebook. Quickly, but I read them all.

Somewhat to my amazement, a story seemed to be unfolding on the pages of the diary. A true story. A story of self-improvement. With a little entertainment and inspiration mixed in. "Maybe it's all here and I just didn't know it," I said to the diary. "Maybe I've been writing up my own recipe for what it means to have it all."

I flipped through the pages again, quickly. Charities. Lipstick. Cakes. Kids. Those are my favorite things, I thought to myself. Doing good for others. Looking good. Making good cakes. Being a good mother. And doing good work. Those were the things I enjoyed working hard to achieve. More than anything else I did. There I was, sitting on the driveway, wishing I could figure out a way to be my free-thinking, hard-working, fun-loving, do-gooding, cake-baking, idea-sharing self without scaring everyone around me. At least not all of the time. Maybe it was all right there, in the diary.

"Maybe, just maybe, I've got something here," I said to myself as

I stood up and brushed off the back of my jeans. I somehow had managed to plant myself right in the middle of one of the girls' chalk drawings.

I shut the front door behind me and I made my way back to my closet. And I jotted down an idea. An idea to wrap up the day. "Kids, cakes, charities, lipstick. And good work. Abracadabra! Put it together and what have you got?" I paused. Maybe, I wrote in the diary, what you wind up with is a fairy tale that celebrates every form of charitable giving imaginable. And still allows plenty of time for baking cakes on the weekends.

I pulled the magic wand out of my purse. "Magic wand," I asked, "can you do that for me? If I waved you over my favorite things, could you create something new and fun and meaningful and rewarding?" The magic wand did not answer.

On another hunch I flipped back a few pages in the pink notebook. To the diary entries from the night before. The ideas I had written down about the magic wand. And I noticed something. I had not identified a single thing that a magic wand *could* do. Not one trick. Not one spell. Not one ounce of magic. No. Not a single idea for what a magic wand could actually do. Only things it could not do.

But I am not a girl who is easily discouraged. "I'll keep trying," I said to the magic wand. "At least until the end of the year. But after that, I might just have to do this myself."

Chapter 11

Yellow is my favorite color. Yellow has been my favorite color since I was 3 years old. I love many things that are yellow. The sun, especially. And yellow roses. And lemons. Especially lemons that are filling up a pretty bowl sitting in the middle of a kitchen table.

Every once in a while I love to bake a yellow cake. A yellow cake, brightened up with a hint of lemon. Today is a good day for a yellow cake, I thought to myself one Friday afternoon. I was standing in my kitchen. Looking at the pretty bowl of lemons on my kitchen table. Summer would be over soon and I could not stand the thought of it ending without at least one yellow cake. "It is always a good idea to celebrate the sunshine while you still can," I said. This time I was talking to the lemons.

"Let's bake a yellow cake," I suggested to my daughters an hour or so later. I was thinking through my options for putting together a meal. Prince Charming would be out late at a dinner for work. This was an opportunity for me to get creative. "Instead of cereal for dinner," I offered, "we can have macaroni and cheese. And bananas. And cake for dessert. We can call it the All Yellow Dinner."

I rather enjoy color-coordinating my meals. Every once in a while it is fun to see whether I can put together a combination of foods, all in the same color family, and still achieve nutritional diversity. I would have to tell my mother about the All Yellow Dinner, I thought. She might like the idea. Especially considering that my mother is, or at least was, such a big fan of the All Toast Dinner. My dad might even like the All Yellow Dinner. My mother could easily substitute grilled chicken and baked potatoes with butter for the macaroni and cheese. Chicken and cheese are yellow enough to qualify.

Betty Crocker is the girl you will need on your team if you want to make a yellow cake. Of course Betty is the girl you need on the team for any cake you bake. When it comes to cake, I have yet to find anything Betty cannot do.

Blend together a box of Betty Crocker yellow cake mix and two-thirds cup of vegetable oil. Slowly add four eggs. Eggs that are at room temperature, of course. And slightly beaten so that the yolks are mixed with the whites. Mix the batter after each addition. Then fold in eight ounces of sour cream.

At this point you get to add the lemon to the batter. I highly recommend using real lemon juice. Lemon extract tastes just a tad bit metallic. I am always sorry when I cut corners on my yellow cake and fall for lemon extract instead of the real thing.

"Who wants to squeeze the lemons?" I asked the girls. The timing was perfect. The princesses were just finishing their yellow dinners. "Me!" "Me!" "Me!" All three girls answered simultaneously. Like they always do. That is why I always buy extra lemons.

A trick I learned once is that lemons produce the most juice if you roll them around on the counter for a couple of minutes. Before you cut them in half and squeeze them over a sieve, collecting the juice in a bowl. The rolling activates the juice. The rolling is also a fun activity for little girls. In fact, it is probably not possible to bruise a lemon, so you can turn the lemon-rolling process into a game. Lemon soccer. Lemon catch. Lemon baseball. Lots of options for activating lemon juice. And it never hurts to add a little physical fitness to the baking process. It helps balance out the calories.

But lemon rolling can get out of hand. Quickly. "Hand over the lemons *now*," I commanded after about six minutes. Lemons are not an appropriate substitute for snowballs in an indoor snowball fight. One of the lemons had just smacked a little girl in the back. And another lemon had landed in what remained of the macaroni and cheese. At least the colors matched.

"And thank you for your help," I added after I had gathered up the lemons. After all, what did I think would happen when I gave the girls an assignment like that? I tried not to think about all the points I had just lost on the good mother scale. What mother in her right mind converts lemon-rolling duties into an indoor sport?

"How much lemon juice should we add?" My oldest daughter is fantastic when it comes to following instructions for making things. She can build an entire spaceship out of teeny tiny Legos in less than three hours. I have no idea how she does it. Lego diagrams scramble my brain. "That all depends," I said to my daughter. Obviously she did not get her talent for measuring precisely from her mother.

It really does depend, though, on what you like. When it comes to adding lemon juice to a yellow cake, you could add anywhere from a couple of teaspoons to a fourth of a cup and I think the cake would still taste good. It just depends on whether you like your yellow cake lightly-lemony or lots-of-lemony or somewhere in between. If you are a true lover of lemon, you can even add a little lemon juice to your vanilla buttercream frosting. In addition to the almond extract. Yellow cake drizzled in lemony almond vanilla buttercream frosting is tasty. Especially when the cake is chilled in the freezer for an hour. Perfect on a summer day.

"How were the girls?" Prince Charming asked when he got home later that night. I was in the closet. Jotting down my notes about the yellow cake. I am pretty sure that 80% of my conversations with my husband occur in our closet. It is a big closet. But it does get a little crowded when it is filled with two people. Especially because the closet is where I keep my treadmill. I had been thinking that maybe I should move the treadmill to the basement. And replace it with a couple of chairs.

"The girls were great," I reported. "They helped me make a yellow cake. With real lemon." I did not mention the rousing game of lemon snowball. My husband would not think that was funny.

Prince Charming sat down on the treadmill to tell me about his evening. "I met someone who knows you," he said. "A really nice lady who runs a nonprofit organization. She said to say 'hi.'" "Which nonprofit?" I asked. "I can't quite remember the name of it," answered Prince Charming. "But it is an organization that helps children." That description was not helpful. I thought about saying something sarcastic. Like "Oh! Got it! Yes, I know her quite well. Lovely woman." But that would have been mean.

"Well that's nice," I said instead. "If you remember her name, or if you remember the name of the nonprofit, let me know. It was nice of her to say hello." And it really was nice of her to say hello. Whoever she was. I looked up from my diary and glanced at my husband. Sitting there on the treadmill. He looked as though he was feeling bad about not remembering the details. "There are lots of great organizations that help children," I commented reassuringly. "It is sometimes hard to keep them all straight."

And it really is hard to keep them all straight, I thought. Kansas City is home to thousands of charitable organizations. And hundreds of them help children. When it comes to keeping track of nonprofit organizations, I have always thought that the best idea is to focus on a handful of charities you really love. Otherwise you could easily get lost in your own world of doing good.

Then it occurred to me that my husband was not the only one who does not always remember the details. "Oh, too bad!" I said. I had just remembered something as I was putting away the pink notebook. My husband was turning off the light in the closet. It was late and we were both turning in. "I missed an opportunity to do good. To do good with that yellow cake. I don't know why I didn't think of it earlier. I could have combined tonight's cake-baking with testing out one of my new ideas for charitable giving."

"Don't worry about it," said Prince Charming. Now it was his turn to reassure me. "I am sure there will be many more opportunities for you to do good with your cakes."

That opportunity arrived sooner than I expected. Much sooner. That opportunity arrived the very next weekend. The girls and I were all in the car. On Saturday morning. On our way to LattéLand. I needed my coffee with Splenda and half-and-half. And the girls were in the mood for bagels with butter. As we pulled into the parking lot my oldest daughter shouted "Yellow car!" Which is something I was used to by now. For months the girls had said "yellow car" every time they spotted a yellow car. I had not really given it much thought. I figured "yellow car" was just a statement of truth. A way to pass the time on the road.

But today my daughter added something new. "That was yellow car number 100. That means I get a yellow car party." A what? "What is a yellow car party?" I asked. I wonder if I am supposed to know what that is, I thought. And then I started to panic that perhaps I had missed a memo from school. Which would not be unusual. But school had not started yet. "I've never heard of that," I said. "What is a yellow car party?"

"Mom, don't you know about the yellow car game? It comes with a prize." I shook my head. I looked in the rearview mirror. The two little girls were listening as intently as I was. The girls in the car are always up for playing a good game. Especially a game with a prize. We listened to every word that came out of my oldest daughter's mouth.

The yellow car game is a competition. A competition where the kids in the back seat compete to count each yellow car they see. The game keeps going until someone hits the magic number of 100 yellow cars. This game can span days. Even weeks. And even months. The yellow car game can last longer than a game of Dogopoly.

"You can't count the same yellow car more than once," my daughter said. She is so good at knowing all the rules. That part I could have figured out on my own, though. It explained all of the backseat cheering and shouting and arguing. The cheering and shouting and arguing that had been going on for months. Every time we drove anywhere. We never went anywhere without cheering, shouting and arguing. Someone is always saying "That's my yellow car!" Even in the short quarter-mile between the coffee shop and the grocery store. Now I understood what they had been yelling about. And now the two littlest girls understood that all along they had been playing a game. They just had not known it at the time.

"What's the prize for the first player to reach 100 yellow cars?" I am always more interested in the prizes than the rules. "Oh," said my daughter, "that's easy. The winner gets a yellow car party." Ah ha, I thought. So that's where the yellow car party comes in.

"Well well!" I said. I needed a minute to process all of this interesting information. The yellow car party idea might actually work for me. A party means cake and cake means fun. I could play this game, too.

Then I remembered my plan to test a few new ideas for doing good. And then I remembered my dad's birthday party. The birthday party with the cake-off, Betty Crocker versus Grandmother. And the Retro Birthday Cake. And the donation our family had made in my dad's honor to the nonprofit organization. The nonprofit organization that was all about fathering. Yes, I thought. I think I can make this work.

"I have an idea," I said. "Let's have the yellow car party. And let's make it a celebration that gives back." Now it was my daughter's turn to ask the questions. "What's a celebration that gives back?" she said. I had to think quickly. "Celebration that gives back" was just something I had made up. "Well," I said, pausing to collect my thoughts, "a celebration that gives back is when you have a party. To have fun, of course. And you also do something nice for others. Like give to charity. Or recycle. Or help a friend. Or turn off lights to save energy. Anything that counts as doing good." Not bad, I thought. Not bad at all, considering that I had put myself on the spot.

"Is that all?" my daughter asked. I am sure she was thinking that her yellow car party was not sounding like much of a prize. At least not yet. So I added "And a celebration that gives back always includes a cake." The word "cake" was something all three of my daughters understood.

Silence in the back seat. I glanced in the rearview mirror. I could tell that my oldest daughter was processing everything I had just said. No doubt she was vetting my idea about a celebration that gives back against the rules for the yellow car game. "Okay!" she finally said.

Whew, I thought. I relaxed a bit, leaning back into the driver's seat. I had not even noticed that I had been sitting straight up, tense and nervous, gripping the steering wheel during the entire conversation. I have to stay on my toes during any sort of negotiation with my oldest daughter. She is smart, smart, smart.

A yellow car party. With a gift to a nonprofit organization. With a cake. A yellow cake. Why not? The giving back part of the yellow car party would be easy as pie. One of my friends runs KidsAndCars.org. KidsAndCars.org is a national nonprofit child safety organization dedicated to preventing injuries and death to children in or around motor vehicles. What a perfect organization to support in honor of a game involving cars, I thought to myself. I would ask the kids to collect a few dollars from their piggy banks. And I would write a check. Kids, cake, charity. I love connecting dots.

We scheduled the yellow car party for Monday afternoon. I could leave the office a little early. And the neighbors would be back in town by then. We could invite them over to celebrate with us. Of course a Monday party meant that I would be baking a cake on Sunday. That made me happy. "Girls!" I said cheerfully as we pulled into the garage. We were all on a coffee-cream-bagel-butter high. "Tomorrow we will bake a yellow car cake. A yellow car cake for the yellow car party."

In fact the cake we baked was so magnificent that it deserved a proper name. We could not call it just "yellow cake." The cake we baked turned out to be a One Yellow Car Cake for 100 Yellow Cars. Yes, that is a mouthful. But this cake really was deserving of an eight-word name. It was six layers tall, made mostly with yellow cake. But in this case the yellow cake sported an interesting spin. Baked into the yellow cake layers were swirls of white cake. It gave the whole thing a marbled effect.

My girls do not get into marbling like their cake-obsessed mother. So the marbling was all for me. Every recreational pastry chef knows that swirled cake is the best kind for bowl-licking because you get two flavors of batter in every spoonful. The batter is so good that you might even be tempted to persuade your children to let you lick the batter off the beaters. Or, even better, you can just take over the whole bowl. "I really need to lick the bowl on this one," I explained to my princesses. "I've tinkered with the recipe and I need to make sure it worked. But you can lick the beaters." I don't really like to lick the beaters anyway. It is too hard to work around the metal. I always end up messing up my lipstick.

Instead of six uniform layers baked in eight-inch round cake pans, I tried something new with this cake. I used three different sizes of round cake pans to bake the layers. I stacked them all up, largest to smallest, on a pretty yellow cake stand. The whole thing looked a little bit like a small wedding cake. Two eight-inch round layers, two six-inch round layers, one five-inch round layer and one four-inch layer on top.

"Girls!" I said. "This cake is a good lesson in physics. Look how the graduated layers help maintain stability." And it was true. I was never very good at physics in school, but even I knew that stacking smaller layers on top of larger layers was a good idea. The cake still tilted a bit, but it was nowhere near falling over. And this was one cake I did not want falling over in the middle of the party. I needed to take pictures. Pictures to send to my friend who runs KidsAndCars.org. Along with our donation.

We decorated the cake with drippy buttercream frosting. And this time we added yellow fondant polka dots in a few different sizes. Then we did something most unusual. Something you will not find in any recipe book. Something the magazines and shows would not recommend. And something my grandmother would probably never have done, although I think she would have loved it. We slid a yellow car right onto the side of the cake.

Of course, before we could do that, I had to get permission from one of the princesses to use one of her Hot Wheels. "Who would like to donate a yellow car to the yellow car cake?" I asked the girls. Silence. "You'll get it back," I assured each potential donor. "And when you do, you'll get to lick off the cake and icing." That did the trick. Within two minutes I had one yellow car. For the One Yellow Car Cake for 100 Yellow Cars. And two minutes after that, the one yellow car was perfectly parked on the cake, between tier two and tier three.

"How was the yellow car party?" Prince Charming asked when he got home the next night. He was in lawyer mode, surveying the party evidence remaining on the kitchen counter. A half-eaten six-layer cake. Yellow paper napkins. Yellow paper plates. Yellow plastic forks. "It was great," I said. "Too bad you missed the party." I showed Prince Charming the photographs on my iPhone. He was impressed. "I don't think I've ever seen a cake decorated with a car," he said. "Neither had I," I replied. "I'm going to post this on my blog tonight."

My telephone rang the next day. It was a wonderful woman who sometimes calls me about public relations opportunities. "Do you want to be on the news this coming Sunday morning?" she said. "I saw that yellow car cake on your website. Could you bring the lady who runs the car safety charity? Where you made the donation?"

What a great opportunity, I thought. I would love to tell people about the celebration that gives back. It was so easy and fun. And any girl could do it. With whatever cake and whatever charity she wanted. "Sure!" I said. Thirty seconds later I realized that I had spoken too soon. I had spoken too soon because the next thing my friend said was "Bring the cake, too. The producer wants the cake on the news, too."

Uh oh. That One Yellow Car Cake for 100 Yellow Cars was now one-half a cake. Oh well, I thought. I will just bake another cake this Saturday afternoon. The Sunday morning news gig was too good to pass up. "What time should I be at the station?" I asked cheerfully. Saying nothing about the one-half a cake.

And that is how the One Yellow Car Cake for 100 Yellow Cars became Two Yellow Car Cakes for 100 Yellow Cars. I had to make two cakes. Cake number one for the party. And cake number two for the show. On Saturday afternoon I fired up my oven for a second yellow car cake. I begged my children to dig out another yellow car from somewhere under someone's bed. The first one was still a little sticky.

And on Sunday morning I left my house bright and early, giving myself plenty of time. I called out to my kids as I juggled my purse and the cake and my cereal and my soda. "Don't forget to turn on the television, precisely at 10:50 a.m.!" And out the door I went. I waved goodbye to the little girls sitting on the steps. And I pulled out of the driveway. On my merry way to drive that six-layer cake all the way to the television station.

I turned onto a busy street. "Please please please do not fall," I begged the cake. The cake that was sitting next to me in the car. The cake made no promises. The road to the television station was full of twists and turns. I took the corners slowly. With one hand on the steering wheel and one hand on the cake. At one point the cake veered sharply to the left. I caught it in the nick of time. "That was close," I said. I pulled into a parking lot to readjust the cake's position. I thought about getting the magic wand out of my purse. To see if I could cast a spell of stability over the cake. "Don't be silly," I told myself. "Surely you are the kind of girl who can handle a yellow car cake!"

As it turned out I did not need the magic wand at all. The cake and I made it to the station, each of us arriving in one piece. The news segment aired without a hitch. The cake looked great in front of the camera. And my friend who runs the nonprofit organization did a great job talking about kids and cars and staying safe in the late summer heat. The entire adventure had been a success.

"I sure am glad *that's* over!" I told Prince Charming and the girls as soon as I got home. I collapsed into a chair in a heap of relief. The return trip had been much faster than the drive down to the station. That was because I had left the cake behind. As brunch for the production crew. The crew was so grateful. I was more grateful, though, because I did not have to drive back to my house with a six-layer cake riding shotgun. I guess it wouldn't have mattered if the cake had fallen over on the way back from its appearance on the news. Except for the fact that I did not want yellow cake and white cake and vanilla buttercream frosting and yellow fondant circles all over the front seat of my car. Unlike beaters, bowls and Hot Wheels, a real car isn't exactly lickable.

Do good, eat cake, I wrote in my diary that night. Eat cake, do good. Catchy! A repeat menu of sorts. Perhaps charitable giving is a secret ingredient, I wrote in the little pink notebook. Mixing in a little good makes any cake taste better.

"I wonder what the smart people I saw in New York a few weeks ago would say about eating cake and doing good," I said to Prince Charming. We were in the closet hanging up our clothes. I was sitting on the floor next to my running shoes, as usual. This time Prince Charming had brought in a chair from the bedroom. I guess the treadmill wasn't as comfortable for sitting as it was for running. "Do you think eating cake and doing good counts as strategic giving?"

My husband smirked. At least I am pretty sure he smirked. Prince Charming usually does not smirk. But this time I think he did. "You are something else," he said. "I'll take that as a yes," I responded. Adding my own smirk.

The practice of strategic giving, sometimes called strategic philanthropy, was gaining popularity among the people I worked with in my day job. Would this practice of baking cakes and donating to charities count as strategic philanthropy? I wrote that question in my diary. Thinking about my husband's smirk, I answered my own question. No, it probably would not. As clever as eating cake and doing good may be, it is probably not strategic. At least not according to the technical definition of strategic philanthropy.

One of the smartest people I know says that to be a strategic philanthropist you ought to first identify a problem you wish could be solved and figure out the best ways to solve that problem. Only after you do that should you pick charities to support with your donations. And even then you should pick only those charities you believe can do the work that will actually solve the problem.

By all means, more power to the strategic philanthropist. Especially where a lot of money is involved. And especially at big foundations where people are responsible for carrying out the charitable wishes of others. Others whose money it was to begin with, sometimes long ago.

That said, after watching thousands of people who are alive and well give to the causes they love, I had made a few of my own observations. When it comes to someone giving his or her own money, most of the time it seems to work just fine for charity to be driven by the giving side of the equation. And not necessarily by what happens on the receiving end. It is just so hard to figure out with any absolute mathematical certainty what really goes on when the donation leaves your hands.

You can spend a lot of time calculating the ratio of administrative costs to program costs. You can analyze fundraising expenses. You can review the audited financial statements of the charities you support. But none of this tells you a whole lot about the human lives the charities are helping to make better. It has always seemed to me that, if you really want to make a difference in the lives of others through your charitable donations, you should bet on the people. That is, you should bet on the skills of the charity's employees and the character of its leader. All of that usually outweighs any evaluation you might make by studying the data.

You have your own reason, strategic or not, for picking the charity you are giving to. And your reason is probably just as good as any other reason. At some point you have to trust the people working for the charities to do their jobs to help the people they are supposed to help. In the end, it is a leap of faith.

No, the yellow car adventure would not rise to the level of strategic philanthropy, I wrote. But that is okay. It was all about the giving. It was all about the fun to be had and the cake to be eaten by the people doing the giving. And it was all about how nice it felt to eat cake and do good at the same time.

I read that last part of my diary to Prince Charming. I cannot imagine what I would do if I couldn't bounce ideas off of my husband. He is the most fantastic resource. "Why did you pick KidsAndCars.org in the first place?" he asked. That was a good question. I had a good answer. "We picked KidsAndCars.org because I adore the woman who runs it. And I know she is very smart and very dedicated."

Just to prove my point I opened KidsAndCars.org's website on my iPhone. This time I was the researcher in the family. I read the results to Prince Charming. "Thanks to KidsAndCars.org all motor vehicles with a trunk sold or leased in the United States now have a glow-in-the-dark internal trunk release, beginning with model year 2002." My husband was impressed. So was I! In fact, I learned, KidsAndCars.org is not aware of any fatalities in the trunk of a car with this safety feature now in place.

"Our yellow car party really did help save lives," I said. "I will be sure to tell the girls about KidsAndCars.org and all of the good that came out of our small donation. And baking that cake. And from their willingness to give up two toy cars." Then I clarified the last part of that statement because my husband is big on the details. "Well, just one car. They got the first one back."

The yellow car party had been a good test, I thought. A good starting point for trying out a few of my new ideas about doing good. "I'll call my mother tomorrow," I said to myself. "She will find all of this so interesting."

More specifically, I was thinking that reading up on a charity after you send your donation, instead of before, is a lot like a great technique invented by my mother. A great technique called retroactive cleaning. Retroactive cleaning is when you do not quite get around to all of the dusting and vacuuming before your ladies' luncheon. To make up for it, you conduct a top-to-bottom, whirlwind scrub down beginning the moment after you wave goodbye to the last guest. Your house will be spic and span exactly six hours after the time you told your guests to arrive. But it is all good. Do the housework before the party or do it after the party. Either way, the house gets clean.

I'll bet it all works out in the end with giving, too, whether you research a charity before you give or after you give. Or even if you do not do any research at all. Strategy or no strategy, the charity gets the money. In fact, interestingly, university experts recently have suggested that if you analyze things too much before you make a donation to a charity, your enthusiasm might deflate when you put your small number up against all of those big numbers and stare into the vastness of the needs. You might get discouraged and decide not to donate at all. And that would be a shame. Because it really does all count.

It is easy to do at least a little good. Whatever that means to you. If you want to recycle, recycle. If you want to drop coins in the kettle, drop coins in the kettle. If you want to donate bedspreads to a shelter, donate bedspreads to a shelter. If you want to buy the cookie dough from the school fundraiser, buy the cookie dough. If you want to give a little cash to someone going through a tough time, give a little cash to someone going through a tough time. If you want to buy tickets to the charity golf tournament, do that. If you want to make a donation to a charity you like, make the donation. It's all good. You can research the numbers and the data later if you would like to give yourself a pat on the back for making the right decision. Because you have.

My idea is that there is no bad decision involved in giving to a cause you love. It's a lot like cake. Eat the cake. Then calculate the calories after you've eaten it.

Chapter 12

Cheerful Chocolate Peanut Butter Cake

"I'm making an A-A-B pattern!" My middle daughter was beaming. "Red, red, blue. Red, red, blue. Six M&Ms." I looked up from my usual spot at the kitchen counter. The spot where I park myself to assemble cakes. I was figuring out that certain places at my kitchen counter had better karma than others. Better karma for ensuring that cakes would stay standing.

"Wow!" I said. I surveyed my daughter's work. I was impressed. "You really did make an A-A-B pattern! And you are right. There are six M&Ms in that pattern." My blonde-haired princess with the big blue eyes smiled and giggled. She was so proud of herself. And she had every reason to be proud. Basic concepts like addition and subtraction are really hard for her to grasp. It's part of Williams Syndrome. Fortunately, though, children who have Williams Syndrome are sometimes able to catch on to math by first learning about sequences and patterns.

Today we were working on patterns. And baking a cake. Just for fun. My daughter was helping out by sorting peanut M&Ms. Peanut M&Ms that I would use to decorate a chocolate peanut butter cake. After I had put it all together on a big silver platter.

"Great job!" I said to my daughter. "Please keep right on sorting! We want only red and blue M&Ms for this cake. And in a minute I will need them." I was testing another idea about eating cake and doing good. The yellow car cake had been such a success. I wanted to find out if eating cake and doing good would work with other cakes, too.

"Today I am making a chocolate peanut butter cake," I answered. Prince Charming had not even had to ask the question. A definite pattern was emerging in our conversations, at least where cake-making was concerned. "Ah," was all he uttered in response as he walked through the kitchen. He did not even slow down to take a look. "I think I will go out to the yard to trim a few bushes," he said, opening the door to the garage. "They've gotten pretty tall over the summer." Chocolate peanut butter cake is not his favorite.

I, on the other hand, do like chocolate peanut butter cake. Chocolate and peanut butter are one of my favorite food combinations. I especially like the chocolate peanut butter combination during times of high emotion. Chocolate and peanut butter mixed together are comforting. "It must have something to do with the high levels of fat and protein in peanut butter," I told my daughter. She had moved on to making a red-blue-red pattern with the peanut M&Ms. "During times of stress," I added, "you need to build up your energy storage and build up your muscles. Plus, chocolate makes you happy."

I stopped what I was doing for a minute to think about that statement. I was pretty sure I was right about the fat and protein part. But I thought I remembered a story about a scientist recently challenging the theory that chocolate can improve your mood. "Oh well," I said aloud. "It works for me." My daughter kept right on sorting the M&Ms, chattering about her new A-B-A pattern. She and I were carrying on a lovely conversation at the kitchen counter. Just not with each other.

"Perfect!" I declared to the cake. The cake was now fully assembled and standing strong. Actually, for this occasion, which was no particular occasion, I had made two cakes. I had made a big cake and a small cake. I had just finished placing both cakes on the silver platter, side by side. Side by side so that the edges were just barely touching, linking them together.

Neither cake was in any danger of falling over. I was going for width on this one, not height. The big cake, which I suppose I could call Cake A, featured four eight-inch round layers, peanut butter cake alternated with chocolate cake.

The small cake, Cake B, needed only two layers, four-inches each in diameter, peanut butter on the bottom and chocolate on the top. The small cake needed only two layers because I had made the four-inch layers extra thick. I had made them extra thick to use up all of the cake batter. Using up all of the cake batter is my self-defense mechanism for avoiding eating cake batter for lunch and dinner. Which was a distinct possibility on that particular day. Especially when the cake batter in question was the high fat, high protein kind. And the happy kind.

It had been one of those weeks, I thought to myself. On the bright side, which is always the best place to start looking at anything, the good girl diary was taking on a life of its own, spilling out of the little pink notebooks and onto my blogs. Onto my blog for my make-believe catering company, One Celebrations. And onto the blog I had started writing on the diary of a good girl domain. It was fun to have two websites.

"You've got quite a hobby on your hands," Prince Charming had remarked earlier that week. At the time he was peering over my shoulder, watching me tap tap tapping away on my laptop. Writing a post and inserting a cake picture. "What exactly are you doing?"

I had thought about saying "Isn't it obvious?" But that would have been rude. And in fact it was not obvious. Not to anyone but me. After all, I was the only one living in my own world. My own world where I filled up pink notebooks with lots of ideas for doing good. And a few ideas for looking good. And lots of ideas for having fun with kids and cakes. And I was the only one in my world who was running a make-believe catering operation. Aren't we all the only ones in our own worlds? I'd have to write about that in the diary, I thought to myself.

Instead of saying all of that to Prince Charming, though, I had made an attempt at the best explanation I could think of at the time. "Well," I had said. "Well" is always a great way to buy time when you aren't quite sure exactly what to say. It is better than "uh." "Well," I had said again, "I decided it was time I started sharing a few of the ideas in this diary of a good girl. This diary about being myself. I thought maybe if I put these things on my websites it might inspire other girls to be themselves, too." I thought that sounded pretty good. "And it might reassure other girls that their cakes are beautiful," I had added. Prince Charming actually nodded. So far, so good.

"And," I had continued. "And" is another good word for stalling. "And, the One Celebrations website is just a place for me to post pictures of all of these cakes. Kind of like an online catalog." I paused. "But you can only look. You can't buy." I wanted to be sure Prince Charming understood that I was not going to convert our kitchen into a commercial cake-baking operation. "The cakes are all from the diary stories about doing good," I said. "I'm not ever going to sell them. It's all a gift. Exclusive catering, you could call it. One of the ways I give a little piece of myself to friends and family. People I care about."

During the conversation I had watched Prince Charming do the math in his head. Very quickly he had assessed that neither of these online publications was making any money. And very quickly he had tallied up the cost of cake mix and eggs and powdered sugar and M&Ms and all of the other ingredients required to operate my not-for-profit venture. And I am pretty sure he had come within 37 cents of the actual total. Prince Charming is a whiz at the grocery store.

Being the Prince Charming that he is, though, he had said nothing about the liabilities side of the hobby balance sheet. "Well," was what he said instead. "Well, if it makes you happy, do it." He really is Prince Charming.

But, like I said, it had been one of those weeks. A week that required a chocolate peanut butter cake at the end of it. It had been one of those weeks because a teeny, tiny downside had begun to seep into the bright side of my diary adventure. It seemed that the more pages I filled in my pink notebook, the more crying I did.

Thankfully it was not a lot of crying. Not enough to ever mess up my six layers of mascara. Just a few little tears every once in a while. And not the kind of tears you get when you smash your finger in the car door loading up the kids for school. Or when you burn your wrist on a hot cake pan. Or when you hear a sad story about a sick child. Not those kinds of tears. These tears were wistful tears. The kind of tears that come from a place deep within you. A place that seems curiously long ago and far away.

The first time this happened I had done a little research on tears. And then I had called my mother to report my findings. "Hi!" I had said. "Hi," she had said. "I think I figured out what's wrong with me," I announced on the phone. "I'm not really sad. I'm just wistful." My mother and I love to discuss the subtle differences between words. A "sad" versus "wistful" discussion was right up her alley. "Yes," my mother said, agreeing that there was a difference. "'Wistful' connotes loss. Like a vague or regretful longing. 'Sad' is more acute." My mother is so smart.

It turns out that tears from emotional crying are chemically different from other types of tears. Scientists can even name the chemicals. Certain chemicals appear in greater quantities in wistful tears than in other kinds of tears. Other kinds of tears like sad tears or tears of joy or pain. A few of the chemicals in wistful tears include prolactin, adrenocorticotropic hormone, something called leu-enkephalin and the more well-known and easier to pronounce elements, potassium and manganese. "I'm convinced," I had told my mother. So was she. We are both easily impressed with research based in biology.

But today was not a day for tears. How could it be? I was staring at a chocolate peanut butter cake. Two of them actually. Two chocolate peanut butter cakes, just waiting to be decorated. "This cake is a happy cake," I told my daughter. "We'll make big, smiling faces out of fondant." That got her attention. "What?" she said, forgetting all about the M&Ms. Kids with Williams Syndrome love to look at faces. It is a fascinating characteristic, no doubt based in genetics and biology. And my daughter loves to roll out fondant and cut it into circles. That's my daughter, not the Williams Syndrome.

"There!" I said as I added the last smiling face to the big cake. It really did turn out to be a cheerful platter. Two cakes, four smiling fondant faces, red and blue peanut M&Ms, red and blue sugar ribbons. And a cherry on top.

"Girls, girls!" I called out to the other two princesses. It was time for our celebration that gives back. "Today we are celebrating a youth mentoring organization. Lots of kids in our community don't get the opportunity to bake cakes with their mothers. Or go to a movie with their fathers. Or have a conversation with a caring adult." Even at their young ages, my girls were beginning to understand that as delicious as cake may be it really does taste better when it is frosted with giving back.

"We'll send our check tomorrow," I said as we cut into the smaller of the two cakes. Otherwise known as Cake B. "And I will send a picture." Of course. I always send an email to the director of whatever favorite nonprofit we were supporting as part of the cake-baking. An email with a link to my blog post about the cake. A blog post about a celebration that gives back. A blog post about eating cake and doing good.

The girls ate a few bites of cake and ran off to find Prince Charming. Probably to convince him to let them watch the Disney Channel while I cleaned up the kitchen. Which gave me the perfect opportunity to park myself at the kitchen counter. And do a little thinking. A little thinking about crying. Not crying for real. Not right then, anyway. Just thinking about crying. More specifically, a little thinking about ideas for how to prevent myself from crying.

"I think I will write a few notes in the diary about all of this," I said to the fork. I was finishing every last bite of my own piece of chocolate peanut butter cake. It was super delicious. My favorite part of chocolate peanut butter cake is the cake-frosting blend. You know, that wonderful thing that happens when the frosting messes up the crumb coat when you spread frosting over the top of cake. That delicious concoction that sits between the cake layers.

There are two tricks to making a chocolate peanut butter cake. One trick is to mix a little peanut butter into the part of the frosting you will use between the layers. That's how you end up with a super delicious cake-frosting blend.

The other trick to making chocolate peanut butter cake is to add a little peanut butter, about a fourth of a cup, to a fluffy white cake batter. Just a little peanut butter is all it takes to convert a fluffy white cake into a super delicious peanut butter cake. The rest of the recipe for chocolate peanut butter cake is exactly like the regular recipe for fluffy white cake and the regular recipe for chocolate cake.

Sometimes one or two tweaks are all you need to create something brand new out of something old.

Yes, I thought to myself as I slid my plate and fork into the dishwasher, it is high time I started jotting down an idea or two in my diary of a good girl for how to stop an onslaught of wistful tears. I really could not afford to break out in wistful tears during a press interview at a coffee shop. Or in a pedicure chair with lots of other people around. Or especially not in the middle of a Very Important Meeting at the office with 27 Very Important People.

My smart psychologist sister with the Ph.D. tells me that awareness is always the first step in any cognitive behavior technique. "Start by observing the circumstances that tend to cause weepiness," she had suggested once. Hello, I thought. Why don't I just call that smart psychologist sister right now? In fact, if she didn't live in North Carolina, I would have invited my sister over that very minute. For a Very Important Meeting. A Very Important Meeting with me and my chocolate peanut butter cake.

"Maybe it has something to do with the first day of school," my sister suggested. Thank heavens she had answered her phone. I was telling her about my week. My week that had ended with an emergency chocolate peanut butter cake. And, as my sister so astutely observed, a week that had included the first day of kindergarten for my youngest daughter. My littlest princess. My baby.

"How is it possible that my baby is in kindergarten?" I asked my sister. I was holding back tears. "She is still supposed to be in a stroller. With me pushing her around the neighborhood. Like the mothers I watch at stoplights as I race through the streets to get to Very Important Meetings on time." My sister understands all about racing through streets to get to Very Important Meetings on time. She has two little kids. A girl and a boy. And an important job at a university. My sister was the perfect person to call on a day like this.

"Maybe you wouldn't have been one of those mothers even if you'd had more time," my sister offered. "Maybe you are getting wistful about something that would never have been part of your world in the first place." Maybe she was right. I rarely ever was a mother pushing a baby in a buggy. This was partly because my babies screamed when buckled into anything. This was also partly because I seem to have an interesting sort of energy. A boundless energy that requires a lot of multitasking. Boundless in the sense that doing just one thing for a long time, even pushing a stroller, has never really been in my DNA.

By the end of the conversation, my sister had convinced me that my wistful tears that week were not really real. That my wistful tears were based on make believe. A make-believe sense of loss. A grief over a reality I never would have had in the first place. I was so glad that I called my sister.

"Think of everything you pull off every morning," my sister reminded me. "Getting the girls filled up with cereal. Getting them and their backpacks into the car. And getting shoes on three sets of feet." She had a point. A big upside victory in my real world happens on the days when each of the girls arrives at school wearing two matching shoes.

"That's true," I said, feeling a little better. "There have only been a few times when one of the girls arrived at school wearing two different shoes." I did not mention to my sister that the mix-ups typically were not blue and black situations. More like flip-flop and cowboy boot. Oh well, I thought after I had thanked my sister and we had said our goodbyes. So what if the occasional sandal gets paired with a sneaker? Even Cinderella wandered around for a while wearing only one shoe.

I set my iPhone down next to the chocolate peanut butter cake. A few pieces were missing but it was still smiling. I smiled back. Then the phone rang. It was my sister, calling back. "I forgot to ask you something," she said. "What is One Celebrations? I've been looking at your blogs and I don't really get it." I started to get defensive. And then I remembered that it was all make believe. My own make believe. How could she get it, even if she tried?

"Funny you should ask," I said. I told her that Prince Charming had asked me the very same thing just a few days ago. "It's my pretend catering business," I said. "It's my hobby. It's just a fun way to package up all of these cakes I've been making. I wrap up pieces of cake in cellophane. Sometimes I wrap up an entire cake. And I tie black ribbon around it. And I seal it with a cute sticker." I paused for questions. There were none. So far, so good. "Then I give the cake away,"

I continued. "As a gift. Nothing is for sale." That all seemed to make sense to my sister. "We both always liked stickers," she said.

In truth, it was a little more strategic than that. At least where the name of the company was concerned. I had dreamed up the name "One Celebrations" for a few reasons. "One" because the test kitchen usually has only one chef, me. And sometimes my mother, but we are so much alike that it still counts as one person. And "one" because even cake for a single person can be a celebration that gives back. And "one" for one dollar, or one hundred dollars or one thousand dollars, because any size donation to charity really does make a difference. And "one" for one hundred. Which is my headcount limit for any gift of my catering services. I had learned my limits with the big rehearsal dinner.

But my sister didn't need to know all of that. She had summarized One Celebrations beautifully with the sticker comment alone. "Now I remember!" she said. "Remember when we were at your house last summer? We had so much fun naming that lemon cake."

Right! I had almost forgotten. That was the time I had hosted a sustainable midsummer luncheon. "I think I made bacon, lettuce and locally-grown tomato sandwiches," I said. And that had indeed been the case. That lunch was one of my first attempts at a new idea for doing good at home. It was a celebration that gives back because it was organic. "As I recall, though," I reminded my sister, "the bacon was pretty salty. We drank a lot of Diet Coke and recycled dozens of cans. I guess it really was an environmentally friendly celebration."

For just a second I had one or two wistful thoughts about having given up Diet Coke six months ago. I had given it up in a moment of organic zeal. Maybe I'll go back to it someday, I thought to myself. At that moment it also crossed my mind that perhaps I should stop making my life harder than it needed to be. And that perhaps I would go back to Diet Coke when I started feeling better about myself. I really missed Diet Coke. I had loved it so.

"Yes! We had bacon and Diet Coke. Lots of it," my sister said on the phone. Thankfully she pulled me away from make-believe Diet Coke and brought me back to the reality of the phone call. "That is exactly right," she continued. "You had also made that delicious cake. That lemony layered nut cake." She paused. And laughed. "The cake we talked about for an hour before we decided that you should name it the Lemony Layered Nut Cake." By now my sister and I were both in tears. Tears of laughter. The good kind of tears. "One Celebrations has come a long way since then," I said. "Remember, now I have stickers."

Actually that Lemony Layered Nut Cake had been really, really good. I have not made it since, though, because the calorie count is outrageous. The Lemony Layered Nut Cake is an every five years sort of thing. "Remember the description I dreamed up for that cake?" I asked my sister. "It was ridiculous. I called it a 'citrus-infused medley of nuts and lemon cream cake molded into a petite tower of endless flavor.' How silly is that!"

My cheerful chocolate peanut butter cake was still smiling back at me from the kitchen counter. "I really have come a long way," I said to my sister. "Today I've been referring to cakes as Cake A and Cake B." "Well," said my sister just before we hung up, "don't suppress yourself too much. You wouldn't be *you* if you didn't dream up funny names for things."

"I have the most wonderful sister," I said to Prince Charming. He had come back inside from trimming bushes and had sat down with me at the kitchen counter. And he had opened up a can of Diet Coke. I tried not to look. Prince Charming still did not want any chocolate peanut butter cake. I was astonished. How could he resist those smiling faces? And those peanut M&Ms? My husband is a strong man. It must be those ten years in the army. But I said nothing. If he didn't want any cake, he didn't have to have any cake.

"You are lucky," Prince Charming agreed. "I am glad you called your sister today. You needed that." And it was true. Where wistful tears are concerned, sometimes a phone call with your sister is an even better remedy than chocolate peanut butter cake.

That night I jotted down the recipe for chocolate peanut butter cake. I jotted it down in my little pink notebook. Under the heading Cheerful Chocolate Peanut Butter Cake. My sister had made a good point about just being who I am. So what if I operate a pretend catering business? So what if I named it One Celebrations? So what if I give each of my cakes its very own name?

"I just need to be myself," I said to myself. In my closet. This time I was sitting on the treadmill. Just to see what it was like. Cheerful Chocolate Peanut Butter Cake. Not over the top, but not boring, either. I liked it.

Just below the recipe I wrote three words: No more tears! At least not for today. Today had been a good day. A good day at the end of a hard week. My little girl was in kindergarten. But so what? She was still my little girl. And I was still her mother. No more tears. And I had not even tried to use the magic wand. "Oh well," I said to myself. "It probably wouldn't have worked anyway."

Chapter 13

Paw Print Cake

Party time! Birthday party time, that is. That is what time it was at our house. Or at least it was time to start planning. I was digging around in the pantry. Making my list and checking it twice. I wanted to be sure my pantry was fully stocked with baking supplies.

The busy season was about to begin. The busy season of baking. And giving. The fall is full of birthdays and holidays. And lots of opportunities for the girls and me to fire up the test kitchen. And to make donations to our favorite charitable organizations. Lots of fun opportunities to eat cake and do good.

"I know what I want to do for my birthday," announced my oldest daughter. Her birthday was still a few weeks away. She is the daughter who is really good at planning things. Planning things well in advance. She plans her own birthday parties. And she runs them, too. It is such a gift.

"We'll ask everyone to bring a donation," she said. "A donation to charity instead of a gift to me. I want to do something nice for the animal shelter." Well, well, I thought. Maybe all of my efforts to practice social responsibility at home were rubbing off on the children.

"That sounds great," I said. "How nice of you! Want to start working on the invitations?" My oldest daughter also is really good at making things with paper and markers and glue and scissors. Once, when she was only 4 years old, she made an entire paper city. It took up most of the space on her bed. I think I still have it somewhere. Somewhere in a box in the basement.

"Maybe you could go get the black construction paper," I suggested. "I have a few blank note cards and envelopes you can use. You could cut out one big circle and four little circles for each invitation. And glue them onto each note card to make a paw print. In honor of the animal shelter." Then I added, "And I'll help you write down the party details on each invitation."

The details matter on birthday party invitations. Especially when you are the mother of the birthday girl. The mother of the birthday girl who will be hosting the party. Details like the date of the party. And the time it will start. And, most importantly, the time it will end. Ten minutes of free time is ten minutes too much. At least when it comes to ten little girls in a basement. I had at least learned that much from the summer cake camp.

Less than an hour later my daughter and I had completed the invitations. Ten invitations, each with a paw print. And a note suggesting to each little girl that instead of a gift she could bring a small cash donation. Or a gift in kind. A gift in kind such as a bag of dog treats or a cat toy.

"I'll make a list of the games," my daughter said. "One game we can play is the adopt-a-pet game. I know all about how to adopt a pet." True enough. That subject has been heavily studied by the girls. By my youngest stepdaughter and my oldest daughter, in particular. Unfortunately adoption of any sort of pet around our house is the make-believe kind of adoption.

I wish that were not the case. I love dogs. I grew up with two golden retrievers. One of those golden retrievers was my running partner. I adored her. But somewhere around the time I was in law school my love of dogs turned into an allergy to dogs. Which was a shame and still is a shame. All five of our girls have always wanted a dog. It is something I have been so sorry not to be able to give them.

"Sure!" I said cheerfully. "The adopt-a-pet game would be great." I had no idea exactly what that game entailed. But I was sure my daughter had it all figured out and I was sure that she would share it with her uninformed mother.

"The game is really fun," my daughter continued, explaining the rules. Just as I had hoped she would. "I will download and print photographs of dogs and cats from the animal shelter website. At the party with my friends we can each pick the pet we would adopt if we could. We can even name our pets." My daughter must have seen my facial expression tense up, ever so slightly. "Not for real, Mom," she assured me. "It's all just pretend."

I breathed easier. Pretend sounded good to me. The adopt-a-pet game sure was better than the party game ideas I had been toying with. Like the cat-and-mouse game. That is when you assign just one party guest to be the cat. The rest of the guests are mice. It is really just another name for hide-and-seek. My other idea was to park the kids in front of a good dog movie. Like *Hotel for Dogs*. Or *Old Yeller*. And then call it done. My daughter's game plan was much better than mine.

"I love your idea," I told my daughter. "Add it to your list for sure." I was having fun watching her write out an entire schedule for the party. The time of arrival. The time to start the first game. The time to start the second game. The time to eat cake. The time to start the third game. And the time to go home. She had covered it all.

"For the second game," she said, "we'll play Dogopoly." I have never played Dogopoly. But my mother, who does play Dogopoly, says it is just like Monopoly. Only with dogs instead of real estate. "And our third game will be a scavenger hunt," my daughter continued. "I will make up clues and hide them around the house."

"You're pretty good at games," I said. "And at making lists," I added as my daughter showed me her progress on the party schedule. "I love making lists," I told her. And I really do love to make lists. My pink notebooks were proof positive of that! I write lists of things to do. I write lists of names of kids to invite to the girls' birthday parties. I write lists of things to buy at the grocery store. I write lists of cakes to bake. I write lists of goals for the month. Goals that always seem to include things like cleaning out the basement and losing two pounds. No matter how messy the basement happens to be at that particular time. And no matter how many pounds I happen to weigh.

Over the years my list-making has taught me a lot of useful things. Things like the fact that basement cleaning is endless. A basement can always be cleaner. Maybe I will never get around to completely cleaning out the basement. Especially if I keep coming up with fun things to do instead. Like baking cakes.

I have also learned that it might not be such a good idea to always write down "lose two pounds" on a to do list every month. It is actually possible to be too thin. Especially when you are racing around. Racing around doing everything you can to keep so busy that you drown out the voices telling you that something is not quite right in your fairy tale. But don't worry. If that happens to you, you will be back to your old self in no time if you just eat a lot of cake. And if you eat a lot of nuts. Whatever it takes so that you don't find yourself someday at the low end of the scale.

"I heard of a woman in Vienna who ate only nuts," my mother had told me one day. One day we were snacking on a can of my favorite roasted almonds with sea salt. We were snacking on almonds instead of cereal. Just for a change.

"Really?" I had said. Kitchen counter conversations with my mother were always so interesting. "Yes!" my mother had confirmed. "This woman ate only nuts. For years. I think even forever. And that is not some European urban myth. She really did it."

I had thought that sounded pretty good at the time. "I love nuts." I had told my mother. "I think I would be very happy eating only nuts, cereal and cake." And then I had paused for a moment to think about that. "Actually, that's pretty close to what I do anyway." And that was true. At least at the time.

"There!" said my daughter. "I've made the list of all of the things we will do at the party." She showed me the finished schedule. It was quite thorough. Her list of party activities even included an allotment of 15 minutes for doing an inventory of the donations to the animal shelter.

"Great! Now," I said, "if you really want to plan ahead, you could make a shopping list. A shopping list of all of the things we will need for the party." Then I added "Including all of the ingredients we will need for the cake." I think I saw my daughter roll her eyes when I said the word "cake." It was an affectionate eye-roll, though.

I started thinking a little bit more about my lists. Some of the lists I write in my diary are probably somewhat unique. Like lists with absolutely no purpose. Such as writing down every email in my inbox. Which is silly considering that the inbox itself is a sort of list itself.

"You can learn a lot about yourself by the things you write down on your lists," I told my daughter. I always try to share life lessons and practical tips with the girls whenever I can. "And you can learn even more about yourself by analyzing why you make lists in the first place," I added. I was thinking about myself, of course. Thinking that the reasons for list-making probably are different for everyone. And wondering about my own list-making reasons.

Maybe I make lists because I love the combination of smooth, lined paper and colored pens. Maybe I make lists because I have a hard time sitting through a meeting without becoming just a teeny tiny bit restless and fidgety. Restless and fidgety no matter how important or how interesting the meeting happens to be. List-making keeps me cheerful and polite and relatively still.

Maybe I make lists because I like the list-making part better than the actual doing part. Way better. I love to make a big, long grocery list and hand it off to my husband. Prince Charming is a talented shopper. He can make a grocery store run faster than anyone I have ever known. Even when the three little girls go to the store with him.

"How is it that Daddy can get in and out of the store with a cart full of legitimate and nutritious items, each one of them on the list, the entire list completed, in less than an hour, with only a single box of Fruity Pebbles as evidence of little girl persuasion techniques?" I asked my daughter. I was talking too fast. And my sentences were way too complicated.

"You know what I mean," I said, slowing down. "When I go to the store, my cart is always piled up with white t-shirts. White t-shirts that are exactly like the other ten white t-shirts in my closet. And brightly-colored paper party napkins from the clearance shelves." My daughter didn't say anything. She can tell when I am having a conversation with myself. Even though I am pretending to talk to someone else.

Once upon a time I had made a shopping list that included a hamster. That was when Prince Charming and I found ourselves, at least for a few hours, without a hamster. A hamster we were supposed to have. It was a unique experience, to say the least, to write "hamster" on a shopping list. A shopping list that otherwise included only normal things. Like cake mix and Cinnamon Toast Crunch.

"Remember when you brought the hamster home from school for the weekend?" I asked my daughter. She was hard at work writing out the grocery list for her birthday party. She stopped immediately when I brought up the subject of the hamster. "That hamster was so *mean*!" said my daughter. "I wish I'd never brought him home. All that hamster did was bite."

"Well," I said. "That hamster did a lot more than bite. That hamster *ate*. I never should have agreed to let it spend the weekend with us in the first place." And that was true. Oh was that ever true!

For the record, you can be a good mother and a socially responsible citizen in lots of ways without bringing a rodent into your home. There are so many other things you can do to volunteer your time to a good cause. And volunteering is a wonderful gift! Especially at school. Sign up to do the games at the class holiday parties. Decorate cookies for the bake sale. Clean up popcorn after the carnival. Even haul a wagon full of 50 water balloons filled from your kitchen sink to field day. "When I was in kindergarten, I volunteered my mother to wash everyone's napping rugs over a weekend," my own father had told me once. How nice! See? There are many ways to help. But never, ever pitch in when the classroom hamster needs a place to stay.

"That hamster project was a big rip off," my daughter continued. "We were only supposed to have to add a little food and water to his bowl in the cage. And, in return for being fed, the hamster was supposed to be fun to play with." That had been the plan, anyway. But the kids had gotten tired of playing with the hamster after the first five minutes of his weekend getaway. And that was because the hamster had not lived up to his end of the deal. That hamster had *not* been fun to play with.

"That hamster bit me 21 times!" My daughter was still irked that her one and only chance to adopt a pet, even temporarily, had been a less than rewarding experience. Hamsters are just plain mean. Twenty-one bites in five minutes had been too much. I had parked the cage on top of the laundry room refrigerator. Where I had planned for that mean old hamster to stay for three days.

"Do you remember what we learned from the hamster's visit?" I asked my daughter, again trying to infuse a little educational value into everyday events. "And I don't mean just the basic lesson that hamsters are mean. There were two science lessons, too." After all, I had to look on the bright side of the whole situation. Specifically, that weekend we had learned the answers to two zoology questions: "What time do hamsters wake up in the morning?" and "What do hamsters eat for breakfast?"

Before we learned the answers to the two science questions, though, there had been a little bit of trouble with the hamster's visit. The first sign of trouble with our volunteer activity had occurred at 10:30 p.m. on Saturday night. Prince Charming had appeared in our closet doorway. I had been hanging up my clothes and getting ready for bed. His expression had been grim.

"We have a problem," he had said. Prince Charmings always seem to start telling you about bad news by using words that are excessively foreboding. You are sure the words to follow will involve physical harm to one of your children. Or a mess in the castle kitchen too big for Prince Charming to want to handle alone. In this case Prince Charming's next words had been scary. "No hamster," he had said.

Naturally I had not immediately believed Prince Charming when he said "no hamster." I had not immediately believed him, partially because he sometimes overlooks things that are really there. As in "I swear the kids' backpacks weren't hanging on their hooks five minutes ago!" And partially because I was desperately hoping he was just flat out wrong.

"What do you mean, no hamster?" I had said that night. Immediately I had rushed to the laundry room to make my own diagnosis. I pulled a step stool up to the refrigerator and tentatively peered into the cage sitting on top of the freezer compartment. Sure enough. I verified my husband's discovery. No hamster.

My daughter was laughing at the kitchen counter. "I didn't know all this happened," she said, enthralled. It was so cute to see her become fascinated with a story about her own childhood. Three years ago really is history when you barely count your age using double-digits.

Truth be told, after I confirmed that the hamster was no longer in his cage, my first thought was one of sheer dread. Sheer dread combined with maternal compassion for all living things. At that moment it had dawned on me that the hamster had dropped six feet from the top of the refrigerator to the laundry room floor. And that he might be lying there, dead or wounded, right under my feet.

"You'd better do the floor check," I had said to Prince Charming. The thought of the hamster's condition had made me a little faint. Prince Charmings are much better equipped than princesses to deal with things like dragons, spiders and rodents.

Alas, though, the hamster had not been in the laundry room. "Oh my gosh," I said to Prince Charming. "Do you think it is loose somewhere in the house?" It made me even more queasy to think about the hamster running around the castle, up to no good.

"It's been a long day," Prince Charming had said calmly. And he was right. Neither one of us wanted to look for a hamster at 10:48 p.m. So, with that, I added "hamster" to my Sunday shopping list. "I'll just buy a new one at the pet store and put it in the cage," I told Prince Charming. "The kids will never know the difference."

And after that we had gone to bed. Telling ourselves the hamster surely must have made his way outside and into the yard and down the street. Down the street to a lawn far, far away where the hamster would be reunited with his hamster family and live happily ever after.

"That was not the end of the story, though," I told my daughter. We were way off the subject of birthday party planning. We were, however, within our general conversation theme about pets. So I kept going with the hamster story. Even though it was getting near her bedtime.

"Everything was fine. At least until 4:13 a.m.," I continued. "That was when I heard a scratch scratch scratch scratch at the bedroom door." In my sleepy fog I am pretty sure I had whispered the names of each of the children. Which had been wishful thinking.

Scratch scratch scratch. That time my husband had bolted out of bed, turning on every light in our bedroom, shouting "That's not a kid! That's the hamster!" Prince Charmings are so good at identifying strange noises in the middle of the night!

"Hamsters are tricky!" I told my daughter. "We could hear it. But we could not see it. And they move so fast! I told Daddy to go get the broom." I had been specific about the broom. I was a little afraid my husband would return with a kitchen knife. Or a sword.

"Hold still while I am gone!" Prince Charming had said. "And scan the room for any sign of movement." In record time Prince Charming returned with the broom. "Stand with the broom above your head for maximum leverage," I recommended. Which was a silly thing to have said. All knights in shining armor know instinctively what to do with weapons. I had not needed to include this in my instructions for conquering the hamster.

The hamster had finally cannonballed himself out from behind a chair, making a dive for that impossible-to-reach spot under the bed. We had known at that moment that it was now or never. "Got him!" Prince Charming declared victoriously. With one sweep of the broom he had catapulted the hamster into the corner of the bedroom where I was waiting with three old towels. Three old towels to throw over the hamster. We had completed the capture.

"I made Daddy put the hamster back in his cage," I told my daughter. "No way was I going to touch that nasty thing. But the glory of duct taping the cage tightly shut was all mine." Women are actually better at duct taping than men. I am pretty sure this is because of so much experience removing lint, cat hair and Rice Krispies from clothing.

After such a heroic, tag-team effort, Prince Charming and I had given each other a high-five in the laundry room. We figured we had achieved a total victory over the hamster. But that had not been the case. That had not been the case because hamsters do not just bite. Hamsters also eat.

"So," I told my daughter, circling back to the science lesson. "We had learned from the scratching sounds that hamsters get up at 4:13 a.m. And then we learned what they eat for breakfast. And it is not cereal. Or pancakes." Indeed, later that morning my husband and I had conducted a thorough search for any signs of hamster damage to the house. What do hamsters eat for breakfast? About 12 inches of the carpet in your bedroom and 1/16 of a jack-o-lantern Halloween costume buried deep in the coat closet!

"Hamsters are not a good idea," I said. "That's the bottom line. "And," I added, "they are no fun." And that was the end of that. I think my daughter had enjoyed the story. Although her only comment was "I still wish we could get a dog." To that comment I had no comment. "Time for bed," I said as we walked together toward the stairs. "Sleep well. I love you."

My daughter's careful planning paid off. Her birthday party was a success. Everything went exactly according to plan. The party started on time. The party ended on time. The little girls loved the adopt-a-pet game. They loved the scavenger hunt. They loved Dogopoly. And they spent precisely 15 minutes oohing and aahing over all of the nice donations to the animal shelter. One little girl even brought a 20-pound bag of dog food. It was a wonderful celebration that gives back.

"The only thing I didn't like," my daughter said when it was all over, "was the cake." Ouch. That hurt.

"Why didn't you like the cake?" I asked. I tried not to get defensive. I thought the cake was fine! More than fine, even. I had called it the Paw Print Cake. I had covered the entire cake with a single beautiful sheet of fondant in lots of colors. Colors like brown and tan and beige and white and black. Colors that are typical of dog and cat fur. I had spent at least 30 minutes rolling out that one big fondant sheet so that the colors would be blended just perfectly. I had even added just a touch of pink fondant. Pink fondant to represent little pink noses. To top it all off I had used circle cookie cutters and black fondant to make paw prints. The cake was stunning! At least I had thought so.

I took a deep breath. I was determined to turn this situation into a learning experience. "What was wrong with the cake?" I asked my daughter. I really did want to know. I wanted to know so that I could improve my cake game. After all, that's what testing is all about. You do not always hit a home run. And you only learn when you strike out. To create anything of real value I guess you have to be prepared to be wrong.

And the truth was that I had tried something different with this cake. Being slightly less of a planner-ahead-er than my daughter, I had waited until the last minute to decide what kind of cake to make. So I had decided to be innovative and use some unusual ingredients.

"Well," I explained to my daughter. "I used fiber-enriched flour to make that cake. And I used sour cream instead of milk. And a little butter. I was improvising."

Then a thought occurred to me. "Did the cake taste too grainy?" I inquired. Maybe the fiber flour had not been such a great idea. Maybe, when it comes to cake, it is best to skip the fiber. Some things are just not meant to be organic. Or even nutritious.

"No," she said. "The cake was really good. I just didn't like all of that fondant all over it. The paw prints were cute but they did not taste very good. They did not taste very good at all."

Ah. So. It was not the inside of the cake she had not liked. It was the outside. All that fondant. I had used all that fondant as a cover up. A cover up for what I thought was a poorly concocted recipe. A recipe that I assumed had baked into a less than delicious cake. "You should have just let that cake be itself," my daughter concluded. "It didn't need any fondant. It was good the way it was."

That day my daughter taught me a lesson, instead of the other way around. I wrote that lesson in my diary before bed that night. Perhaps it is better to be beautiful on the inside than it is to be beautiful on the outside.

Yes. As I put away my pink notebook I decided my daughter was right. If you do not like what is on the inside, nothing on the outside can ever make up for it. Not fondant. Not frosting. Not lipstick. Not mascara. You can wave the magic wand all you want but in the end you still wind up with yourself.

Chapter 14

Recycled Cake

"There you are! I've been looking everywhere for you."

I glanced up at Prince Charming. I glanced up from where I was sitting. Which was on the basement floor. Which was where I had been sitting for the last four hours. Surrounded by 30 years and 30 boxes. Boxes of Christmas cards. And finger paint drawings. And term papers. And law school exams. And newspaper clippings. And report cards. And photographs. And even a few particularly adorable items of little girl clothing. Little girl clothing so little that it was sized by the month and not by the year. I was spending the morning attempting to make a dent in cleaning out the basement. Cleaning out the basement instead of baking a cake.

"I decided Labor Day was the perfect day to go through a few of these boxes of memories," I told my husband. Funny that he had not even thought to look for me in the basement. It was a place I rarely visited. "I can no longer stand the thought of all of this stuff sitting down here in these boxes, just taking up space. Surely I can throw most of it away."

Throwing most of it away was my plan, anyway. But throwing most of it away was proving to be more difficult than I had thought it would be. I had opened the first box before 8:00 a.m. The next thing I knew four hours had gone by and Prince Charming had hunted me down. "I didn't expect to be sucked in by a box of things from grade school," I explained to my husband. "Somehow, though, I have found myself buried in old photographs and papers. Photographs and papers from when I was a little girl."

True enough. I was lost in my own history. "Send the girls down to help," I suggested to my husband. "I am looking for a book I wrote. A book I wrote when I was five. I just know it is in here somewhere. The girls would get a kick out of it. And I might even be able to use it to teach them a lesson. A lesson about starting early with your hobbies." I have always loved to write. Even in kindergarten I loved to write.

Prince Charming headed back upstairs to recruit the princesses. What I had not admitted to Prince Charming was that I was lonely down there in that basement. Down there in that basement with all of those boxes. All of those boxes reminding me of who I used to be.

Besides, I have never much liked to take on a big project alone. A big project is so much more fun with a friend. Especially a friend who is someone in your own family. Like daughters. Or a mother. Or a sister.

My sister would tell you that she has many memories of cleaning out my closet when we were growing up. I always asked her to help me. I asked her to help me in exchange for letting her have her pick of any or all of the things from my closet that I no longer wanted. Today I planned to negotiate a similar bargain with any or all of my daughters who showed up to help me in the basement.

"Now where could that be?" I asked myself. I distinctly remembered that the first book I had ever written was somewhere in one of those boxes. I was determined to find it. Not that I needed it. I just wanted it. The book had happened to cross my mind. And therefore I wanted it. The same thing sometimes happens to me with cake. Sometimes white cake with vanilla buttercream frosting just happens to cross my mind and therefore I want it. In the case of cake, though, I can always make one. I could not make another one of those books. So I continued to look.

"Girls, girls!" I said five minutes later to the two princesses who reported for duty. Two out of three! Not bad. I would have to be sure to thank my husband later. And find out exactly what he had promised the princesses in return for their hard labor.

"We are looking for a book," I continued. "Not a real book," I clarified. "Not a real book like the kind we read before bed. A book I made myself. With paper and magic markers. I think it is about ten pages long. Ten pages all stapled together."

"When did you last see it?" A very good question from my oldest daughter. "When I was your age," I answered. My daughter visibly retreated. "That was a long time ago, Mom. Why do you want that book?"

"Actually it's two books," I said as the memory became a little more clear. "There are two books." And there *were* two books, I thought to myself. It was all coming back to me. Once upon a time when I was in kindergarten I had written two books. I had titled the first book *People I Like*. I had filled it with pictures I had drawn of my friends. I had written their names neatly in crayon underneath each of the faces.

I was so proud of that book. I got a good grade! A good grade, as in a big smiley face written in blue magic marker by the student teacher. I enjoyed writing the first book so much that the next day at school I had released a sequel. The sequel was called *People I Don't Like*. That book got a bad grade. A frown face. A frown face dashed off in a stroke of disappointment on the cover page in bright red pen by the student teacher. It was the first bad grade of my academic career.

"Those books are not in these boxes," the girls declared. Two hours had gone by and still there was no sign of either of the books. We had dumped out the contents of all but just three boxes. And the last three boxes were full of the princesses' own school papers. Quite astutely my daughters assumed that two paper books, thirty-plus years old, would not be in a box of artifacts that were recent. Recent, relatively speaking.

"Well, maybe we should give up on finding the books," I admitted. I had to let it go. "Anyway," I reassured the girls, "looking for those books forced us to clean out these boxes. Look at how much we are throwing away!" And it was true. We had made great progress in our frenzy to find the books. We had filled up five yellow trash bags. "We made a dent in cleaning out the basement!" I continued cheerfully.

"Let's all go upstairs and have lunch. I just bought a brand new box of Life cereal."

Still, I was a little sad. A little sad, for the next 15 minutes anyway. I wonder why I wanted those books, I thought. "It was probably nothing more than a temporary challenge. A game of sorts. A way to make cleaning the basement seem more fun." Now I was talking to myself. "*People I Like*," I said aloud as I poured the milk over two bowls of Life, "*People I Don't Like*. What funny names for books." Maybe, I thought, I wanted to look at those books to find out. To find out in which of those two books I would find myself. "In that case," I said to the Life cereal, "it might be a good thing that those books seem to be gone forever."

"You're back," said Prince Charming. He had walked into the kitchen to eat lunch. "I wondered how long you could stand to be in the basement," he commented as he pulled a box of Total from the pantry and got out the skim milk. "Those kinds of projects usually put you in a bad mood."

"Well I'm not going back down there today," I assured Prince Charming. "I think I am done with the basement for a while. Maybe even forever." "I'll handle the basement," he said. "If you get some of that stuff out of our closet."

Ah. Good point. Our closet had gotten a little bit crowded. What with the treadmill and all of my work clothes and my four pairs of running shoes and my cookbooks and my logo stickers and my pink notebooks. And a handful of things that belong to my husband.

"Girls, girls, girls!" I said to the team of princesses. "Come help me clean out my closet. Someone grab a big yellow trash bag and we'll get to work. I will teach you how to recycle, re-purpose and re-use. It will be a lesson in giving back. Practicing a little social responsibility at home." If I couldn't teach the girls a lesson today about my writing hobby, I thought, I'll just teach them a lesson about my doing good hobby.

I knew that I would have to make the closet project fun. That I would have to make the closet project into a game. Or a dramatic production. Or a fairy tale. Or a little bit of all three. Otherwise I would be doing it alone. Which I did not want to do.

"Let's use my closet as a place to test the magic wand," I suggested.

I still had the magic wand in my purse. And I still had a vague sense of uneasiness. Of wistfulness. Of longing. Of questioning. Of searching. Of not being good enough. The magic wand still was not working.

I had the girls' attention. At least for now. They all took a seat in my closet, lining themselves up, side by side, on the treadmill. I stood on stage, four feet in front of them, my dress pants and silk blouses a backdrop. I stood near my running shoes. It is always a good idea to be in the vicinity of your running shoes. Just in case you need to go somewhere in a hurry.

I started with an educational statement. "A very wise man once said that all suffering is caused by that of which we must let go." I surveyed the audience. They were still with me. So far, so good. "That is all the more reason why it is a good idea to clean out closets and cabinets at least once a year. Before things really start to pile up."

I waved the magic wand over an entire section of my closet. The section of my closet full of eight clear plastic boxes. Clear plastic boxes full of dress pants, mostly black, in three different sizes.

"And it's not just the things themselves that pile up," I continued, as dramatically as possible, "but also the dust that goes along with it. By the way, that dust isn't magic fairy dust. It's called dirt."

Three little girls wrinkled their noses. "Ew," they said. "We see it! That's gross!"

"Yes. That is gross. Thank you. Now, let's all make the dust go away. Repeat after me. 'Abracadabra, dusty old pants, get out of this closet while you still have the chance!'" I waved the magic wand. Nothing happened.

"Now blow really hard, girls," I said. I had to make something happen here. "Blow really hard at the dust. Like you are blowing out the birthday candles and making a wish." That worked. The dust circled dramatically above our heads. It was better than a powdered sugar cloud.

"Wow, Mom! That's fun!" The girls were dazzled.

I kept going. After the dust cloud I figured I could lean a little bit harder on the curriculum side. "When you are cleaning out your closets and cabinets," I began in the most professorial voice I could muster, "you may use a magic wand to determine whether to recycle, re-use or re-purpose the item. Or, on occasion, resort to the yellow trash bag."

They were still listening. Excellent! "To do this," I said, "examine the item in question by holding it at arm's length while closing one eye and squinting with the other." To demonstrate this technique I held up one of the boxes of dress pants. Size 4. Black. "This allows you to ensure that you have the necessary objectivity to ask the right question. Such as 'Will I ever eat enough nuts and cereal and cake to wear a size 4 again?' Then wave your magic wand, close your eyes, let the answer appear in your head."

Still listening. Good.

"Now let's talk about social responsibility," I said. I was getting braver. "My opinion is that social responsibility must be practical. It must be easy. If it is too hard, you might not do it at all. And that would be a shame." Two out of three princesses nodded their dusty heads. I kept going. "After you've waved your magic wand and you open your eyes to deal with the item you are holding, you are allowed to first look around to see if anyone is watching. For example," I said to the girls "it is okay, every once in a while, when no one is watching, on a day when you are particularly overwhelmed or restless, to toss a cereal box into the trash instead of carrying it out to the recycling bin in the garage."

All three looked a little relieved. "No worries, girls, if you occasionally do not recycle. It is just fine to be good but not perfect. That still counts as good. Now, are you ready to learn the basic rules for recycling?" They all nodded.

"Okay," I said. "The basic rules involve a few simple questions. Is it paper? Is it glass? Is it plastic? Or is it a Something Else?" The rules for paper, plastic and glass are pretty easy to follow because the rules are printed right on top of most recycle bins, with pictures even. But it is not quite that simple because so many things seem to fall into the category of Something Else.

"What's a Something Else, Mommy?" my middle princess asked. "Is that like a Cat in the Hat? Or a Lorax?" Clever girl.

"Not quite," I said. "But there are similarities. A 'Something Else' is vexing. Let's try a quiz."

I could tell I was heading into dangerous territory. I might lose them at the quiz. But that would be okay. There was only so much throwing away the past I could deal with in a day. During the lesson I had already managed to fill an entire yellow trash bag with the contents of six of the eight boxes of dress pants in the wrong sizes.

"How should you classify hybrids. Hybrids such as half-eaten Tootsie Pops? Is it paper? Glass? Plastic? Or is it a Something Else?" Three blank stares.

"What about a plastic baggy? A plastic baggy that was used to hold a peanut butter sandwich? A plastic baggy that is still covered in peanut butter?" Three blank stares.

"That's okay, girls," I said. "Used food containers are tricky. Used food containers are tricky because you are tempted to believe that you need to re-use them, rather than recycle them."

In fact, I find that used food containers are very stressful when it comes to practicing social responsibility at home. This is because re-purposing or re-using an item trumps recycling it. An example of a used food container is an old sour cream carton, wholesale size, from Enchilada Night three years ago. An old sour cream carton that you have stored in the pantry ever since. It is just begging to be re-used for leftover meat sauce from the meat sauce that you have not had time to make. Or pleading to be re-purposed for a child's butterfly project at school. This is the same carton that for years has fallen off the shelf every time someone reaches for the toaster. But there it sits. A go-green guilt magnet. The solution for this type of food container is to recycle it immediately and do not even bother to store it for future re-use. Controversial? Perhaps. Sanity-saving? Yes. Save your sanity before you save the planet.

I surveyed the three faces. They were bored out of their minds. I had to stop immediately. I did not want to give my daughters the idea that doing good was a boring activity. "Okay girls, that's it for today. But tonight, in honor of our recycling lesson, we will have Recycled Cake for dessert."

"That doesn't sound so good, Mom," said my oldest daughter. "Recycled from what?"

Good question. "Oh, don't worry," I said. "I'm being dramatic. Giving things proper names, just for fun. Recycled Cake is simply another name for leftover cake. The leftover cake that is in the back of the freezer. We'll make it fun, though. Maybe we'll wave the magic wand over the top of it and serve it with a little ice cream."

By the time 8:45 p.m. rolled around that day I was ready to go to bed. Reviewing the past can be exhausting. "I wonder when it was that I gave up on the books," I asked Prince Charming in the closet. The closet was now much cleaner. Prince Charming was happy. And not just because of the closet. I had fixed him a special version of Recycled Cake. A special version of Recycled Cake that included not only ice cream but also strawberries.

"Gave up on the books?" He was confused. "You mean the ones you gave up looking for this afternoon? That was only seven hours ago."

"No," I said. "I mean books. As in all books. As in all the books I had planned to write. After the books I wrote in kindergarten." Maybe going through those boxes had been a good thing, I thought to myself. Maybe going through those boxes had reminded me that once upon a time I had been a little girl who wanted to grow up and write books.

"Well at least you are writing things down in those notebooks of yours," Prince Charming pointed out. "And you seem to be posting more often on your blogs. The diary blog and the cake blog. Doesn't all of that count?"

"Yes," I said. "Yes it does." I was thinking he had a point. Maybe I still *was* that girl who wrote those books in kindergarten. "I don't need the books themselves," I agreed. "I don't need any of those things in those boxes, actually."

Prince Charming nodded enthusiastically. He has been longing for years to clear the clutter from the basement and the closet. "Far better to invest your time and energy in your future than to spend it cleaning up your past," he said. Prince Charming is so smart.

As I fell asleep that night I thought to myself that I just might be right about not really needing all of those things. Even if you recycle things or re-purpose things or re-use things or throw things away or even lose things, those things are still part of who you are. No one can ever really take those things away. Not even the recycling people.

Cleaning out basements. Cleaning out closets. Recycling. Re-purposing. Re-using. Over the years I have learned a lot about all of those things. One thing I know for sure is that every year or so you should ask someone who loves you to help you clean out your basement or your closet or your cabinets. Or wherever things have piled up in your castle. This someone who loves you could be a sister. Or a mother. Or a daughter. Or three daughters. Or a good friend. Ideally this someone who loves you will have a magic wand. Not necessarily because it works but because it makes it fun.

Not long after I cleaned out my own closet I had an opportunity to help a good friend clean out her closets. Actually, her mother's closets.

"Why don't I come over in the morning and help you go through your mom's things," I offered to my friend. One of my very best friends. One of my very best friends whose mother had recently passed away. "I'll bring salads for lunch," I suggested. "And I will bring my magic wand," I added, laughing.

"Thank you so much for doing this," my friend said after I had arrived. We were starting in the kitchen. The kitchen is always a good place to start.

"Oh I am glad to help," I assured her. "This is good for me. I can test a few of my ideas about social responsibility and doing good at home." And then I added "Plus, I'd like to run a few things by you. I need your ideas on a few things. A few things about work."

I had known my friend's mother. She had been an absolutely wonderful woman. And a socially responsible girl for sure! My friend's mother was organic before organic was cool. She was ahead of her time.

"Look at all of these herbal supplements," I said as I surveyed the pantry. "Your mother was amazing. So health-conscious!" I moved a few of the bottles aside to get to what was behind them on the shelf. "And look at this!" I announced. "Your mom's sack lunch bags. How sweet."

"My mom was amazing," agreed my friend. "She used the same brown paper bag for her lunch every day. Until the bag fell apart. She hated the thought of filling up the landfills with things that still had a purpose."

My friend's mom had kept her cabinets and closets nice and neat. And she had not saved much. Still, my friend and I were a little overwhelmed at how we would get all of this done. It was, after all, an entire house. And we had been in the kitchen for four hours already. Sorting and recycling and re-purposing and re-using and occasionally throwing things away.

"Here is a good idea," I suggested. "Let's not do this in the regular way. The regular way, as in the sort method. The sort method where every item is separately evaluated for save-worthiness." I could use complex sentences with my friend. She is a lawyer, too. Sometimes it is fun for us to talk to each other like lawyers. "Instead, let's use the extract method. The extract method in which every item is presumed discarded unless specifically saved for a specific, articulateable reason."

"Great idea," my friend agreed. "That will make all of this go so much faster."

Indeed, some reasons for keeping things are good reasons and some are not. I try very hard not to keep things for reasons like: My kids will want this. Or: I'll pass this down to my grandchildren. Or: Someone, unnamed, might want it. When we say these things to ourselves, I am pretty sure that what we really mean to say is "I want this because it makes me remember who I am." I was beginning to figure out that it's okay to let these things go. That you are who you are without them.

"I think I am done," I said to my friend. We were in one of the bedrooms. Cleaning out the desk drawers.

"Already?" she asked, amazed. "Those drawers were packed full! How did you extract every important paper so quickly?"

"No, not the drawers," I clarified. "I am not done with the drawers. I think I am done with my job."

"Oh! Well that is interesting! Why? You love your job." My friend has known me for a long time. Since law school. She even helped me get my job. The wonderful job at the charitable foundation. The wonderful job I loved.

"I think," I said, considering my words carefully. I was speaking much more slowly than I usually do. "I think," I said, "that I have done everything I set out to do." And that was true. All of this cleaning out the past was helping me review my own history. My own recent history. As in the last six years I had spent as president of the Greater Kansas City Community Foundation.

"When I started as president, I promised myself that we would do five things," I continued, thinking it through. "We would find the right talent to run the financial administration side of the foundation.

The right talent to focus on providing charitable giving services to individuals, businesses and families."

I continued. "And I promised myself that we would figure out a way to help nonprofit organizations see how the foundation is designed to work for the giving side of the doing good equation. Working for the people who want to give money to charities and who want to give it away in the ways that are meaningful to them."

"We've done those two things," my friend agreed. "Plus, the staff at the foundation does such a great job gathering information about the nonprofits. The expertise is best in class."

"That is a good point," I said, nodding. "I also wanted us to figure out a way to offer services to other people and other foundations across the country in a way that does good and returns an investment for Kansas City. And I wanted to inspire the team to create a handful of extraordinary giving experiences for people of all demographics and all generations. Experiences they can't get anywhere else in the country. Like the breakfast for bedspread idea."

"And," I added, "I wanted to make sure the foundation is a place where innovation and creativity can thrive into the future."

"That's an important one," agreed my friend. "That will mean that my children and their children and your children and their children will get to experience giving at its best, right here in Kansas City, just like we do today." She paused for a moment, putting down the stack of papers she had extracted from a filing cabinet. And she looked at me thoughtfully. "You might be right," my friend said. "You might be done."

"There's just one more thing I need to do, though," I said. "I need to help make sure the foundation is in good hands. In the hands of the right people who will take care of it and love it as much as I do."

"The board is smart," my friend assured me. "They will know just what to do to find the right person to take your place. Everything will be fine."

I drove home that afternoon from my friend's mother's house. "I am so lucky," I said to myself in the car. "I have the most wonderful friend." And she really is the most wonderful friend. I hang on her every word. Especially today, I thought. Especially her words today. Especially what she said about work.

I repeated my friend's words. "Everything will be fine." It felt so good to say them out loud.

Chapter 15

In a burst of lightheartedness one morning, I dashed off a diary entry. I had finished drying my hair a couple minutes ahead of schedule. With all that extra time I thought I might have a little fun with the pink notebook. Mirror, mirror on the wall, I wrote, sitting in my closet. Have I reached good girl status, once and for all?

I laughed. I laughed about my poor attempt at poetry. And I laughed about the whole thing. "What a funny journey I've been on!" I was talking to my running shoes. "Months and months of writing about being a good girl. Writing about being a good girl in my diary and in my blogs." No comment from the running shoes. "What in the world am I going to do with all of this material?" I asked. I was not laughing anymore. That question was not funny. At least it did not sound funny when I heard myself say it. It sounded like a real question.

I put the diary back into my purse. Back into my purse next to my iPhone. My iPhone that was tucked into the same pocket with my keys. The keys I would need in five minutes to drive three little girls to school. I checked my purse for the other essentials. Wallet? Check. Lipstick? Check. Magic wand? Check.

I was still holding out hope that the magic wand could do something. Something like arrange all of the good things in my life. Arrange all of the good things in my life in a way that would actually make me feel good about myself. That was not happening. At least not yet.

Twenty minutes later I had dropped the girls off at school. And I was driving to work. I was thinking about the diary. And the cakes. And the charities we had supported already with our celebrations that give back. And all of the charities we could support in the future. I thought about all of those good things as I munched on my cup of fiber cereal.

It is not a bad little hobby, I thought to myself. Baking cakes. Doing good. Having fun with the girls. Taking pictures. And writing it all up on my blogs. "I could do this," I said to my can of all-natural grape soda. "I could do this for a long time. As in forever." The can said nothing. But I could tell it was wondering whether there would be any place for it in that particular version of forever.

"Don't worry," I said to the can, reassuringly. "The cake thing is just a hobby. I will still have a real job. So you will still get to ride to work with me every day."

I decided to call my mother. I get a little tired of hearing my own voice. Besides, I wanted to tell her about my new idea. My new idea that I had shared with my friend. My new idea about possibly having done what I set out to do at my job. She would find that interesting.

"Hi!" I said to my mother. "Hi!" she said. "I had an idea," I said, after my mother and I had checked in on the essentials. My dad. The girls. My sister. Her kids. My brother. His kids. "I've been thinking that I might be ready to move on to something new." Silence from my mother. Ready to move on to something new? That pretty much applied to me all the time. I am always up for something new.

"I've been thinking that I might be ready to move on to a new job," I clarified. "Oh!" said my mother. "Well that *is* an idea!" She paused. "What would you do?" "I have no idea," I said. "Maybe I would just be myself."

My mother laughed. Even though I had not been joking. "Write that one down in your diary," she said. "That might just be the best idea you've ever had."

I started laughing, too. Then I had to stop. "I am laughing so hard. You're making me cry," I said to my mother. I pulled down the sun visor and flipped open the mirror. I had to make sure my mascara had not been damaged by the tears of laughter. It was so very simple. Be myself. It was so very simple that it was very funny.

"I am serious about this job thing," I said to my mother. I had returned to my serious voice and I was speaking as convincingly as I could. "Let's talk about it when you come over for the birthday party this weekend."

One of the many benefits of raising five girls is that you get to host a lot of birthday parties. I love birthday parties. To end the telephone conversation with my mother on an upbeat note I signed off with something bold. "I am going to see if I can make an eight-layer cake," I told her before we said our goodbyes.

I wonder if I could do that, I thought to myself after I hung up the phone. I wonder if I could put together eight layers without the cake falling over?

The answer to that question would be no. At least for that particular birthday cake.

I do not expect perfection in cakes. I never have. I never will. Not every cake produced by One Celebrations can be perfect. In fact, not a single one of them is perfect. Not even close. And that is okay. That is how it should be, actually. A cake is baked to cheer on a celebration. A cake is supposed to be delicious. A cake is a symbol of fun. A cake is created to be eaten. A cake is meant to be whatever the cake-baker wants it to be. A cake is not meant to be perfect.

"Good but not perfect," is what I always say. Good but not perfect. In cakes. In children. In life. Why, then, could I not apply that principle to myself? The pages of my pink notebooks were filled with ideas for being better. Ideas for being a good mother. A good stepmother. A good daughter, sister, wife, friend. A good socially responsible citizen. "I have no idea what to do about myself," I said as I pulled into the parking garage at work. I was talking to the can of all-natural grape soda again. I think the can appreciated the attention. What to do about myself? The cans of all-natural grape soda and I talked about it all week on the way to work.

"Girls, girls, girls," I declared on Friday night. "It is time to make a really big cake. This time we will try eight layers." The birthday party was the next day. I was excited about the party. I was excited about testing a really big cake. I was excited about celebrating my daughter's birthday. I was excited because the guest list included more adults than children. Which meant that I could add wine and beer to my birthday party repeat menu of cake and apple juice.

The girls, on the other hand, were not too excited. They were not too excited about my call for help with yet another cake. Not a single one of the princesses came running. I wandered around the house until I found all three of them working on a Lego project.

"Please let us finish this," my oldest daughter said. "We only have an hour before bedtime. We'd rather play Legos than bake a cake." Then she added, "Not everyone likes cake as much as you do, Mom." That hurt. Just a little bit. But I was learning not to take comments like that personally. Especially comments related to cakes.

I made my way back to the kitchen. I looked at the clock on the oven. Wow. My daughter was right. It was getting late. 7:34 p.m. "I'll be cutting it close," I said to myself. "But I can do it."

Eight layers is bold. Eight layers is actually more like nine layers, I thought. I would have to bake three cakes, three layers each, to get enough layers to make an eight-layer cake.

I calculated all of this in my head as I got out the ingredients and arranged them on the kitchen counter. One box of white cake mix. One box of dark chocolate cake mix. I stopped. "And then what?" I asked out loud. I wanted the eight-layer cake to have an equal number of white layers and chocolate layers. That would mean four layers of each flavor of cake.

"One box of cake mix only makes three layers," I reminded myself. "You'll have to make two cakes in each flavor to get the numbers to work out. You'll have to make four cakes." When it comes to doing cake math I have found that it helps to do the calculating out loud.

The eight-layer birthday cake. That was how it had started. It had started at 7:34 p.m. The night before the birthday party. Twenty-four hours later, the story would have a happy ending. But the middle of the story is a little messy.

"I'll just deviate a bit from my usual recipe," I had said to the boxes of cake mix. "Just this one time. It's getting so late." And that had been my big mistake. A recipe deviation can lead to a cake crisis.

Of course a recipe deviation that precedes a cake crisis will always occur late at night. Late at night when you are tired and desperate and behind schedule. And when you are directing every last drop of your energy toward the will power required to stick to your self-imposed limits on calorie-rich taste-testing.

In my experience the most treacherous recipe deviations involve eggs. Either failing to add them to the batter slowly, half an egg at a time, or failing to warm the eggs to room temperature before they go in. Eggs are scientifically critical to the baking process.

Eggs in poor condition will result in weak layers. Unfortunately you will not know your layers are weak until the entire cake has been fully assembled. And decorated. And sitting on the kitchen counter for at least eight hours. Weak layers do not immediately break down. But break down they do.

If you are a girl who loves cake, every member of your household will know your boundaries. For example, Prince Charming will know that any cake anywhere in the castle is off limits and cannot be eaten. At least it is off limits without your express permission. The cake is off limits whether it is on the counter, in the freezer, hidden in the pantry or stashed behind a flower arrangement.

My own Prince Charming has developed a sixth sense about cakes. He knows that a cake in the castle is my private property. He knows that the cake was baked for a party. Or baked for a friend. Or baked for a neighbor. Or baked for me. Or even that the cake was baked for him, but that he is not allowed to eat a piece. Not allowed to eat a piece until after I have taken enough pictures of the cake to get a decent image to post on my cake blog. The princesses, even the one who is most clever at getting what she wants, will stay away from all cakes, too. Unless and until the cakes are served to them by their mother, the Queen of Cake.

Given all of this, I knew immediately that something was terribly wrong the next morning. I knew something was terribly wrong when my most conscientious princess charged into my bedroom. The little princess was desperate to get my attention. She waved her hands wildly, trying to get my attention over the screaming of the hairdryer. Of course, the Queen of Cake must be perfectly coiffed for the afternoon birthday party. For if she is not careful the gorgeous cake will outshine her.

"Something bad happened." My daughter did not mention the cake. The princesses know to stay away from cake! And none of my princesses would ever dare to include the word "cake" in the same sentence as "bad." That's kind of like saying that any form of charitable giving is anything other than good.

Naturally, because I wisely dwell in a place of optimism and possibility, it did not immediately occur to me that anything bad had happened to the cake. After all, I was certain that the eight-layer cake was still sitting prettily on the kitchen counter. On the kitchen counter where I had left it the night before. Having enjoyed a full night of beauty sleep, I had completely forgotten about cutting corners with the eggs. But it all came rushing back to me like an unfriendly gust of wind when I followed the princess into the kitchen.

"Look, Mommy, look!" she said. I gasped. And then I froze. The other two princesses ran up behind me. And they froze, too. There we were. Frozen. The ice queen and her three ice princesses. We could not move.

I stared, disbelievingly, at the array of fluffy white, chocolate and buttercream displayed, in all its glory, on my kitchen floor. Oddly, though, I was not entirely horrified. I was not entirely horrified because, incredibly, the cake was still beautiful. Even artistic. Artistic in its chaotic and deconstructed state. "The birthday party is in four hours," I said quietly after three full minutes of icy silence. "Obviously we will have to go to Plan B."

The eight-layer structure I had so carefully built the night before was now a thing of the past. It was gone forever. And now I had a challenging, exhilarating, pressure-cooker of a challenge in front of me. Literally. Could I possibly reconstruct a cake out of the shapeless bits and pieces that were spread out all over my otherwise very, very clean kitchen floor? "Of course you can," said the optimistic voice in my head. "Anything is possible."

If you happen ever to find yourself in this situation, I will tell you precisely how to handle it. First, remember that children and other innocent bystanders come in very handy. Instruct each of them to use plastic cups to scoop cake and frosting from the floor into a large mixing bowl that you have lined with strips of parchment paper sprayed with nonstick baking spray. Smash as much cake into the bowl as possible. Cover the bowl and put it in the freezer.

Next, assign one child to find a Barbie doll somewhere in her bedroom, the basement, her backpack or the car. Every house containing girls always contains at least one Barbie doll in at least one of these places. Assign the other children to floor duty, giving them an entire roll of paper towels and an extra-large trash bag. While the Barbie search and the floor cleaning are underway, pull that handy-dandy extra fondant out of your pantry. This is a good reminder to never, ever, ever let your fondant supply run out. Make as many pretty little flowers as you possibly can by rolling out the colored fondant and using cookie cutters.

After about an hour has passed from the time you smashed the cake into the parchment-lined bowl, pull the bowl out of the freezer. Overturn it onto a serving platter, the lovelier the better. Gently pull off the strips of parchment paper and decorate the cake structure with the fondant flowers. Let the princesses help you with the flowers as a reward for the clean floor.

The next-to-last step is to stuff the Barbie doll into the cake so that she rises out of the top from the waist up. You get to do that part. It is really fun to stuff a Barbie doll into a cake. Way more fun than shoving Hot Wheels into a cake. And way, way more fun than duct taping a hamster cage.

As the grand finale, use a few extra bits of fondant to dress Barbie in a makeshift halter top to complete her outfit. Presto! Barbie will be wearing a lovely dress with an uber-flowery skirt. The cake will be even more beautiful than the cake you made the night before. A happy ending. Indeed, the universe is benevolent.

Sometimes, though, the cake crash is not the end of the story.

"We've got to run to the store," I told the girls excitedly. Our moods were gleeful! The Barbie Cake was gorgeous. But there was more work to be done. "We still have to get a few things for the party. Including beer."

Remember the beer? The beer I planned to serve at this particular party? The beer for the adults? The adults who would outnumber the children? We had to go get the beer. Along with a few groceries.

We made the round trip in record time. "Are you speeding, Mom?"

my oldest daughter had asked at one point. "No, I am not," I replied truthfully. It just seemed like we were going too fast. I think all of our heads were still spinning from the cake disaster.

I was in a big hurry to get everything ready for the party on time. So I tried to unload the groceries from the trunk by making only two trips from the garage to the kitchen. Via the laundry room. I should have made three trips. On the second trip I dropped an entire case of Boulevard Pale Ale onto the laundry room floor. Shattering all but five bottles.

"Nobody move!" I immediately shouted to all three of the princesses. All four of us were in the laundry room. For the second time that day we struck our ice queen and ice princess poses.

"Carefully walk out of the laundry room," I ordered. "And go down to the basement. And do not come back up until I say so." Broken cake is not dangerous. Broken glass *is* dangerous. I would have to take on the beer mess all by myself. The three princesses tip-toed past the washing machine and then scampered across the kitchen floor, heading for the basement stairs.

First cake. Now beer. The pressure was on.

"Never fear," I told myself. I was alone in the laundry room. "You have two secret weapons. Make them work for you!" I loved the confidence I heard in my own voice. My own voice that seemed to echo a bit in the laundry room. Maybe the sound waves were bouncing off of all that glass.

And it was true. I did have two secret weapons. My first secret weapon was the big hunk of cake stashed in my freezer. I ate it. *Before* I dealt with the beer. A sugar rush and carbohydrate-induced serotonin surge will get you through even the most messy beer disaster.

The second secret weapon was a pile of old towels. Old towels that I had wisely not thrown away. I had not thrown them away out of a sense of loyalty and gratitude. Those old towels had saved my bacon during the hamster capture. Besides, I would have felt funny about recycling the towels by donating them to charity. That would have been a little yucky. And that might not have qualified as doing good. Or even being nice.

I pulled out every towel. I threw them all onto the laundry room floor into one big heap. I pushed the towel heap around the laundry room to mop up the beer and the glass. And I tossed the whole mess into a big yellow garbage bag.

"This isn't so bad," I said to the towel heap. I actually did not mind doing this. It was good exercise. And the fragrant beer evoked fond memories of college parties. "What a youthful glow I'll have for the party!" I cheerfully told the towels. "Thank you!"

"You look beautiful!" my mother said, 40 minutes later. She and my father had just arrived for the party. They had arrived a few minutes early, just as my mother and I had planned during our telephone conversation. They had arrived early so that my mother and I could discuss the idea about my job. "Is that a new color of lipstick?" she asked. My mother was wondering what it was about me that looked different.

"No," I said. "This is still that Mary Kay color I really like. It is called Give Dreams. I think maybe what you are noticing is the beer." My mother looked a bit bewildered. She does not drink beer. Except once she did. When we were in Germany. "It goes with the bratwurst," she had said.

But I did not get a chance to explain about the beer. At least not at that moment. The princesses had come running. Chattering about the cake. "The whole cake fell down!" they exclaimed. "It was a big mess! We cleaned it up and used it to make a new cake!" My mother looked a bit taken aback. "The cake was in a million pieces," the girls continued. "It landed right *here*!" They pointed to the spot on the kitchen floor. The spot where the cake had been just a few hours before.

I could tell my mother was looking at the floor wondering how clean it had been. Wondering how clean it had been before the cake had landed on it. I read her mind. "You know I wipe down my kitchen floor six times a day, Mom," I reminded her. "It is a nervous habit." Then I thought about it a little further. "Actually it is a form of exercise."

"Okay," said my mom. I am not quite sure she was convinced about the clean floor. But she decided not to pursue it. My mother is so polite. She even ate a piece of cake an hour later during the party.

And it was true. I really do exercise by cleaning the floor. So many household chores can serve double-duty as exercise! The very best example is pushing a wet dishrag around the floor with your feet in a combined lunge-slide motion. This works wonders for toning the inner thighs. And it is even better if you are a little obsessive-compulsive about having a clean floor because you naturally complete five sets without even thinking or wincing or flinching.

My favorite form of exercise, though, is running. I love to run. I run three miles. Every morning. I run three miles every morning on a treadmill. A treadmill that has a little place to hold reading material. I study my pink notebooks when I run. Just to keep me on track with reaching my goals for being better.

I had just learned from a friend, a friend who is also a runner, about an organization called Girls on the Run. Girls on the Run inspires girls to be joyful, healthy and confident. It is a really wonderful organization that encourages positive development. Emotional, social, mental, spiritual. And physical. There is running involved! I was so happy to have learned about it.

I was thinking about Girls on the Run when it was my mother's turn to read my mind. "What charity are you supporting today?" my mother asked. She was switching subjects. Switching subjects from cleaning the floor to doing good. "What kind of celebration that gives back goes with a Barbie Cake?" So I told my mother about Girls on the Run.

"That's a great idea!" my mother said. "Girls these days need to get out and get moving. Now shall we talk about *your* next move?" Just then the doorbell rang. My brother, sister-in-law, niece and nephew had arrived for the party. "Showtime!" I called to the princesses. "Run over and open the door. Let's get this party started!"

I turned back to my mother. "We can talk about my big idea some other time," I said. "It is not an emergency or anything. I'm not going anywhere anytime soon." The truth was that I was getting cold feet. Well, maybe not cold feet. More like tepid feet. My latest idea was so big that I had to warm up to it a bit before I could really talk about it. Changing jobs is a big deal. It was not something I did very often.

That night I gave myself extra time with the pink notebook. "Today has been quite a day," I said in my closet. "So much food for thought. So much to write down in my diary of a good girl."

I jotted down a few notes. A few notes about the Barbie Cake. Which had actually turned out to be a beautiful and delicious cake. One of my prettier cakes, I wrote. But I should have listened to my instincts, I added. My instincts were telling me not to cut corners with the eggs. But I did it anyway.

Well before a kitchen disaster or a job that needs changing, I continued as I turned the page, there are often little voices telling you what you ought to do. Sometimes you will ignore the voices. And you will choose instead to carry on.

I stopped to think about carrying on. Carrying on is probably easier than making a change, at least in the short term, I wrote. But the key is knowing when to settle for something better than good enough. Then I stopped to think about that a little bit more. Good enough might be good enough for little things, I wrote. Little things like cakes. After all, carrying on with the plan to shortcut the eggs had worked out just fine in the end. But I felt compelled to finish writing the thought. Maybe, though, it is not such a good idea to carry on, settling for good enough, when it comes to bigger things. Bigger things, like jobs.

I thought about writing a little bit more in my diary before I went to bed. Maybe adding a little bit more about my big idea. My big idea about being done with my job. But I decided against it. I was not quite ready to have that conversation with the pink notebook.

I decided to wrap up the diary entry with something safe. And lighthearted. Something safe and lighthearted, like cakes. Good but not perfect, I wrote just before I put away the pink notebook for the night. Bottles will break. Cakes will collapse. Eight layers will turn into one big layer of Barbie. But you, the Queen of Cake, are unbreakable. I laughed as I wrote it.

Unbreakable. Now that was funny! But maybe I believe it, I thought. Maybe I am unbreakable. Not in every way, of course, but in some ways. In some ways, as in being who I really am. Being who I really am no matter what life throws my way. Just like Barbie, always smiling in her plastic state of optimism and beauty, the Queen of Cake may fall down. But she always gets back up.

Chapter 16

"That's okay. Maybe Daddy can fix it."

My sweet little girl was in tears. Her princess tea set was broken. Well, not really broken as in shattered. It was broken as in the teapot did not work anymore. At least the teapot did not work like it used to work. The teapot had stopped playing music.

I kind of doubted that Prince Charming would be able to do anything to restore music to the teapot. It was a few years old. And I saw no compartment for a battery anywhere on it. No, I thought, nothing short of magic can fix this teapot. Prince Charming is good. But he is only human.

But I did not say any of that. Instead I tried my best to make my littlest princess feel better. "Maybe it just wore out," I suggested. "You've had that tea set since you were practically a baby. And you've played with it a lot. Maybe the teapot is just tired and doesn't want to play music anymore."

I stopped for a moment to come up with something slightly more hopeful. "But you can still play with it," I told my daughter encouragingly. "The teapot still has a handle. It still has a spout. You can still tip it over and pour out the tea." As long as that tea is imaginary tea,

I thought to myself. No real liquid is allowed in any toy teapot in any castle of mine! But I kept my mouth shut about that, too. I was trying to stay positive.

My daughter studied the teapot. I could tell she was carefully considering what I had just said. "I want a new one," she declared after a minute or so. "It is time for a new teapot." And she was probably right. There is only so much fixing up a girl can do to something that is just plain finished. Sometimes you really do need a new one. When it comes to cakes, though, I was learning that almost anything can be fixed.

"Let's go have a little tea," I said cheerfully. "We'll get out the left-over cake and have that, too." On this particular day the leftover cake was not just any old leftover cake. The leftover cake was leftover Mummy Cake. No one had ever heard of a Mummy Cake. At least not until I had made one.

"I want a dog and kitty cake for my play date," my princess had said earlier in the week. She had been inspired by the Paw Print Cake. The Paw Print Cake that I had made a few weeks before, for my oldest daughter's birthday party. My youngest princess is the princess who actually likes fondant. And she is the princess who wants to do everything just like her sister. My youngest daughter absolutely adores my oldest daughter. She wants to be just like her.

"Okay!" I had agreed to make a dog and kitty cake. "But this time I will decorate the top and the sides of the cake with cute little orange and yellow paw prints. Instead of black and brown. Just for a change." That seemed to sound good to my little girl. "And I want a big cake," my daughter had said. "Really big!"

Really big. That could be a problem, I had thought to myself. At the time I was still reeling a bit from the Barbie Cake. The Barbie Cake that had not started out as a Barbie Cake. "Oh well," I said to myself. "What are the odds of history repeating itself?" I could not resist my princess's request. "Okay! A big cake!" I had sealed the deal with my daughter. A big cake. Famous last words.

Fast forward to the day of the play date. More specifically, one hour before a neighboring princess would ring the doorbell. Ring the doorbell and be ready to play. And be ready to eat cake.

"You did it again?" My oldest daughter was staring, incredulously, at the seven-layer cake. The seven-layer cake that had just collapsed onto my kitchen counter. I could hardly believe it myself. "At least this one didn't fall on the floor," I had said. I really was trying to be more optimistic. Even where falling cakes were concerned.

Just then Prince Charming had walked into the kitchen. He had heard the commotion. "You did it *again*?" Those words sounded familiar. Like daughter, like father. At that point I had become less cheerful. But not less optimistic. "Everyone please leave me alone," I had said. "I will fix it."

One big cake, one big counter top, one big mess, one short hour before a little guest would arrive. What to do? If this ever happens to you, this is when you will need a recipe for a Mummy Cake.

Run, do not walk, to your pantry. Dig out that extra box of white fondant you keep handy for emergencies. Roll it out and tear it into strips that look like bandages. Strips that look so much like bandages that the edges are even a bit frayed. Frayed edges happen automatically when you tear up a big sheet of white fondant.

Next, as best you can, re-assemble the cake. Re-assemble the cake on the most gorgeous cake stand you own. Better yet, use a shiny silver cake platter. You will need all the beauty you can possibly scare up if you really want to balance out the beast in this cake.

Use the fondant strips to wrap up the cake. Wrap up the cake just as you would bandage up a broken arm. Or a paper mache piñata. Or, of course, a mummy. If you just so happen to have any on hand, add two little candy eyes to the top of the cake. To the top of the cake where they will look directly at you. After all, everyone will be staring at this cake. So the cake might as well stare back. Mummies are supposed to be spooky.

It is a good idea to add a bright garnish to the all-white Mummy Cake. To do this you can tear up what remains of the orange and yellow fondant paw prints and sprinkle the pieces around the bottom of the cake. This will draw the viewer's eye away from the mummy's eyes and down to the shiny silver platter. But the mummy's gaze cannot be broken.

Ta da! Within just 27 minutes after the cake crash you will have a repaired cake. A repaired cake that looks like a brand new cake. It will not be the dog and kitty cake requested by your daughter. But it will be the Mummy Cake. And everyone will love it.

And everyone *had* loved it. Especially because the inside of the Mummy Cake had been delicious. I had played with the recipe a bit, using a combination of white cake layers and yellow cake layers. I got creative with the cake-frosting blend, adding fresh banana and a little rum. And peanut butter. It had all been quite yummy.

"I love this cake," said my daughter. We were enjoying our imaginary tea. And our real leftover cake. We were sitting at the kitchen counter. And we were talking about mummies. My princess had forgotten all about the broken teapot. "What is a mummy, Mommy?" my little princess asked.

I wondered how I could answer that question without getting gruesome. "Well," I said, stalling. "A mummy is a human body. A human body that has been all wrapped up. A human body that is no longer living."

My daughter was fascinated. Instead of getting into greater detail, though, I told her a story. A story about when I was a little girl. A story about mummies. "Once I did a project in school about mummies," I said. "I made a big poster and listed lots of facts about mummies. And then I glued mummies onto the poster."

"You glued cake onto the poster?" my daughter asked, puzzled. After all, the only mummy she had ever seen in her entire life was the cake kind of mummy.

"No," I said. "These mummies were made out of play dough. White play dough. White play dough that I made all by myself out of flour and salt and water. White play dough mummies that I baked in the oven so they would be hard enough to glue onto the poster."

That was a fun project, I thought to myself. And funny, too. I did not tell my daughter the funniest part. Which was that the first batch of mummies had burned. I had not pulled them from the oven in time and they had turned brown. So I had made another batch. I guess I have a history of kitchen projects where the mummy returns. Just like the movies.

"Tell you what," I told my daughter. "We can't see a real mummy. But how about we take a field trip this weekend? And learn a little bit more about how families keep memories alive? Memories of relatives who have died?"

Why not? I thought. I could pull this off. I had an invitation sitting on my desk for just such a field trip. An invitation to a fundraiser. A fundraiser in a cemetery. To raise money for the cemetery. The cemetery was one of Kansas City's most significant historical sites. And the fundraiser was a picnic. And kids were invited. A field trip. A field trip that does good. Perfect!

Looking back, I really should have been paying more attention to what the universe was trying to tell me. We did indeed attend the picnic in the cemetery. We attended the picnic in the cemetery on a gorgeous Saturday in the fall. A gorgeous Saturday in the fall when my diary entry at the end of the day appeared under a very interesting heading. A heading titled How to Gracefully Exit a Picnic in a Cemetery After a Granite Headstone Falls on Your Toddler's Leg.

Yes! That really happened. How could I possibly dream up something like that? I simply could not. The outing began happily enough. It is so inspirational to witness the commitment of civic leaders to preserving a community's heritage!

"We can learn so much from the people who were here before us," I told the girls. Just two of the princesses were with me that day. The middle princess was at a birthday party. "This cemetery is really important," I explained. "People were buried here nearly 150 years ago. That was when your great-great-grandfather came to Kansas City to start a business."

And that was true. My mother's family has been in Kansas City since the 1870s. My mother and I love to explore family history. So the picnic was right up my alley. I only wished I had thought to invite my mother. Then again, it is a little odd to invite someone to go with you to a picnic in a cemetery. Even your mother.

The girls were having fun. So far, so good, I thought. "What child would not find it fascinating to look for the names of their own deceased relatives on headstones?" I said to myself as the girls explored. Well maybe that is a bit of an exaggeration, I thought. "Regardless, this is the perfect activity to set the mood for Halloween." No one was around to hear me talking to myself. No one above ground, anyway.

I watched the girls participate in the scavenger hunt. They scampered about, from tombstone to tombstone, looking at names and dates. One princess scampered about in her sneakers. The other princess scampered about in her cute little pink kiddie cowboy boots.

"Come look at this one!" called the older of the two princesses. "This tombstone has the dates we need for the scavenger hunt!" The younger of the two princesses, the one wearing cowboy boots, was still too young to really catch on to the scavenger hunt. But she ran over to her sister anyway.

I looked away for just a moment to say hello to a photographer who was walking by. A photographer who was taking pictures for the newspaper. "Your girls are darling," he said. I smiled proudly. "That would make a great picture," he continued, referring to the princesses.

The photographer and I turned our heads to a spot six feet away. Six feet away where my oldest princess had found the winning date on a headstone. And then I saw something happen. I saw something happen that I would never have imagined could happen. I could hardly believe my eyes. The headstone tipped over. The headstone tipped over and fell right on top of my littlest princess. The headstone was so big that I could only see my princess from the shoulders up.

I gasped. I felt faint. I could not move. I could not think. Everything in the cemetery started spinning. I might as well have seen a ghost.

Without an incident like this one to illuminate what is true, you might mistakenly believe that cowboy boots are useful only for demonstrating your prowess as the fashion-forward, trendy and hip type. Or for working on an actual ranch. As it turns out, though, cowboy boots are the ideal defense for a toddler. Cowboy boots are the ideal defense for a toddler when a headstone falls on top of her. I love cowboy boots. I love cowboy boots! Cowboy boots look good. Cowboy boots do good. Cowboy boots are just plain good.

Those cute little pink kiddie cowboy boots had everything to do with those cute little legs escaping their predicament. Escaping their predicament, unscathed. Unscathed but for one tiny scratch. The cowboy boots had broken the fall of the headstone. The cowboy boots had been strong enough to hold up the bottom one-third of the headstone so that the top two-thirds of the headstone had barely even touched my daughter's legs and midsection. Incredible.

"Thank you, thank you, thank you!" I hardly knew what to say to the photographer. So I just kept saying "thank you." What else could I do? I was saying "thank you" because within two seconds of the collapse, that brave and strong photographer had swooped in with mighty arms and lifted the toppled slab of stone right off of that princess. He was a hero. I will forever defend the press! Especially photographers! These photographers surely must spend long hours training in a gym. Or a quarry.

"Thank you, thank you, thank you!" I hardly knew what to say to the physical therapist, either. Other than "thank you." Who knew that physical therapists have a passion for historical places? I was saying "thank you" because that physical therapist had been just 10 feet away when the headstone fell. A good physical therapist who is in the right place at the right time can calm even the most heart-wrenching tears. While simultaneously checking for broken bones and dislocated joints.

"Thank you, thank you, thank you!" And I hardly knew what to say to the mounted policeman. Other than "thank you." And I said "thank you" to his horse, too. The irresistible draw of an animal in the eyes of a person under the age of 10 is a lifesaver. A lifesaver when you are trying to forge a path to a picnic exit accompanied by one frightened princess and one stunned sister princess. If this happens to you, just remember that the picnic exit will be located conveniently adjacent to the mounted officer. You can take the children's minds off the whole episode. Just by chattering about how lucky they are to get to see a real horse. Instead of the ones on television.

"Girls, girls!" I said when we were all back in the car. Safely. Safely in the car and buckled into our seats. There would be no more falling over today. Not if I could help it, anyway. I breathed a huge sigh of relief. "Surely you must believe in miracles." I was still a little stunned. But by that time I was so relieved that I was giddy. I was talking way too fast. But I kept going. It was the only way I could calm myself down. "What is the likelihood of finding King Arthur disguised as a paparazzi, a physical therapist disguised as a picnic guest and a child-friendly horse, all within ten yards of each other? In a graveyard? Something like this definitely calls for ice cream."

Ice cream, indeed! We all needed it. "McDonald's, here we come!"

And we were off. On our merry way. On our merry way out of the cemetery. To the drive-through. Where ice cream was waiting for us.

Prince Charming was waiting for us when we got home. "You have got to be kidding!" he said after I told him the whole story. And after the princesses had related their version of the whole story. "You have *got* to be kidding!" He repeated it a few times. Just as I had repeated "thank you" more than two dozen times back at the cemetery. It really is difficult to find the right words in a situation like this. Even for two lawyers.

"I only wished I had thought to get their names," I said to my husband. It was the only other thing I could think of to say. I was so grateful that my little girl was okay. I was so grateful to the nice people who had helped us. "The photographer, the physical therapist, the policeman. All in a graveyard. What are the odds of that?" Prince Charming agreed. "That never happens. Not even on Halloween." But it had happened that day.

That night I needed cake. I did not just need cake. I *really* needed cake. Once upon a time, many years before the picnic in the cemetery, I had invented an idea I called the Cake Overdose Diet. The idea is a bit unconventional. The idea is based on the benefits of occasionally eating a little too much cake.

"Tonight I will go on the Cake Overdose Diet," I said to Prince Charming after an all-cereal dinner. I was too wiped out to even consider warming up macaroni and cheese in the microwave. "After I get the kids to bed, I am going to get out the rest of the Mummy Cake and finish the whole thing. Care to join me?"

Prince Charming was not interested. Which was just as well. That meant more cake for me. Besides, the Cake Overdose Diet is best undertaken alone. Especially tonight, I thought, when I have so much to think about. The cemetery incident had been eerie. Had it been some sort of sign? A metaphor for things falling over and breaking? Cakes, teapots, tombstones?

"I really do need to think about my job," I said to myself after Prince Charming had left the room. "I need to decide whether to change it or get out from under it. Fix it or make a new one." Tonight was a good night for cake. So often it is true that with cake comes awareness.

The Cake Overdose Diet. Before you attempt this diet for the first time you have to decide how much you care about precise calorie counting. There are those of us who do and there are those of us who do not. Either way works. Because I am one of those who does, during this diet I prefer to eat cakes I bake myself so that I can count the calories with as much accuracy as possible.

It is far easier, though, to purchase a cake from a local grocery store or bakery and check the Internet for nutritional information. You can purchase a food scale and weigh your cake hunks to decode calorie information reported in grams on the websites. Personally, though, I have always drawn the line at weighing cake. Or any other type of food, for that matter. Weighing food is a bit extreme. Even for me.

The best time to go on the Cake Overdose Diet is when you desperately need a little stress relief. An obvious time is the evening following an afternoon at the cemetery. An afternoon at the cemetery when a granite headstone falls on top of your daughter.

You can also go on the Cake Overdose Diet when you are gearing up for future stress. Such as anticipating a Very Important Meeting scheduled to occur at your office the next day. Or Prince Charming getting ready to head out of town for five days. Or an old washing machine that is making funny noises.

Present stress is also a perfectly fine reason to try the Cake Overdose Diet. Examples of present stress include a washing machine that just broke. Or a husband who is already out of town. Or a Very Important Meeting that is occurring via conference call. In that case you could even eat cake during the meeting. Just hit the mute button.

Past stress is also decent justification for going on the Cake Overdose Diet. Letting down can be just as taxing as gearing up. This means that you can do the diet when Prince Charming finally returns from his business trip. Or after you have survived the Very Important Meeting. Or when the new washing machine has just been delivered. ·

The Cake Overdose Diet is really easy. Just pull the cake, the whole thing, out of the freezer. Or out of the Tupperware container. Or out of wherever you happen to stash your cake. Incidentally, most cake stays fresh and tasty for five days if it is wrapped up carefully and stored in your pantry. You can freeze cake for weeks, too, as long as the cake is not the fruity kind. Cake probably even freezes well for up to two months. It just depends on how badly you want to ensure that you always have a decent supply of cake. There really is nothing more comforting than sitting at your kitchen counter, all alone, with a whole cake and a plastic fork.

Counterintuitive as it may seem, going on the Cake Overdose Diet every few weeks actually promotes weight maintenance. I cannot explain why this is, but it is true. Maybe it is because an hour spent eating a full third or more of a cake satisfies cravings in advance. So that when you finally throw away that plastic fork, along with the demolished cake, you are so sick of cake that your soul is screaming for carrots and tofu. Or maybe it is because the freedom to eat the whole thing, even if granted just for an hour, is such a blissful exercise of free will that it inspires proper eating for at least ten days after that.

And feel free to go ahead and finish off the entire cake. Especially when you are searching for solutions and answers and prizes to your life's most vexing challenges. Just do not expect to find any solutions or answers or prizes at the bottom of the cake. Cakes are not like boxes of sugar cereals. The only thing you will find at the bottom of a cake is a shiny silver platter. And the only thing you will find in that shiny silver platter is you. You, staring back at you.

Chapter 17

"Thirteen layers."

"What?" said Prince Charming. He looked over at me to see what I was doing. I was putting on my lipstick. "Thirteen layers of lipstick?" He asked the question and gave me a funny look. A funny look that meant that he had realized immediately after he asked the question that he was out of his league. Out of his league when it comes to lipstick. Which is true.

"No," I said, finishing off the third layer of lipstick. The third layer of lipstick in a great Mary Kay color called Give Joy. "No, not lipstick. Cake." Prince Charming is not out of his league when it comes to cake. He has eaten so much cake that he is as much of a recreational cake expert as I am.

"Oh!" he said. "Thirteen layers? You're not actually thinking of making a thirteen-layer cake, are you? I thought even your six-layer cakes were collapsing."

Then it was my turn to shoot Prince Charming a look. A look that said "Watch what you are saying, mister. As you recall I have made many six-layer cakes that stayed standing. And, in the case of each of the cakes that fell over, I salvaged them beautifully." But I did not say any of that.

"Yes, I am thinking of making a thirteen-layer cake," I said instead. "A thirteen-layer cake, as a gift."

Prince Charming gave me another look. This time the look said "Please do not tell me you are catering a wedding reception." We were exchanging a lot of looks on a Monday morning. On a Monday morning in early November while we stood in front of our mirrors getting ready for work.

"No, no," I assured him, looking him straight in the eyes so that he knew I was sincere. Then I turned back toward the mirror to add a dab of lip gloss to three layers of lipstick. And I was pretty sure I saw myself turn pale at the very thought of catering a wedding reception. I added extra blush to my cheeks.

"No, not a wedding reception," I explained. "A regular reception. My friend asked me to make a cake for a charity. A charity she runs. Called PIPELINE. PIPELINE is hosting a VIP reception in a couple of weeks. For 75 people. I think I will need to make a thirteen-layer cake to be able to serve everyone."

Prince Charming is used to my declarations of bold ambition. And usually he does not comment when I make a boldly-ambitious declaration. My husband has learned over the years to trust that there is always a method to my madness. A method to my madness in every single one of my bold ambitions. My bold ambitions begin as impossible goals, adapt to reality somewhere in the middle and then end up with everything turning out just great.

This time, though, Prince Charming felt compelled to comment. "Are you sure you want to attempt that?" he asked. Nicely, of course. My husband is always nice. "It seems a little risky to put together a thirteen-layer cake and drive it to a reception and have it stay standing. Your cakes don't seem to be all that mobile. Remember how hard it was to get the cake to the television station a few months ago? The yellow cake with the car stuffed into the side? That cake was only six layers. How would you transport a thirteen-layer cake?"

"Gee, I hadn't thought of that," I snapped. And immediately I felt bad about being sarcastic. Sarcasm is ugly. I try so hard not to be sarcastic. But I am not always successful. I quickly self-corrected.

"I'm sorry," I said. "You do have a good point about mobility. And I think I have that figured out."

Prince Charming had disappeared into the closet. Disappeared into the closet to put on his shoes. And probably also to get away. I followed him into the closet. "That is a good point, really. And I really do have a plan. First of all, I am not going to try to drive the cake to the reception as a thirteen-layer cake. I plan to assemble it on site."

My husband seemed to be listening. I think he was genuinely interested in how exactly I planned to pull this off. He is very good at transportation logistics. Traveling from city to city on vacation. Moving from apartment to house and house to apartment and apartment to house. And navigating the aisles in grocery stores. Naturally Prince Charming would be good at thinking through transportation logistics where cakes were concerned.

"That would work to get you there," he nodded. "Load the cake into your car in pieces, not assembled. But how will that help you keep the cake from falling over at the reception?"

"That is where my second idea comes in," I continued, "I plan to use different sizes of layers. Like a wedding cake. Like I did with the yellow car cake. So that smaller layers are stacked onto larger layers. That is a much more stable structure." Prince Charming nodded again. The plan was making sense to him. So far, so good.

"Third," I continued, "I am going to get some help. Some help from two people. One is my mother. We will deliver the cake together and my mother will help me set it up before the reception. The other is my friend who makes cakes. The one who owns the Cake Girl. She makes really good cakes. And she makes them with a recipe that is sturdier than mine. So her six-layer cakes are really solid. They do not even tilt."

I looked over at Prince Charming. His dress shoes were on his feet and he was now sitting on the treadmill. Listening carefully. So I sat down on the floor next to my running shoes. We had time for a real conversation. We had a whole three minutes. We had three whole minutes before we had to gather up the princesses from the kitchen counter, brush Apple Jacks off of their clothes and load them all into my car to go to school.

"How does all of that add up to 13 layers?" he asked. What a good question, I thought. I was so happy. How kind of my husband to take a genuine interest in my cake and charity hobby.

"That is a very good question!" I said enthusiastically. "I am going to ask the Cake Girl to make a big six-layer cake. A six-layer cake that will form the bottom of the thirteen-layer cake. Cake Girl cakes are so strong that all six layers can be nine-inch rounds and the cake will not even lean to one side." Prince Charming was still listening. I kept going. "And I will make my own seven-layer cake to place on top of the Cake Girl's cake." I paused to study my husband's face. He looked skeptical when I mentioned seven layers.

"I know that is dangerous because of my less-than-perfect track record with even six-layer cakes," I said, "but I think I can do it if I stack the layers in graduated sizes. Two nine-inch rounds, two eight-inch rounds, two six-inch rounds and a four-inch round to top it off."

My husband considered what I had said. "That will be a pretty tall cake. But I think you can pull it off."

"So do I!" I said cheerfully. "I will do it!" I checked my purse to be sure I had my keys and my iPhone and my pink notebook. "I'll call the Cake Girl today," I said to my husband as I hurried out of the closet and out of our bedroom and toward the kitchen to collect the girls. That three-minute conversation in the closet had turned into a three-and-a-half minute conversation. I needed to step up the pace.

"And I will call my mother," I added. "Actually, I will call my mother first. If my mother can't help me, then I will have to go to Plan B. I cannot transport and assemble a thirteen-layer cake without my mother." I may be boldly ambitious but I am not a fool.

"Hi!" I said. "Hi!" said my mother. She answered the phone on the first ring. I was just turning out of the school parking lot after a successful drop-off. Three girls, three backpacks, three pairs of matching shoes.

"What are you doing next Thursday evening?" I asked. "I am completely open!" my mother said. I breathed a huge sigh of relief. Game on, I thought. Thirteen layers, here I come! "Great!" I said. "Want to help me cater the cake at a reception?" "Sure!" said my mother. My mother is wonderful. "What time? And where is it?"

"The reception is downtown," I answered. "Downtown in the studio of a local sculptor. I can meet you in that grocery store parking lot," I said. "That grocery store right off the exit you would take to go downtown. Let's meet right after work. I'll have the cake in the car. And the supplies. And the frosting."

"Okay," agreed my mother. She paused for a moment. "What exactly is this for?" she asked. My mother was probably thinking some of the same thoughts that my husband had been thinking earlier that morning.

"I promise this is okay, Mom," I said, trying to read her mind. "This is not like the rehearsal dinner. This is a reception to benefit a nonprofit organization. A nonprofit organization that runs an entrepreneurial mentoring program. This time we do not need to cook chicken or bake cornbread or toss salad. I am only in charge of cake." And then I added, "A real caterer is catering the dinner."

"Oh!" said my mother, sounding relieved. "Well that's good. What's the headcount?" asked my mother. For a non-caterer, my mother sure was getting pretty good at caterer lingo. "Seventy-five. I am making a thirteen-layer cake." And I explained to my mother all about how I planned to pull that off. How I planned to ask the Cake Girl for help and how I planned to assemble the cake on site. "I'll need your help, of course," I said.

My mother was silent on the other end of the phone. I wonder if she thinks this is a bad idea, I thought to myself. "Do you think it will work?" I asked.

"Oh yes," she said. "I think we can easily stack the cakes on top of each other once we are there. And if the kitchen has a microwave, it will be easy to warm up the frosting and pour it over the top of the cake after it is assembled. All of that should be fine. I am just worried about the numbers. I don't think 13 layers is enough cake for 75 people. Especially if the top layers of the cake are small."

I quickly did the math in my head. I had no way to write down numbers. I was driving to work, attempting to juggle the phone and the cereal and the soda. Which was too much juggling as it was. Six layers on the bottom would serve about 24 people, I thought. But the seven layers on the top would serve only about twelve people because the layers would get smaller as the cake got higher.

My mother was right. My thirteen-layer cake would serve only 36 guests. Assuming it stayed standing.

"You are right," I said to my mother. Now I was nervous. Me and my bold ambition, I thought to myself. When will I ever learn? And then I had an idea. "Wait," I said. "Why don't I just make four cakes? One thirteen-layer cake for a dramatic effect, and three six-layer cakes for volume? That would be more than plenty of cake. Some people could even have seconds."

"I think that will work," said my mother. And then I could tell she was thinking about it a little bit more. And she decided to be definitive. "That will work."

"Problem solved!" I said to the can of all-natural grape soda after I hung up the phone. Of course, I thought to myself, this would mean that I would have to bake a lot of cake next week. And make a lot of frosting. I would have to bake eight cakes, to be exact. Four boxes of Betty Crocker Devil's Food cake mix and four boxes of Betty Crocker white cake mix. Thank heavens for Betty. Made from scratch would be truly frightening at this point.

"No worries," I said as convincingly as possible to the can of all-natural grape soda. "As I always say, the more layers the better." And it is a good thing I believe that. A thirteen-layer cake. Flanked by three six-layer cakes. In a sculpture studio.

"Now there's an idea." I continued chatting with the can. Actually chatting *at* the can would have been a more accurate statement. "I've never thought about this before, but these cakes of mine are a lot like sculptures. Only instead of clay or bronze or wood, I use cake and frosting and fondant as my raw material."

I kept talking. "Four cake sculptures. How fun! How creative! How bold! How ambitious!" No reply from the can. Cake sculptures. Was I being too bold? Was I being too ambitious? Maybe, I thought to myself, but I am going to go for it. Who ever said a sculpture cannot be made out of edible material? The cake people on television do it all the time. At least that is what I hear.

"I don't care what you think," I said to the can of all-natural grape soda as I pulled into the parking garage at the office. "These cakes will be works of art. I will collectively name them Studio Cake. All four of them, together." Studio Cake. It sounded pretty good to me.

So far, so good, I thought to myself. I was standing in the second-floor kitchen at the sculpture studio. Pretending to be a caterer. On a Thursday evening in mid-November. My mother was also there, standing a few yards away. Wiping up a little frosting from the gorgeous granite counter top. My mother was pretending to be a caterer, too.

It turned out that the sculpture studio was more of a museum than a studio. The whole place was absolutely stunning. So absolutely stunning, in fact, that the studio doubles as an art gallery. The studio belonged to a local sculptor named Tom Corbin. And the building was built in 1912. It started out as a firehouse and then it turned into a city hall and then it turned into a private residence. And now it is a beautifully restored artist's studio, gallery space and office. It even has a gated sculpture garden to display Tom Corbin's work. And the brass fire pole still works, too. For quick escapes I suppose.

Everything was going according to plan at the kitchen counter in the sculpture studio. My mother helped me assemble the thirteen-layer cake on top of a blank 16 × 20 artist's canvas. And the three smaller cakes were ready to go, too, each on its own blank canvas. I had decided that silver platters were not quite artsy enough for the Studio Cake. So we were using artist's canvases instead of cake platters and cake stands.

"The frosting looks gorgeous, dripping over the sides!" my mother said. And she was right! The cakes looked so pretty.

"Here I go!" I said to my mother. I lifted up one of the canvases. The canvas holding the thirteen-layer cake. And I started to slowly make my way across the kitchen. So far so good. The cake was still standing.

"Good thing I've been lifting weights," I said to my mother. "This cake is heavy!" I successfully crossed the kitchen. And I started to make my way across the room toward a table in the corner. A table in the corner of the gallery where my mother and I would display the four cakes. The four cakes collectively known as Studio Cake.

And then I felt something shift. I knew enough to know exactly what that meant.

"Mom!" I called out across the room. "Come quick!"

My mother ran over from where she had been wiping frosting off of the hardwood floor. The hardwood floor in the absolutely stunning gallery. The absolutely stunning gallery that did not need any frosting to make it look better. The gallery was perfect. At least it had been perfect until a little frosting had hit the floor. Thanks to my mother and her paper towels, though, the gallery was perfect once again.

My mother and I both gasped as the cake in my arms lurched to the left. "That was close!" I said. It was a brief sentence. A brief sentence that had started in a shriek and ended in a whisper. While I was shrieking I had remembered that I was in an art gallery. Not in my own kitchen, where shrieking is allowed. That was close, I repeated, this time in my head. My mother had caught the edge of the canvas just in time. Thirteen layers. Still standing.

My mother and I were shaken. We shuddered to think of what 13 layers of fluffy white cake and Devil's Food and an awful lot of vanilla buttercream frosting might have done to the absolutely stunning gallery.

"Can I help?" asked a woman standing nearby. She was part of the team of caterers. The team of real caterers. The real caterers had just arrived to set up the real dinner. "We've got it handled. But thanks!" I said. And then for some reason I added "My mother and I do this a lot."

"That was dumb. Why did I say that?" I mumbled. I must be trying to justify all of this, I thought. Even to complete strangers. Trying to justify why on earth a former lawyer and a current executive at a charitable foundation would be carrying around a thirteen-layer cake in an art gallery on a Thursday evening. With her mother. It would make no sense. At least it would make no sense to someone who knew me in my real job. It all made perfect sense to me, of course. And to my mother. I suppressed a chuckle.

I looked across the cake at my mother. She looked as though she had just suppressed a chuckle, too. At that point we had to try really hard to keep ourselves from laughing. We held on to the canvas for dear life. We held on for dear life so that we could make it the rest of the way across the gallery floor to install the cake on top of a table. On top of a table where the Studio Cake belonged. Not on the floor, thank heavens. That would not have been funny.

We made it.

"Wow," I said. "That was scary." My mother just nodded. We stood, staring at the cake, for almost a minute. We were too relieved to move. Then we sprang back into action. We had three more cakes to install to complete the Studio Cake. "Now for the easy part," I said. It did not take us long to move the three smaller cakes from the kitchen to the display table. Although I suppose after hauling a thirteen-layer cake across a gallery, hauling just about anything else across a gallery would have been easy. It is all relative.

"Time for the photo shoot," I said. Studio Cake. Worthy of a photo shoot, for sure! A thirteen-layer cake towering majestically in the corner of an art gallery. Leaning artistically to the left but not leaning enough to create a risk of collapse. Three smaller cakes. Each cake decorated with red, orange and yellow fondant. Red, orange and yellow fondant cut into strips in the shape of a big "P." A big "P" that stood for PIPELINE, the name of the nonprofit organization. Red, orange and yellow were the theme colors of the event.

"This is a beautiful cake," my mother said after we had completed the photo shoot with our iPhones. "All four of them." And it really was. I had worked hard on the Studio Cake. Trying to make it all hang together with the art theme. The big cake even featured a paintbrush leaning against one side. So that the fondant looked like it had been painted on. By a real artist. Okay maybe not by a real artist. But definitely by a real pretend caterer. And at that particular moment I was really proud to be a real pretend caterer. Even though it was not really my job.

"It smells good, too," I said. The whole gallery smelled like cake. It was a beautiful studio that now smelled as good as it looked. Perfect! "I am sure the cake is delicious," said my mother. "Your cakes really are delicious." And the cake was delicious. At least it was delicious according to my friend. My friend who runs PIPELINE. The morning after the reception she posted on Facebook that the real caterer had said that the cake had been the best cake he had tasted in eight years. I could not imagine a higher compliment to my cake. I was so grateful. And so relieved that the cake had not fallen over.

"We'd better get out of here, Mom," I said. It was time for us to stop admiring the Studio Cake. A few of the guests were starting to arrive. "I can't risk being seen. This hobby is just way too hard to explain."

"Eat cake, do good. Do good, eat cake. What's so hard to explain about that?" my mother asked 11 minutes later. We had managed to escape the studio without any awkward moments. And we were safely in my car. Getting on the highway. The highway that would take us out of downtown Kansas City and back to the suburbs and back to where my mother had parked her car. "I hope you at least left your business card," my mother continued. "Just in case someone wants to know who made the cake."

"No way!" I said, laughing. "The president and CEO of the Greater Kansas City Community Foundation does *not* make cakes. But just for fun I did sneak a One Celebrations sticker onto one of the canvases. And I will post the cake pictures on my website. Besides," I continued. "I didn't want to detract from PIPELINE. Or from that sculptor. Or from that caterer." I paused to think about all of that for a moment.

"You know, Mom," I said. "That PIPELINE organization is a terrific organization. It helps entrepreneurs make their businesses bigger. And that sculptor is a real artist. He makes things for real. Not as a hobby like me. He is famous. And that caterer was a real caterer. The best caterer in town."

And then I thought about the whole thing a little bit more. "In fact," I said, "we should consider ourselves pretty lucky to have gotten out with only a couple of people even knowing we were there. I was way out of my league." It was so nice to have the time in the car with my mother. The time for a real conversation. A real conversation in person, not just on the phone. It was almost as good as sitting with my mother at my kitchen counter snacking on cereal. Or eating cake.

"What kind of a place do you think of when you think of the word 'work'?" I asked my mother. Installing a total of 31 layers of cake in an art gallery had boosted my confidence. This would be a perfect time to begin to discuss a few preliminary ideas with my mother, I thought to myself. Preliminary ideas about a new job. Starting with the easy parts of work. The easy parts, like where to work and what to wear to work. Not the hard part of work. Which is what to do.

"That is a good question," my mother said. "It is interesting, actually, that some people seem to define work as an activity conducted sitting behind a desk. Maybe that's because we all spent so many years sitting at desks in school."

"You are so right," I said. "It is curious! Really, think about the fact that many jobs have nothing to do with a desk. Think of all of the other places good work is performed. In a studio if you are an artist. In the operating room if you are a heart surgeon. In the kitchen if you are a cake-baker. In your laundry room if you are either cooling down or heating up a lot of chicken. In the ductwork if you are an HVAC engineer specializing in eradicating bacon grease. In the cemetery if you are a newspaper photographer assigned to cover the civic picnic. At the gym if you are a personal trainer or if you are the one being trained. In the coffee shop if you are a barista or if you are a customer writing down ideas for doing good in your diary of a good girl."

I caught myself. And I stopped talking. I was trying so hard to break my habit of talking too fast. And using too many words. And throwing out too many ideas all at once. Being the good mother that she is, though, my mother had listened to every word.

"You are absolutely right," my mother said. "Good work should be defined by productivity. By results. Not by where the work is performed." "Right!" I said. "And, on a related subject, think about what people wear to work. That is interesting, too."

My mother and I looked down, simultaneously. We looked down to see what we were wearing. Nice skirts. Nice shoes. Nice blouses. Nice bracelets. Nice lipstick. And then we started laughing. There we were, two non-caterers, dressed in office clothes, driving home from delivering a thirteen-layer cake and three six-layer cakes to a roomful of VIPs at a charity event. We had not been dressed for that work!

"We could have worn jeans," I said, wiping away a few tears of laughter. "Or capes," said my mother. She was wiping away tears, too. I laughed harder. "Those aren't called capes, Mom," I said. "Those are called smocks. Or aprons. Real artists and real caterers wear smocks and aprons. They do not wear capes!" "They wear capes when they need to escape quickly, unseen," laughed my mother.

Now we were in hysterics. In the car. Driving down the highway. Driving down the highway after pretending to be caterers. I flipped down the sun visor and checked the mirror. I had completely ruined my mascara. I did not care. It had been so much fun. And so funny. Unlike wistful tears, tears of laughter are worth ruining six layers of mascara.

"How did the cake thing turn out?" Prince Charming asked that night. I was hanging up my skirt and blouse, studying them closely as I put them on the hangers. Amazingly, there was not a spot of frosting on either one.

"We pulled it off," I reported proudly. "Completely unscathed." I told my husband about how my mother and I had escaped down the stairs in the nick of time. And I told him that the cake was beautiful. But I did not want to talk to my husband about cake. Not this time, anyway.

"Where do you think I should work?" I asked Prince Charming. Now it was his turn to be sarcastic. "Don't you work at the community foundation? In an office? Downtown?"

"No, no," I said. "That's not really what I meant. What I mean is, someday, if I work somewhere else, where should I work? Should I work at a desk? Should I work in a coffee shop? In a studio? In an office in an office building? In the car pool line? In the office here at home? At the kitchen counter? Where should I work?"

My husband laughed. "You are so funny," he said. "You ask all kinds of questions. But you rarely ask the question you really need to answer."

"What do you mean?" I said.

"Never mind," he said. "You could work anywhere you wanted to work." And he really meant it. In every sense. My husband is wonderful.

After I got home from work the next day I took the time to sit at my kitchen counter to record my ideas about work. In my diary of a good girl. In my pink notebooks I am always honest with myself. I am honest with myself about things that make me happy. And things that make me laugh. And things that make me uncomfortable. Or embarrassed. And things that make me feel like I am not good enough. As I jotted down a few notes about work that night, I was honest. In that diary entry I had to admit that my worries about work probably had nothing to do with the physical location of where I did my work. But I thought it was worth exploring. Just a tiny bit further.

I called my mother from my kitchen counter. It was after 6:00 p.m. and so my mother was probably at her kitchen counter, too. It was one of our kitchen-to-kitchen calls. "Do you think there is something wrong with me because I can't seem to be as productive as I would like to be when I am sitting behind a desk all day?" I asked. "I am beginning to think that sitting behind a desk is not a very good place to do good work."

Much to my surprise, my mother disagreed. "Sitting behind a desk is a very good place to do good work," she said firmly. "I love my desk. I love sitting in my office at work. I have a window with a pretty view and a print of my favorite Monet on the wall. I would never want to give up my desk."

Wow. Maybe I really was unusual. "Maybe you are right," I said, thinking it over and talking it through all at the same time. "Maybe the problem is with me. Maybe I am someone who cannot sit still for more than five minutes. And maybe I annoy people around me with my enthusiasm. Maybe my colleagues wish they had a magic wand to make me go away."

"Oh now you are just being hard on yourself," said my mother. "You should stop feeling so bad about just being you." "Well," I said. "Okay." I felt a little childish for saying all of that. Then again, I was talking to my mother. And I was still her child. "But," I added, in a far less whiny voice, "I really do like to move around a lot during the work day. It helps me think." And that was the truth. For me, productivity requires movement. And I love to move.

Mobility is a gift. I always remind my daughters to be grateful to be able to move around. I often think about our daughter with Williams Syndrome. Our daughter who is not likely to ever be able to ride a bicycle or drive a car. But she sure can zip around on her little pink trike, her curly blonde hair blowing in the breeze behind her as she pedals her little heart out on the sidewalk in the cul-de-sac across the street from our house, oblivious to the whispers of other children who wonder why she is still riding on three wheels designed for a child half her age. But she is alive. And she is outside. And she can get around.

"If you absolutely must work in an office all day," I told my mother, "at least go outside every once in a while. It is how you really know you are free." I was still sitting at my kitchen counter. With my pink notebook. On my iPhone. Talking to my mother. But I was eating no cake. And I was eating no cereal. The subject of work was giving me plenty of food for thought these days.

"Now you are making a little more sense," my mother said. "You've even made cake mobile, hauling around the Yellow Car Cake and the Studio Cake." That was an interesting point, I thought. Even a cake sometimes needs to get up and move. "See if you can do something with that idea," my mother continued. "That idea about mobility being a gift."

I laughed about the cakes. It really was funny to drive around with a big cake in the car. "Okay, I will," I said. "I will do something with that. Mobility is a gift."

We said our goodbyes. I switched my iPhone from phone to email. Well, well! I thought to myself as I scrolled through my inbox. What a coincidence. Sitting in my email was a message from a friend. A friend who runs a terrific organization. A terrific organization called Variety, the Children's Charity.

My friend knows a thing or two about freedom and mobility. Variety is an international, volunteer-driven organization with 52 active chapters worldwide. Variety is committed to bettering the quality of life for special needs children.

Once upon a time my lucky princess got to participate in Variety's "Kids On The Go!" mobility program at school. She was so excited! Her special education class tested an adaptive bicycle that helps kids like my daughter who have difficulty with balance. When you have a hard time getting around, just going from point A to point B can be a lot of work. Thank heavens Variety provides mobility in many forms, including vans with lifts, wheelchairs, adaptive bicycles, prosthetic limbs, medical procedures and more. "I'll make a donation tomorrow," I said to the kitchen counter. "In honor of my love of mobility. Even when it comes to cakes."

"Have you decided where you want to work?" Prince Charming asked a little later. I was putting away my pink notebook and my iPhone. Putting them away in my purse. My purse. Now that is a good place, I thought. "I can't exactly work in my purse," I said. Not realizing that I was talking out loud.

"What?" Prince Charming gave me that look. That look that says "Hello there, lovely lady, you are talking to yourself again." "Sorry," I said. "I guess I am starting to get a little slap happy. Sitting here on the floor all the time next to my running shoes."

For a moment I even wondered whether all of the ideas I had been writing in the diary of a good girl might have been better had I not written most of them sitting in a closet. Sitting in a closet next to a purse and a pair of Nikes. Staring up at a treadmill. Oh well, I thought. It is too late now. The diary was huge. I was beginning to think it might be almost done. At least the first one. I could always write another.

"I know what you are thinking," I said to Prince Charming. "You are thinking that I need to stop spending so much time thinking about *where* I might work and instead start thinking about what I might actually *do* at work." Prince Charming just smiled. He loves it when I am brief, logical and direct. And accurate. Especially all at the same time.

What would I do? I asked myself that question over and over as I tried to fall asleep that night. I thought about getting out of bed to study my pink notebooks. Just to see if I could find an idea. Sometimes that works.

But I did not even think about getting out the magic wand. I was pretty sure by now that figuring out what I was going to do with my life was something I would have to do all by myself.

Chapter 18

Chocolate Chip Cookies with a Twist

A little change can be a very good thing. Like tossing change into the drive-through window box on an ice cream outing. Or a little change discovered between the sofa cushions just in time for a coffee run. Or a little change dropped into the red kettle during the holidays to make the season brighter for people who need help. A little change is sometimes good for recipes, too. Even though a little change in a recipe can lead to a big change in your baking plans.

It had been a couple of weeks since I baked the Studio Cake. The Studio Cake that was really four cakes. Four cakes baked from eight boxes of cake mix.

"Girls, girls, girls!" I called out from my favorite spot at the kitchen counter. "Who wants to help me make a cake?" Today was a day that called for a cake. A cake to kick off the holiday baking season. This time two princesses came running right away. Evidently my daughters were missing cake as much as I was. The girls climbed onto their favorite spots on the kitchen counter.

"Who wants to get a box of Betty Crocker white cake mix out of the pantry?" Both of the princesses volunteered. I helped them off the counter. They disappeared briefly into the pantry. And they emerged proudly when they had completed their task. The girls love to help.

"Okay, that's fine," I said, glancing quickly at what the princesses were placing on the kitchen counter. There were two boxes, not one. "We'll just make two cakes," I said. After all, I thought, the more layers the better. "Go right ahead and climb back up onto the counter and pour both cake mixes into the mixing bowl." I was so proud of my girls. They were really catching on to cake making.

We were off! Vegetable oil blended into the cake mix? Check. Eggs at room temperature? Check. Milk at room temperature? Check. Egg whites and milk added to the bowl, alternating and mixing between additions? Check. Vanilla? Check. Almond? Check. A pinch of salt? Check. "Perfect!" I declared. And speedy, too, I thought. We were all getting very good at making cakes!

"Maybe Gran was right," I told my daughters. "These cakes are so good. Maybe I really should tell more people that I bake cakes. Instead of keeping it a secret. Maybe I should expand my cake and charity hobby beyond just friends and family. Even beyond a few wonderful people who look at my websites." I was feeling bold! Too bold, as it would turn out.

"Can we lick the bowl now?" The girls were staring longingly at the cake. The cake that was still in batter form in the pink mixing bowl. "Sure!" I said. "I will even join you. I am in the mood for cake." I poured the batter into six eight-inch cake pans. Eight-inch cake pans that I promptly placed in the preheated oven. And I got out three spoons. "Here we go!" I said to the girls. And we dove into the bowl with our spoons.

Ooops. I knew immediately that something was not quite right. The cake batter was a little dry. Actually it was very dry. And a little stiff. And a little too unsweet. And too sticky. In fact, the cake batter did not look, feel or smell like cake batter. And it did not sound like cake batter, either, when we scraped it off of the sides of the mixing bowl with our spoons. The cake batter tasted a lot like cookie dough. Actually the cake batter tasted exactly like cookie dough. Only not nearly sweet enough. And then it dawned on me. I had not paid any attention to the boxes the girls had pulled from the pantry. This mystery was about to be solved.

"Girls," I said, "would you please get the cake mix boxes out of the recycle bin?" I asked nicely. "We threw them in the trash," my middle princess said. "The green box was all full." Ooops again. This cake was looking less and less good all the time. "Well, okay, get them out of the trash, then." And I added "Please." At the very least I should use good manners.

The girls produced the evidence. Sure enough. One box of cake mix, one box of cake flour. And the box of cake flour was still more than half full. That explained it. "Well, well!" I said to the princesses. "It looks like we have ourselves a change of plans!"

If it walks like a duck and quacks like a duck, it is probably a duck. The same goes for baking. If it looks like cookie dough and acts like cookie dough, it is probably cookie dough.

"Stay right there," I said to the girls. "Do not move. I will be right back." I dashed out of the kitchen and into my bedroom and into my closet. I grabbed the magic wand out of my purse. And I dashed back to the kitchen. The girls had not moved. They were dutifully still sitting on the kitchen counter. What good girls.

"Today," I declared, "we will not be making a cake. We will make cookies!" I said this as enthusiastically as possible. Smiling broadly as if I was on candid camera for a secret cooking show. A secret cooking show that was catching recreational pastry chefs on videotape to see how well they reacted to a recipe mishap. I thought I did a pretty good job.

Quickly I pulled the six cake pans out of the oven. The batter was warm but it had not yet started to bake. Perfect. "Not so fast," I said to the batter. "Who do you think you are, anyway?" I dumped the contents of each cake pan back into the pink mixing bowl. "Watch this, girls," I said to my daughters. I pulled out the magic wand. I waved the magic wand dramatically over the top of the bowl. In a mystical, raspy voice I chanted a spell.

There once was a cake in a bowl.
A cake, not feeling quite whole.
Of cake, the queen was quite fond,
But along came a magic wand.
And converted the cake's very soul.

"Abracadabra!" I said, giving the magic wand a final flourish. "You are not batter," I said to the batter, "you are dough! *Poof*!"

The girls watched with great interest. I think they were also a little afraid of my scary voice. "Mommy, are you magic?" they asked in a whisper. "Yes, girls. Yes, I am!" I said. I was still using my mystical, raspy voice. But I tried to make it sound slightly more friendly. I did not want my daughters to develop a fear of baking. The three of us peered into the bowl. It looked about the same as it had before I cast the spell. Maybe slightly less runny. The batter had cooled off just a bit.

"I am magic," I said, switching back to my regular voice, "because I have the power to fix this recipe." And then I added, "I have the power to fix this recipe even without a magic wand. That spell was just for fun." I could only imagine what Prince Charming would think if he knew I was giving our children the impression that magic wands can fix cake recipes. My husband would not have been very impressed.

My daughters were watching with great interest. "Don't worry, girls," I said cheerfully. "This will all be fine." And I meant it. I can make this work, I said to myself. And there really was no point in being upset. The little girls simply were not old enough yet to read and understand the difference between a box of cake mix and a box of cake flour. After all, each of the boxes is covered with a picture of a big piece of cake.

I searched my memory for a glimmer of a recollection of a recipe from my past that might work in this situation. This situation in which cake flour had been combined with cake mix. No luck. Then I thought about the magic wand. "I wonder if the magic wand could help me channel Grandmother," I said. "I could try to conjure up a recipe from Grandmother's past." Then I started laughing. And so did my daughters. They had no idea what I was laughing about. But I guess they did not want me to be laughing alone. They are so sweet.

I had drawn a complete blank on a recipe that called for both cake mix and cake flour. So I did what any girl would do under the circumstances. I made something up. Making something up is a great idea. If you draw a blank on a recipe and you are facing a bowl full of dough that thinks it is batter, just make up a new recipe. Even when you are staring at a big bowl of batter-dough. Go with your instincts.

And the best instincts involve chocolate.

"Girls," I said. "This will work. I am going to add a magic ingredient, wave the magic wand and turn this cake into cookies." Now the princesses' eyes really lit up. They had never seen their mother do anything quite like this before. Turn heaps of cake and frosting into a new cake, yes. But turn cake into cookies? This was something they wanted to see. Especially since casting the spell over the batter had not seemed to change things much.

When you are making something up in this kind of situation, use the highest quality chocolate you can find. The higher the quality of chocolate, the better off you are. Dig around in your secret chocolate stash. Cobble together enough broken up pieces of half-eaten dark chocolate bars to generate approximately one and a half cups of chocolate. Dump the chocolate pieces into the mixing bowl. Stir by hand until it is all blended together.

"Now for the moment of truth," I said to the girls. Actually, it would have been more accurate to have said "moments of truth," plural, because there are two here. First, test the dough for taste. It should taste good. It will be slightly bland because of all that extra flour, but that is okay. The chocolate makes up for lack of sweetness. If the dough tastes bad, you had better throw in the towel, throw out the dough, go ahead and panic and then send Prince Charming out to buy a cake.

If the dough passes the taste test, though, it is time for the second moment of truth, which is the structure test. See if you can form the dough into little balls that hold their shape. If you can, that is great. Form the dough into balls, arrange them on a greased cookie sheet with a little room between each one and gently punch a shallow thumbprint into the center of each ball. Then bake them as if they were normal cookies. Normal cookies bake at 350 degrees for 10 to 12 minutes.

The results of the structure test depend on how much cake flour ended up in the bowl in the first place. If the dough is too loose to form into balls, it simply means that the dough is a little light on extra cake flour. No problem. Just convert your baking goal from cookies to bars. Bars are a convenient cross between cookies and cake. To complete the cookie-to-bar conversion, grease a 9 × 12 baking dish, fill it with the dough, bake it for about 25 minutes at 350 degrees and cut the finished product into bars while it is still soft and warm enough to slice.

"Thank heavens for chocolate!" The girls and I were putting the finishing touches on our thumbprints. Our cookie dough balls had met the structure test. Our creative chocolate chip cookies were shaping up nicely! I was practically dancing and twirling and spinning around the kitchen counter. "Chocolate has saved the day!" I sang.

Our cookies were actually pretty good. Good enough that we decided to turn the whole adventure into a celebration that gives back. Even though there was no cake involved. Cookies were good enough. Cookies can do good, too. Even if they are not super-delicious.

"Let's write a check to the Down Syndrome Guild," I suggested to the girls. I had always been impressed with the woman who runs the organization in Kansas City. My middle princess is friends with a darling boy at school who has Down Syndrome. And I thought we could package up some of the cookies and give them to him and his family. With, of course, a One Celebrations sticker on the cellophane wrap. A One Celebrations sticker right next to the black ribbon. The black ribbon that would tie it all together. The packaging was becoming my signature.

"Girls, girls," I said. "We are so fortunate to have so many wonderful organizations in Kansas City that help children with special needs and their families." My littlest princesses are too young to catch on to that. But I wanted to be ready for the day that they do catch on.

"It is really important to support organizations like the Down Syndrome Guild. Organizations that offer information and education to promote positive awareness and acceptance for people with disabilities," I continued. Pretty big words for little girls. But someday they will be big enough to understand.

Well, I thought a few hours later. I was in my closet. Working on the diary of a good girl. Writing up my new recipe. Well, I thought, that had worked out nicely! The Queen of Cake and the Cake Princesses had successfully completed a conversion of fluffy white cake to Chocolate Chip Cookies with a Twist.

The chocolate really saved the day, I wrote in the pink notebook.

Really good chocolate holds its own. Even when it is surrounded by cake flour, cake mix, milk, oil and eggs that have been combined into a slightly odd formulation.

I wondered what I would have done without my secret stash of dark chocolate. If chocolate is not available, I wrote in the diary, you really might be out of luck. In that case I suppose you could park the mystery batter in the refrigerator and immediately go to bed. Willing yourself to dream up a new recipe that will solve everything the moment you wake up.

"I think I will have a little piece of chocolate this morning," I said to the girls the next day as we began to load backpacks, a purse, a cup of cereal, a can of all-natural grape soda and ourselves into the car. "It sounds good right now." I tossed my purse into the driver's seat and went back inside to get my cereal out of the pantry. And eat a piece of chocolate, while I was at it.

"Delicious!" I said to the pantry, popping into my mouth half a square of 70% cacao left over from making the cookies the day before. And it was the very best kind, too. Christopher Elbow. The best. Why not chocolate for breakfast, I thought. After all, they make chocolate cereal. Chocolate is a perfectly good breakfast food, I assured myself.

Just that little bite of chocolate made my morning a lot sweeter. The morning drive was almost as delicious as a whole bar of 70% cacao. A pleasant drop-off at school. My reliable cereal and soda. Life was good.

"How's work?" I asked my friend. My friend and I sat down with our coffees at my favorite table. At my favorite table at my favorite coffee shop, LattéLand. I had not seen this friend in months. Starting the work part of my day with my friend was a perfect complement to my delicious drive. I was looking forward to catching up.

"Work is great," she said. "Well it must be great because you look great," I replied. And she did! She was glowing. "I joined Rodan and Fields," she said. "I've been using the products for a few months and I love them." I had never heard of Rodan and Fields. "What is that?" I asked.

"Innovative skin care," my friend answered. "The company was founded by a couple of world-renowned dermatologists. The anti-aging products are terrific. But the best part of my work is the opportunity for women to share something that makes them feel good about themselves."

"Interesting," I said. I reached into my purse to pull out my pink notebook and a pen. I wanted to write that name down. I am always looking for new ideas for looking good. And for making other girls feel good about themselves. Plus, my friend had given me an idea. An idea about work.

"You know," I continued. "I've been testing lots of ideas. Lots of ideas about doing good and helping others, mostly at home. But maybe the general idea of doing good and helping others applies to work, too. Kind of like you just said."

My friend nodded. "I love my work," she said. "In fact, my work is a form of giving, in a way. I think that the people who give to charities sometimes experience more fulfillment than the charities themselves. And I have that same feeling when I do my work, introducing my company to someone new. I honestly feel it is a gift."

Well said, I thought. I wrote that down in my notebook. I wrote down the idea that work can be a gift. And the idea that giving can be part of work.

"How is work for you?" asked my friend. "Work is great," I answered, still thinking over what my friend had just said about work and giving. "But I am thinking about a change," I added. I might as well test the waters, I thought to myself. It felt so good to say it out loud. To say it out loud to someone who was not my mother or my husband or my pink notebook.

"What exactly would you do?" she asked. "I'm still thinking that through," I admitted. And then I remembered what my mother had said a few weeks ago on the phone. About being who I am. Her words had stuck with me. I decided to try it out on my friend. "Actually," I said, "I am thinking I might just be myself."

We both laughed. "That is always a good idea!" my friend said. Always a good idea. I repeated the words to myself. She was probably right, I thought. In fact, when is it *not* a good idea to be yourself? I would have to think about that some more. "Well," I said as we wrapped up our conversation. "I am so glad work is going well for you. That is great!"

My friend switched subjects. "Before we go, what's with all the cakes?" Evidently my friend had visited my personal websites. "Oh," I said. "That's my hobby. The girls and I bake cakes. And we give them away. And we do something good for others, like give to charity. And sometimes I let the girls put on a little lipstick. Just for fun. So that we all look good for the photo shoot."

I could tell that I had lost her at the part about the photo shoot. I laughed and tried to explain. "It's just all for fun. I take pictures of my girls and the cakes. And I post the pictures on my blogs. I post the pictures and the stories on my blogs to inspire other girls to do good. In their own ways."

My friend was smiling. But she was still a little bit lost. "It's all just my way of doing good at home," I said. "Oh!" she said. She got it. "That is fun! What a good idea." "I've got the hobby thing down, at least for the most part," I said, thinking about the cake-to-cookie episode. Best to keep the cakes as a hobby, I thought. "Now," I said to my friend, "I just have to work on the work part."

Work, work, work. I was thinking about work a lot these days. I thought about work as I said goodbye to my friend and threw my coffee cup into the recycle bin. I thought about work as I drove downtown to the office. I was thinking about work so much that I took a little break later that day and actually wrote a diary entry about work. At my desk. In my office. At work.

"Hello," I said to the pink notebook. "Welcome to work." I was pretty sure this was the first time I had ever written anything in my diary of a good girl while sitting in my office. It was a nice change of scenery, actually. Much better than the closet. At least for this particular topic.

Choose carefully where you work, I wrote. And then I decided to have some fun. Some fun with all of this work. I added a catchy title for the entry. How to Determine Whether a Potential Employer Is Good Enough for You, I wrote at the top of a new page.

And then I left the next six lines blank.

And then I wrote: That's the end of the formula for How to Determine Whether a Potential Employer Is Good Enough for You. Maybe the company you're about to go to work for is good and maybe it's not. Take the job either way. A paycheck is your number one priority. How else are you going to afford that cute loft apartment and still get coffee every morning and manicures once a month? You can go for good when you are older and richer and still happy and gorgeous.

Okay that was not very nice, I thought. That was not something a good girl would write. Especially not at work. "Just kidding," I said to the diary. I was talking to the pink notebook. I was the only one in my office. Unless you counted the pictures of my girls sitting on my desk. Perhaps I would talk to them next.

"It is worth a little more analysis than that," I said to the little girls smiling in the pewter picture frames. "After all, this is your life and you get only one of those. And it is more fun to work for a company that does at least a little good."

I decided that I would make amends for having written something so snippy in my diary. A diary that was supposed to be good. I turned to a new page. And then the ideas started to flow. Probably because I was sitting at a desk in the office of a very good place to work.

I started a new heading, Ways for a Company to Do a Little Good. Underneath it I wrote down as many ideas as I could think of, in no particular order. A recycling bin next to every desk. A rain garden on the roof. A scholarship fund for fellow employees who need help. A program to encourage time off for volunteering. Disaster relief funds to help employees make donations to tornado victims. Organized clothing drives and canned food drives. A corporate foundation. A donor advised fund for every employee. The gift of a giving card to each employee on a birthday or anniversary of employment. Annual donations by the company to a few favorite charities. Purchasing tables at charity events. A matching gifts program. Lights that turn off automatically. Credit to employees for service on nonprofit boards of directors. A special place in the break room to post cookie order forms and sell fitness bracelets and collect pop tabs and display a list of all of the charities that the employees collectively support and the impressive tally of total donations. Employee participation in the grant making decisions of the company's foundation. A program where the company pays half of the cost of season tickets to support employee attendance at local performing arts productions.

Well, that was interesting! I reread the list. Not bad, I thought.

And then I remembered what my friend had asked me earlier that day. "What are you going to do?" she had asked. That was such a good question. And I had said that I was thinking about just being myself.

I wonder, I thought, if all of this fits together somehow? Doing good, at home and in the workplace, and being myself? And work? "I'll have to sleep on that one," I said to the pink notebook as I put the diary back in my purse. And I got back to work.

I have always believed that the mind has magical powers that will work on things for you while you sleep. Without a magic wand, even. Relatively minor things, like recipe challenges. But also lots of other vexing dilemmas about kids and jobs and work and offices and desks and true callings and other things that are just part of life. All while you are slumbering away, enjoying sweet dreams of cakes and castles and fairy tales. It is amazing how you can go to bed as a person asking questions and wake up as a person who has answers.

"I have so many ideas about work," I told Prince Charming that night. We were back in the closet. It really is such a good place for a conversation. "Especially, today, ideas about doing good at work. The ideas are spinning in my head. I can't quite figure out what to do. I am hoping a good night's sleep will help."

"Have you done any research?" asked my husband. That was a very good question. Usually the answer to that question is "no." That is because I usually rely on my husband to do the research. But this time was different. I had, in fact, researched the idea of doing good in the workplace.

To demonstrate my research savvy I jumped into my lawyer role. I also wanted to impress my lawyer husband. "Most companies and their employees are already doing a lot of good," I said. "Which is good, because consumers and employees are becoming increasingly focused on this sort of thing."

I could not resist sharing a few statistics. I love numbers. "In fact," I continued, "almost 94% of consumers will choose to purchase a product that supports a cause instead of a product that does not support a cause. At least where price and quality are equal. That's up from 74% of consumers only a year ago! Plus, 56% of 20- and

30-something employees will *refuse* to work for a company that is not socially responsible. Can you believe that? *Refuse."*

"Interesting," said Prince Charming. He looked impressed. "What are you going to do with all of that?" "I am not sure yet," I admitted. "But I love to write about corporate social responsibility. And, remember, sometimes I am asked to speak about it or teach a class about it. I love to talk about it." The talking part was pretty obvious. Prince Charming said nothing, passing up a golden opportunity to be sarcastic. Prince Charming is wonderful.

"I really think most companies should celebrate all the good they are doing," I continued. "It is so inspiring! Talk about creating employee loyalty and a positive customer experience!" At this point I could tell that Prince Charming was reaching enthusiasm overload. I have learned to watch for the signs. So I stopped talking.

"Maybe you should just get started," Prince Charming said. "It seems like you have all of the ingredients for what to do in a new job. You just don't have the recipe yet. But that's never stopped you before."

My husband paused and sat down on the treadmill. He sat down on the treadmill to look at me directly. Instead of looking down on me from his chair. I was sitting on the floor. Next to my running shoes. "Actually," he said thoughtfully, "you never follow the recipe anyway. I think you should just do something." And then he added, "As long as it makes money. I don't exactly want our family to go broke baking cakes." He was only half-joking.

"Don't worry," I said with a wink. "I would never give up my financial independence." I, too, was only half-joking.

I laid awake that night and thought about what my husband had said. I thought about it a lot. What would I do? If I did what I loved to do, I would spend my days meeting interesting people. People who are doing good. And I would spend my days finding talented people who want to help me build something new. And I would spend my days inspiring. And writing. And talking. And celebrating all of the ways a person can do good in the workplace. And I would still have time to be home in the evenings and on weekends to do good there, too, baking cakes and giving to charity and having fun with the girls.

At 3:41 a.m. I sat up in bed. It had just hit me. Meeting interesting people. Finding talent. Building something new. Inspiring, writing, talking. "Those are the things I do anyway!" I said out loud. But my husband was sound asleep. I was only talking to myself. "I just need to do what I do," I said, this time using a softer voice. Two little princesses were asleep on the floor and I did not want to wake them, either. "I need to do what I do. In a new way." By then I was whispering. I would keep that secret to myself. At least for now.

I stayed awake for a while, thinking it over. Something new. A new recipe. A change. Like when you think you are making a cake. But the cake changes its mind and decides that it does not want to be a cake after all. The cake changes its mind and decides that what it really wants to be is a batch of cookies. Even a cake sometimes must discover its true calling.

And then I thought about LM Associates. The company I had started when I was a little girl. I had started a company then, I thought. Why couldn't I start a company now? I could start a company that inspires other companies celebrate doing good in the workplace. I could do what I do. I could work for myself. I could be myself. I could do it! No, I thought. That is not quite right. I *will* do it.

Maybe the cookie episode yesterday was a sign, I thought as I fell asleep. A sign of change. A signal that something new lay ahead. A hint that I have the power to change the recipe. The power to change the recipe for my future. *I will do it*, I thought. Now it was only a matter of timing.

Do what you do, I told myself in my dreams. Do it well. There is no point in doing anything else. And that is when the activity formerly known as work disappears altogether and, *poof*, it magically becomes fun.

Chapter 19

Happily Ever After

"Hurry, Mommy! We'll be late!"

I glanced at the clock. We had plenty of time. A full 17 minutes, to be exact, until I would have to start loading everyone into the car. My conscientious daughter had nothing to worry about. I was in no real danger of making the princesses late for school.

And I was not in the mood to hurry. It was a beautiful day. It was a beautiful day already, even at 7:43 a.m. The forecast called for perfect early spring weather. The morning sun was pouring through the windows, bouncing off the shiny colored metal on six tubes of lipstick. The six tubes of lipstick sitting on my vanity. Sitting on my vanity next to my favorite mascara. All of which lipstick and mascara I still needed to put on.

"I'll try to hurry!" I called to my daughter, thinking now that she might have a point. Seventeen minutes can go by pretty quickly if you start slowing down your normal routine, even just a tiny bit. My daughter left the bedroom to find her shoes and her backpack. I figured she and her sisters had already eaten breakfast because I had heard the familiar clink of spoons and cereal bowls coming from the kitchen a few minutes earlier.

But I still was not in the mood to hurry. I was standing in front of my mirror. Putting on lipstick. Six layers. And putting on mascara. Six layers. And while I was putting on my lipstick and my mascara I was thinking about all of the good things that had happened since the first of the year. All of the good things, starting with a good thing about my name. A name is always a good place to start.

"What's up with your name?" Prince Charming had asked me a couple months ago. A couple of months ago when we were both in the closet. My husband was sitting on the treadmill. Again. He was back to sitting on the treadmill. The chair in the closet had made it too crowded.

"What do you mean?" I had said. I looked up from the floor. I was sitting next to my running shoes. Again. I still liked that spot.

"Your new personal website says 'Laura Wells McKnight.' Instead of 'Laura McKnight,'" my husband observed. "Why did you switch your name?" That was a good question. And I had a good answer.

"First of all," I said, "that's not a switch. That's really my name." Which was true. Wells is my middle name. Wells is my mother's maiden name. Which, of course, Prince Charming already knew. And I knew that I had not answered my husband's question. "Second," I continued, answering the question this time, "the domain for 'lauramcknight' had already been taken." Which was also true. That was okay, though. There are a lot of Laura McKnights. But I am pretty sure I am the only Laura Wells McKnight floating around out there.

"Oh," Prince Charming had said, thinking it over. Thinking over the part about the domain. And the part about my name. And then he had asked, "What are you going to do with it?"

"Be myself," I said.

My husband had laughed. And he decided to play along. "When will you start?" he asked.

"I'm still working on that," I said. I had laughed, too. And, just for fun, I had added, "I am waiting for a sign from the universe." I had winked at Prince Charming. He loves my references to the universe. He loves them so much that my wink had been the end of that conversation. The end of that conversation in my closet a couple of months ago. The end of that conversation about my name.

As I recalled that conversation I started laughing at myself in the mirror. Then I forced myself to stop. I forced myself to stop because laughing does not mix well with keeping lipstick inside the lines of lipliner.

"Mom! Are you coming?" Now my oldest princess was at my bedroom door, urging me to hurry. "We'll be late for school!" I looked at the clock. We still had plenty of time. Nevertheless, I was impressed by the diligence of my children this morning. Two out of three!

"We still have 14 minutes before we have to get in the car," I said reassuringly. "You could go clean up your room," I suggested. My daughter scowled ever so slightly. "Or eat more cereal." At that suggestion my daughter quickly left the room, wisely deciding to take me up on the cereal idea instead of the room-cleaning idea. Or whatever idea I might come up with next that was likely to be even less fun than the room-cleaning idea.

Yes, I thought to myself, the website with my name was a good thing. I had already begun to post even more ideas from my diary of a good girl. Ideas about my hobby. My hobby celebrating good at home. And I was beginning to think about what I might write about celebrating good in the workplace.

I had been telling my mother all about the idea for my new venture. The one I had dreamed up after the cookie episode. "I am going to build a business," I said. "A business that inspires companies to celebrate social responsibility. A business that inspires companies to look as good as they deserve to look." This time my mother and I were not talking on the phone. And we were not sitting at my kitchen counter. This time my mother and I were meeting for lunch. We had just sat down at a table for two. A table for two at one of our favorite restaurants.

"That sounds good!" my mother said after we had ordered. "You can take everything you know about doing good and use it to help companies."

"Exactly!" I nodded. "I really have seen first hand the positive impact that doing good can have on employees and customers. I think I'll start by doing a little consulting, inspiring business leaders to make the most out of all of the charitable giving and doing good and giving back that is already going on in the workplace. And then I'll see where that leads."

My mother and I love to have lunch at André's Confiserie Suisse, a delightful Swiss bakery. A delightful Swiss bakery that serves delicious quiche and beet salad with a special vinaigrette dressing. A Swiss bakery that is famous for its cakes and pastries and tarts and tortes. To die for! With every lunch, you get to pick out your own pastry, your own little cake, for dessert. You get to pick it out, right off of a tray they bring to your table after the quiche plates are cleared and after your coffee has been refilled. The pastry comes with the lunch. You have no choice; you must eat cake for dessert. It is a wonderful experience.

"I'll bet you can offer some good advice to companies," my mother had remarked as we finished our lunches. We both were scanning the room for the lady with the pastry tray. And trying not to look like we were scanning the room for the lady with the pastry tray. "Advice about making their giving programs effective and practical. And advice about community image." My mother had been on board with my idea. Which was a good thing. Which was a good thing because at that time I was about ready to put my idea into action. I was just waiting for that sign. "And, of course," I had said, "I will make sure it is all good for the company's bottom line."

My mother and I had picked out our pastries. And we had switched subjects. "How's the good girl project going?" my mother asked. It had been a few weeks since we had talked about the diary of a good girl. My mother knew that the diary had consumed me for months and months. Ever since the day I heard the story about pumpkin pancakes.

"That's coming along, too," I said as I took a bite of Linzer torte. Linzer torte at André's is so good! "I'm not going to quit the good girl hobby. I'll keep right on writing. And baking. And doing good. Even when I start the business. That good girl hobby has been good for the girls. And," I had added thoughtfully, "it has been good for me."

My mother looked at me. And she nodded. "You do seem happier," she said. "You seem more like *you*. Maybe the diary of a good girl idea was exactly what you needed. Maybe it was exactly what you needed to get you to the new business idea." My mother is so smart.

A few weeks had passed since that conversation at André's with my mother. But I found myself reflecting on that conversation, too, just as I had reflected on the conversation in the closet with my husband. Such good conversations, I thought to myself. I was still standing in front of my mirror, leaning over my vanity. Putting on makeup. And watching the clock to be sure I would get the girls to school on time.

"It is true. The diary of a good girl *has* been good for me," I said to myself as I added a fourth layer of mascara. A fourth layer of mascara from the tube of one of my all-time favorite beauty products, MAC's Haute & Naughty mascara. By the way, do not let the name scare you. MAC's Haute & Naughty mascara is fantastic. It is a product worthy of a good girl.

I continued talking. "And that diary is not over yet," I said to the mascara. "That diary is just beginning!" And that was true, too. I would keep writing. The diary of a good girl was not over. And neither was the mascara. I still had two layers to go. And I still had 12 minutes before I had to round up three princesses, six shoes, three backpacks, a cup of fiber cereal and a can of all-natural grape soda.

My name. My new business idea. My diary of a good girl. Those were all good things. And good things were happening with the girls, too. Good things like changing bad situations into good situations. Or at least into educational experiences.

I almost started laughing again when I thought about a particularly funny diary entry I had written. A diary entry I had written under a heading called How to Exterminate Reptiles from the Castle Chandeliers and Simultaneously Teach Children the Value of Honesty. I had written that entry one night after I ventured upstairs to tuck the girls into bed. One night when I found myself in the pretty pink room occupied by two of the princesses, staring at a suspicious pile of pillows and chairs in the middle of the floor. "What's all this?" I had asked.

"Oh we were just playing," one of the princesses said, quite convincingly. So I kissed them goodnight. As I made my way to the bedroom door, though, the older of the two princesses piped up. "Mom, wait. I am going to tell you the absolute truth."

It is always a good thing when a child says that she plans to tell you the absolute truth. What will happen next is that the truth will come out in one long sentence. So you have to listen carefully.

"We were playing a game with the sticky worm I got from the

dentist and throwing the worm into the air and trying to catch it and playing baseball with the worm and somehow on accident the worm got stuck up on the ceiling and we tried to get it down but we couldn't and so we built a tower to try to climb up and get it but we still couldn't reach it and we are so sorry and now the worm is stuck up on the ceiling. *Right. There.*"

Sure enough, dangling from the ceiling three feet above my head was a sticky, yellow worm. The the kind of worm used for fake fishing bait. Prince Charming had to get the ladder to get it down. And then all had been well in the castle. At least for a few days.

But the sticky worm had not been the end of the story. Two weeks later another one of the princesses in the kingdom hunted me down in my closet. She said, "Mommy, come quick, something is yucky!" To which I responded, "In a minute, honey." Which was not what I should have said because fifteen minutes later Prince Charming leaped down the stairs, three at a time, and made a valiant dive for the light switch on the wall by the front door.

I heard the commotion from my spot in the closet. And I came running out to see what in the world was going on. And I gasped when I saw a nasty, serpent-like plume of rubbery-smelling smoke circling up, up, up into the eaves of the entry way.

You really do not ever want your Prince Charming to have to ask "Who threw the squishy dinosaur into the chandelier?" If that happens, make sure your princesses remember what they learned from the worm on the ceiling. What they learned from the worm on the ceiling about telling the truth. Prince Charmings love to slay fire-breathing dragons with real weapons like knives and swords. But they are not too keen on the idea of having to use messy fire extinguishers in their castles. And they become very disagreeable when the littlest subjects in the kingdom do not own up to their less-than-ladylike deeds.

Now I was really laughing. I was really laughing, standing there in front of my mirror, trying to prevent tears of laughter. Tears of laughter that would get in the way of the final layer of mascara. I was really laughing because the squishy dinosaur had not been the end of the story, either. Just one week later, I had to teach a third lesson about telling the truth. One week later when I noticed that a very large section of hair was missing from one of the princess's long, golden locks. "Did you cut your hair?" I had asked. Mothers sometimes ask the most obvious questions! "No," my princess said confidently. "An alligator did it." Naturally. Still slightly exhausted from the sticky worm talk and the squishy dinosaur talk, I now had to have the alligator talk. I had to have the alligator talk at the kid salon while the princess's shag look was being repaired.

For the record, rarely are there happy endings to stories that involve slimy creatures. Two weeks after the emergency visit to the salon and the alligator lecture, a little voice piped up from the back-seat of my car on the drive home from school. "Mommy," my princess announced brightly, "the alligator went away." Equally brightly I asked, "Where did he go?" The answer: "He ran into the street and got hit by a car." Oh my.

I suppose it really is true. One way or another, every dragon and worm and dinosaur and demon and alligator and serpent in the kingdom eventually meets its match. Especially in the victorious imaginations of beautiful and shrewd princesses.

I was still laughing. I was still laughing, standing there in front of my mirror. "All of that was so funny!" I said to the mascara. Fortunately I prevented tears of laughter. The sixth layer on my lashes was safe. "These girls are so wonderful," I added. I looked at the clock. Good! I still had ten minutes. Plenty of time for a little more lipstick. And a little more conversation with my makeup. It was so nice to have a few minutes to myself. To myself and my lipstick and my mascara. And to my own good ideas.

"A good mother knows," I said to the tube of a great color of lip-stick called It Girl. A great color called It Girl that is slightly mauve and slightly pink. I love that color! "A good mother knows when to teach little girls a lesson about honesty." And that is true, I thought to myself. How bad a mother could I be, really, if I could convert hanging worms and burning dinosaurs and haircutting alligators into educational experiences? Surely any mother who can do that is a good mother, I thought to myself. "That counts," I said out loud. "Even without the pumpkin pancakes."

So far, so good, I thought to myself. I was getting somewhere. I kept right on talking to the tube of It Girl. The tube of It Girl kept right on listening. "A good mother knows exactly what kind of birthday cake each of her princesses likes best. A good mother knows what a joy it is to love princesses who are stepdaughters every bit as much as they love princesses who were placed in their arms at birth. A good mother knows when it is okay to let little girls sleep on her floor and in her bed instead of upstairs in their rooms. A good mother knows when it is okay to serve cereal for dinner and when her children need something from the stove or the oven."

I stopped talking. All of that seemed to be a bit much for the tube of It Girl to absorb. So I directed my next set of comments to the tube of Give Joy lipstick. And I dabbed another layer of color onto my lips. "A good mother knows when something is different about her baby," I said to Give Joy. "Long before anyone else does." And that was true. I had known. Even before she was born I had known something was different about my blonde curly-haired princess. The nine months were perfect. The tests were perfect. The birth day was perfect. And the baby was perfect. It just turned out to be a different kind of perfect.

Before the blonde curly-haired princess had arrived in our family I had regarded mothers of special needs children with admiration. Mixed with a little bit of pity. And mixed with a lot of guilty relief for having a daughter and two stepdaughters who each fit the perfect definition of a good girl. The perfect definition of a good girl that I assumed existed. That I assumed existed somewhere out there in the filing cabinets and report cards and checklists of the universe. In the filing cabinets and report cards and checklists where the universe keeps all of the standards set by everyone else. The standards set by everyone else that we are all supposed to meet if we want to qualify as good enough.

"But that is not how it works," I said to myself, somewhat tentatively. Just to see if the mirror in front of me would shatter. It did not. I studied my reflection. The lipstick and the mascara were still fully intact. So far, so good. "That is not how it works," I repeated, this time with emotion. And with confidence. And with sincerity. "That is *not* how it works. A good girl is a girl with special needs," I urged the lipstick. "A good girl is a girl without special needs." The tube of Give Joy seemed to be listening.

I stopped. I looked in the mirror. And I looked at myself. I really looked at myself. For the first time in a long, long time. "A good girl is any girl of any chronological age," I said to myself in the mirror. "A good girl is you. A good girl is me." And for the first time in a long, long time—maybe the first time ever—I actually believed that.

I put down the tube of Give Joy. And I paused. And I took a deep breath. And I did something I probably do not do as often as I should. I admitted to myself that I had been wrong. Months of writing. Months of analysis. Months of striving to be good. Months of questioning and judging and grading and evaluating. And there I was. Looking at myself in the mirror. I *was* good enough. Could I be better? Absolutely. But there is a big difference between being good enough and being better. "Good enough is an identity thing," I explained, this time to the mascara. "Being better is aspirational, a goal thing."

"Mommy? Are you coming?" This time it was the blonde curly-haired princess. The one who has Williams Syndrome. Now 100% of my princesses had tracked me down. Tracked me down to make sure we would not be late for school. I was impressed!

Anyone who has met our blonde curly-haired princess will nod in agreement with the scientific research showing that children with Williams Syndrome are quite charming, especially with adults. One look into her blue eyes will have your heart melting and your face smiling and your arms extended with a really big hug. Unfortunately, though, peer friendships and long-term relationships are difficult for people with Williams Syndrome. They crave social experiences, but their cognitive challenges sadly prevent them from picking up on social cues, like when to stop talking and how to not stand quite so close to another person. This makes for a lot of confused and hurt feelings on the playground and a lot of days that end with reports of "no one will play with me at recess" and "I don't have anyone to sit with in the lunchroom." Which is heartbreaking. That is a downside of Williams Syndrome.

Another downside of Williams Syndrome is that too-small blood vessels can cause big problems. Big problems like fainting spells and heart failure and cardiac arrest and emergency procedures. All of which are very scary. But wishes can come true! Our blonde curly-haired princess is alive and well and sunny and bright. Just like her golden hair and blue eyes. Happy and cheerful, at least most of the time. And learning all of the things she is supposed to learn in school. At least most of them, anyway. She is sunny and bright and alive because of a talented cardiologist and a valiant heart surgeon and all of the brave doctors and nurses and pharmacists and therapists and other kings and queens and princesses and princes and ladies and knights in shining armor at a top pediatric medical center in Kansas City, one of the tip-top children's hospitals in the country.

"I'll be ready in just a few minutes," I told my daughter, looking her squarely in the eyes to give her the best chance of understanding what I was saying. "I just have to finish my mascara. And then I will get my purse. And then I will come into the kitchen. And then I will get my cereal and my all-natural grape soda. And then I will make sure you and your sisters have your backpacks. And then I will make sure you and your sisters have your shoes on. And then we will all get in the car."

You have to use a lot of "and thens" when you are talking to a child with Williams Syndrome. And it usually works. And it worked this time. My daughter understood what I had said. And she ran off to find her backpack.

I finished up my lipstick. "Now there's another good thing that has happened in the last couple of months," I said to myself. "The birthday party." Our blonde curly-haired princess just had a birthday. I had baked a cake. Of course. A Cheese Cake. Not a cheesecake, but a Cheese Cake. A fluffy white cake molded into the shape of a wedge of cheddar and a wedge of Swiss cheese. The birthday princess loves cheese. Kids with Williams Syndrome are often picky eaters. Which means that repeat menus come in very handy. And our daughter is one of those picky eaters. She prefers foods that are orange. And foods that involve cheese. Especially Cheetos. So I had nestled the Cheese Cake into a big bowl of Cheetos. She had loved it.

The birthday party had been a celebration that gives back. Of course. We honored the Williams Syndrome Association. The Williams Syndrome Association is a comprehensive resource not only for the people and families living with Williams Syndrome, but also for the doctors, researchers and educators who work with children and adults who have the condition. New research is always emerging to help improve the lives of people living with Williams Syndrome.

Our family loves to celebrate the Williams Syndrome Association. I have the most wonderful sister-in-law who planned the most wonderful birthday party for her daughter, my niece. Once upon a time my sweet niece celebrated her birthday by inviting the whole family on a walk in the park to raise money in honor of Williams Syndrome Awareness Week. We all met bright and early, coffees in hand, to take a 1½ mile stroll before heading back to the birthday girl's house for pizza, birthday cake, a pinata and even a dance competition. What a nice gift from a little girl, sharing her birthday celebration with all of the kids across the country who will be better off, even with Williams Syndrome, thanks to lots of support.

"*Mommy!!* Are you coming?" The littlest princess was back. More insistent this time. And with good reason. I looked at the clock. It was 7:59 a.m. We had to get moving.

"Let me get my purse," I said. My youngest daughter followed me into my closet. She loves the closet almost as much as Prince Charming and I love the closet. And she has many opinions about my wardrobe. Opinions which she shares freely. She is quite the fashionista.

"I'll carry your purse, Mommy." My youngest daughter loves to carry my purse. It is almost as big as she is. But she can pull it off. She lifted my purse up off the floor of the closet. And then she put it back down. "Wait, Mommy," she said. "Look at this. In your purse. It's the magic wand. The one I gave you." I watched as she lifted the magic wand out of my handbag. "This is mine," she said. "I want it back."

There it was. The seven-inch silver wand topped with a glittery star. The seven-inch silver wand topped with a glittery star that, while beautiful, had not helped me much. Still, though, the thought of giving it back nearly brought a few wistful tears to my eyes. The magic wand had become a friend. The magic wand was a symbol of the gifts in my life. And a reminder that every day begins and ends with its very own magic. And the magic wand was a metaphor for my belief that anything is possible. The wistful tears began to well up. The magic wand and I had been through so much together.

I started to cry. And then I remembered the mascara. No tears, I thought to myself. Always protect the mascara.

"You can have it back," I told my daughter. I managed to regain my composure. "And thank you for letting me borrow it," I added, as graciously as possible. What I did not say was that the magic wand did not work. But that was okay. It was better that my little princess figure that out on her own.

My daughter carried my purse out of the closet. It was so heavy that her whole body was leaning to one side. Bless her heart. She looked so cute with a giant gold leather purse on her left shoulder and a silver magic wand in her right hand. That girl was ready to take on the world! She headed for the kitchen. I surveyed my closet to be sure nothing was out of order before I left for the day. Maybe, I thought to myself, that magic wand really did do its job. Maybe, I thought, just having it in my purse was all the inspiration I had needed to make a change. To make a leap. To jump into my own fairy tale. To leave my job.

The sign from the universe had arrived. It had arrived one day a few weeks ago. One day a few weeks ago when just about every single thing that happened added up to a sign that the universe was trying to tell me something. No single thing that happened was big. But, as so often is the case with signs from the universe and last straws and nudges, it is usually not anything big that motivates you to act. It is lots of little things. Lots of little things that add up to one big sign that now is the time. That now is the time to make your move.

At 4:00 a.m. on that deceivingly ordinary day, one of the first Sundays of the new year, a child crawled into bed next to me. This itself was not unusual. But she crawled into bed smelling like butter. And chocolate. Those were the first signs that the day would be colorful. Later that morning, the daily gratitude recitations with the kids on the drive to the coffee shop had not been quite as cheery as they are supposed to be. Not even close. I was pretty sure that I completely undercut the benefits of expressing gratitude when I told my oldest princess that she should not keep saying "I am grateful to have a house" over and over, day in and day out. My not-so-gentle recommendation resulted in a big, ugly debate over the rules for expressing gratitude. Then, at the coffee shop, I looked up from my iPhone just in time to see a little princess spill an entire cup of water on the floor. And, alas, back seat fighting broke out on the drive home. The oldest princess was nothing short of apoplectic over the alleged unfairness of her sister getting a donut when she had gotten a bagel. I remained calm the entire time, a major point of pride. But when I pulled into the garage and calmly asked the grouchy princess to go to her room, she refused. I repeated the request. She refused again, this time belligerently. On my third request my voice bordered on almost-witch-mom tone. So I dialed up reinforcements from my iPhone. While I was still sitting in my car in the garage. Prince Charming answered on the first ring and promptly came to the rescue. And he physically removed the princess-turned-grouch from the car. I hustled the remaining two princesses into the house to finish a holiday craft project. That was when one of the little princesses began throwing stickers and Skittles and then a stapler. The metal weapon was the last straw. The stapler-wielding princess joined her older sister on the second floor of the castle. Prince Charming later reported that the little princess whacked 20 dents in the wall upstairs during her punishment time. Using the stapler I could have sworn I had hidden away in my secret closet with my chocolate and my Sharpies. All of this caused me to eat way too many pistachios and wheat puffs for lunch. And, later, we had cereal for dinner, which was perfectly fine, except for the fact that most of the Apple Jacks and Go Lean and Total and Cinnamon Toast Crunch ended up on the floor. Which I had to wipe down five times. And I had not wanted the exercise.

Yes. That deceivingly ordinary day was the day when I had finally decided that it was time to resign as the president and CEO of the Greater Kansas City Community Foundation. To resign as the president and CEO of the Greater Kansas City Community Foundation and start my own business. Start my own business to inspire companies to celebrate doing good in the workplace.

Yes. I had made up my mind at the end of that day. After I had cleaned the floor five times. And after I had ended the day with cake, topping off a day full of little signs from the universe by diving into a multi-layered grand finale of Betty Crocker and vanilla buttercream. Which was a total calorie debacle because I polished off the last third of the leftover birthday cake stashed in the back of the freezer.

It had taken me a full 30 minutes at my kitchen counter that night to eat the rest of that birthday cake. A full 30 minutes of thinking time. A full 30 minutes to think about the big decision I had just made. The big decision I had just made to leave a job I had loved. To leave a position I had loved for six years. At a place I had worked for 11 years. And a place I had loved for even longer than that. And a place I would love forever. But it was something I had to do. It was something I had to do to be myself. Just like I have to bake cakes in my own way. Just like I have to give to charity in my own way. Just like I have to define good girl in my own way. I have to define work in my own way, too.

"It is hard to step into the fairy tale when you give to someone else's favorite charity that is not your favorite charity," I had said to the last few bites of cake that night. "Or when you wear a color of lipstick you do not really like but it is supposed to be all the rage. And you are not living the fairy tale when you try to make a cake that looks like the ones on television when you really love the excitement of knowing that your cake might fall over. Or when you try to change yourself from a cereal mother into a pumpkin pancake mother. You live the fairy tale only when you play the part of you."

I was jarred back to reality by all three princesses. "Mom!" the oldest princess had come running. "Why are you still in the closet? We need to go!" Yikes, I thought. She's right! It was 8:02 a.m. I had been lost in my very own closet. I had been lost in my very own closet, in my very own thoughts.

But I was not quite finished in the closet. Almost, but not quite. "I was right about the fairy tale," I said to my running shoes as I started to close the closet door. "Once you start playing the part of *you*, nothing can stop *you* from becoming even more of *you*." The running shoes said nothing. But they did not run away. "Eventually you will find yourself packing up your old business cards and your old office," I explained. "But you will do it with so much love that you will be overwhelmed and nearly lose your six layers of mascara to tears of joy and even mess up your lipstick, too. And you will walk out the door wearing layers and layers of gratitude for the experience and for the friendships and for the people who supported you. And even for the people who did not support you, for we all learn best in adversity."

I pulled the closet door halfway shut. And I looked intently at the running shoes. They were standing at attention, listening to my every word. "And, finally," I said, "all of this means that you will embark on a new adventure. But you can still eat cereal for dinner. And bake your cakes. And sometimes a cake will fall over." That statement did not seem to surprise the running shoes. "But even that is good," I said. "Just because something falls over or ends does not mean that it was not beautiful, good and delicious. It is never too late to bake a new cake. And who knows? Someday you might just decide you like yourself even more than you like cake."

And with that, I closed the door. And I hurried toward the kitchen.

"Girls, girls, girls!" I said. "Time to get in the car!" I looked around the kitchen. No princesses. I looked around the laundry room. No princesses. I opened the garage door and looked in the car. And there they were. Three princesses. Three backpacks. And, I suspected, three pairs of matching shoes. Like magic, the princesses were ready to go.

"Thank you so much for doing such a great job getting ready for school today!" I said as we backed out of the garage. "I am so grateful. I was running a little behind this morning. And you girls saved the day. I love you!" I looked in the rearview mirror. I looked in the rearview mirror at three beautiful faces beaming with pride. I blinked away tears of joy. I could not possibly be any happier than I am at this moment, I thought to myself.

"We're off!" I said to the girls. We were all in the car. We were on time. And we were off. Off on our merry way to our busy day. Ten minutes later the princesses were successfully deposited at school. And I was on my way to the coffee shop. On my way to the coffee shop to review a few manuscripts.

I reached for my can of all-natural grape soda.

Uh oh. No can of all-natural grape soda.

I reached for my cup of fiber cereal.

Uh oh. No cup of fiber cereal.

I had forgotten my breakfast. I had forgotten the same breakfast I had eaten for years. The same breakfast I had eaten for years on my drive to work. In my haste to get to school on time I had left the can of all-natural grape soda and the cup of fiber cereal sitting on the dryer in the laundry room.

No breakfast.

Then I had an idea. I turned around in the nearest parking lot I could find and I drove back home. I pulled into the garage. I got out of the car. I went inside the house and opened up the freezer. I pulled out a piece of fluffy white cake. A piece of fluffy white cake with vanilla buttercream frosting. A piece of fluffy white cake with vanilla buttercream frosting that I had been saving for just such a celebration. I got a Diet Coke out of the refrigerator. And I got out a plastic fork. And I sat down at my kitchen counter. And I called my mother.

"Hi!" I said. "Hi!" she said. "I won't bother you for long," I said. "I know you are getting ready for work. But I wanted to call to tell you that there is no such thing as too much cake. Just in case you were wondering."

"Oh!" said my mother. "Okay!" She sounded a bit puzzled. She paused. And then she asked, "Are you okay? Where are you? What are you doing?"

I laughed. "Oh I am fine!" I said. "I am good!" I took a bite of cake. It was delicious. I took a sip of Diet Coke. It was delicious, too. "I am at home," I said. "I am sitting at my kitchen counter. And I am eating a piece of cake. And drinking a Diet Coke."

"Oh!" said my mother, relieved. "What a good idea!" she added enthusiastically. My mother is wonderful. "And then what are you going to do?" she asked.

"And then," I said, laughing, "I am going to live happily ever after."

featured in

Cereal for Dinner,

Barbie Cake

Cheerful Chocolate Peanut Butter Cake

Coffee Cake

Fluffy White Cake

Lemony Layered Nut Cake

Mummy Cake

One Signature Birthday Cake

One Yellow Car Cake for 100 Yellow Cars

Paw Print Cake

Retro Birthday Cake

Studio Cake

For these recipes and more,
please visit www.diaryofagoodgirl.com

Five Ideas for Celebrating Good at Home

1. Make your next birthday party a Celebration That Gives Back. Cake is even more delicious when it is sweetened with a dash of doing good! Visit www.celebrationsthatgiveback.com for a step-by-step guide to make your party easy, fun and rewarding.

2. Start your own Diary of a Good Girl to inspire you to be yourself. Fun resources are available online at www.goodgirldiaries.com.

3. Create one or two Spaces That Give Back in your home to celebrate all of the ways you and your family are doing good and striving to be socially responsible. Visit www.spacesthatgiveback.com for ideas to get you started.

4. Bake your own signature birthday cake. The more layers the better! Take pictures! For ideas and inspiration, visit www.onecelebrations.com.

5. Put together a plan for teaching your kids about the joys of giving back. Just an hour or two every month does the trick. Especially if you promise cake. Visit www.eatcakedogood.com for a step-by-step guide.

My Charities

Down Syndrome Guild of Greater Kansas City
Down Syndrome Guild of Greater Kansas
City is featured in Chapter 18.
To learn more, or to get connected with a similar
organization near you, visit www.kcdsg.org.

Euphrates Gallery
Euphrates Gallery, Inc., is a philanthropic venture with a mission
focused on cross-cultural, cross-discipline cultural education
content, based in the urban core in Kansas City, Missouri. To support
Euphrates Gallery by purchasing the poster featured in Chapter
8, please contact the author at laura@diaryofagoodgirl.com.

Girls on the Run
Girls on the Run is featured in Chapter 15.
Learn more at www.girlsontherun.org about its nearly
200 councils worldwide. If there is not a council near
you, find out how you can get one started!

KidsAndCars.org
KidsAndCars.org is featured in Chapter 11.
KidsAndCars.org is a national organization based in
Leawood, Kansas. Learn more at www.kidsandcars.org.

PIPELINE
PIPELINE is featured in Chapter 17.
PIPELINE is a nationally-recognized regional
entrepreneurial immersion program based in Kansas City.
Learn more at www.pipelineentrepreneurs.com.

Ronald McDonald House Charities

Ronald McDonald House Charities Kansas City
is featured in Chapter 1 and Chapter 7.
To learn more, visit www.rmhckc.org.
Or, learn about a Ronald McDonald House
near you by visiting www.rmhc.org.

Variety, the Children's Charity

Variety of Greater Kansas City Charity is featured in Chapter 17.
To learn more about Variety's work in Kansas City,
please visit www.varietykc.org.
Or, learn about one of the 52 chapters near you by
visiting www.varietythechildrenscharity.org.

Williams Syndrome Association

The Williams Syndrome Association is featured in Chapter 19.
To learn more about the work of the Williams Syndrome Association
across the country, please visit www.williams-syndrome.org.

About the Author

Laura Wells McKnight is a mother, stepmother, wife, daughter, sister, friend, entrepreneur, cake sculptor, giver to charity, writer, connoisseur of coffee and mascara, fairy tale chaser, lover of wine (limited to three-fifths of a glass unless it is a special occasion), non-practicing lawyer, self-proclaimed recreational pastry chef, socially responsible citizen-in-training, lipstick's biggest fan and, depending on the day, an aspiring good girl (lots of humor intended), which is an endeavor she documents on her Diary of a Good Girl blog. Laura recently served as president and CEO of the Greater Kansas City Community Foundation in Kansas City, Missouri. The foundation administers more than 3,500 charitable accounts, totalling more than $1 billion, established by individuals, families and businesses to pursue the charitable causes that are most important to them. Laura and her husband live in Leawood, Kansas. They have five daughters who are most forgiving of a dinner menu that sometimes includes not much more than cereal.